OpenMind

Upper Intermediate
Teacher's Book
Premium Pack

Robyn Brinks Lockwood
Jaimie Scanlon

Concept development:
Mariela Gil Vierma

B2

Macmillan Education
4 Crinan Street
London N1 9XW

A division of Macmillan Publishers Limited
Companies and representatives throughout the world

ISBN 978-0-230-45858-1

Text, design, and illustration © Macmillan Publishers Limited 2015
Written by Robin Brinks Lockwood and Jaimie Scanlon
The authors have asserted their rights to be identified as the authors of this work in accordance with the Copyright, Designs and Patents Act 1988.

This edition published 2015
First edition published 2010

All rights reserved; no part of this publication may be reproduced, stored in a retrieval system, transmitted in any form, or by any means, electronic, mechanical, photocopying, recording, or otherwise, without the prior written permission of the publishers.

Designed by MPS Limited, India
Cover design by emc design limited

The publishers would like to thank the following educators and institutions who reviewed materials and provided us with invaluable insight and feedback for the development of the *Open Mind* series:

Petra Florianová, Gymnázium, Praha 6, Arabská 14; Inés Frigerio, Universidad Nacional de Río Cuarto; Alison Greenwood, University of Bologna, Centro Linguistico di Ateneo; Roumyana Yaneva Ivanova, The American College of Sofia; Tán̆a Janc̆ar̆íková, SOŠ Drtinova Prague; Mari Carmen Lafuente, Escuela Oficial de Idiomas Hospitalet, Barcelona; Alice Lockyer, Pompeu Fabra University; Javier Roque Sandro Majul, Windmill School of English; Paul Neale, Susan Carol Owens and Beverley Anne Sharp, Cambridge Academy of English; Audrey Renton, Dubai Men's College, Higher Colleges of Technology, UAE; Martin Stanley, British Council, Bilbao; Luiza Wójtowicz-Waga, Warsaw Study Centre; Escuela Oficial de Idiomas de Getxo; Cámara de Comercio de Bilbao; Universidad Autónoma de Bellaterra; Escuela Oficial de Idiomas EOI de Barcelona; University of Barcelona; Escuela Oficial de Idiomas Sant Gervasi, Isidro Almedarez, Deniz Atesok, Monica Delgadillo, Elaine Hodgson, Mark Lloyd, Rufus Vaughan-Spruce, Kristof van Houdt, Rob Duncan, James Conboy, Jonathan Danby, Fiona Craig, Martin Guilfoyle, Rodrigo Rosa.

The authors and publishers would like to thank the following for permission to reproduce the following materials:

Figures taken from 'Booktrust Reading Habits Survey 2013' published by Booktrust.

These materials may contain links for third party websites. We have no control over, and are not responsible for, the contents of such third party websites. Please use care when accessing them.

Printed and bound in Spain by Edelvives

2019 2018 2017 2016 2015
11 10 9 8 7 6 5 4 3 2

CONTENTS

	INTRODUCTION TO THE COURSE	page iv
	KAGAN STRUCTURES: A MIRACLE OF ACTIVE ENGAGEMENT	page xviii
	STUDENT'S BOOK SCOPE AND SEQUENCE	page xxii
	GRAMMAR REVIEW AND REFERENCE	page xxvi
UNIT 1	WHO DO YOU THINK YOU ARE?	page 1
UNIT 2	GLOBAL VIEWS	page 11
UNIT 3	FAME AND FORTUNE	page 21
UNIT 4	UPS AND DOWNS	page 31
UNIT 5	SOMETHING IN THE WATER	page 41
UNIT 6	LIVING TRADITIONS	page 51
UNIT 7	DESIGNED TO PLEASE	page 61
UNIT 8	A FAIR DEAL?	page 71
UNIT 9	COMPETITIVE EDGE	page 81
UNIT 10	RISKY BUSINESS	page 91
UNIT 11	THROUGH THE LENS	page 101
UNIT 12	BRIGHT LIGHTS, BIG CITY	page 111
	AUDIOSCRIPT	page 121
	WORKBOOK ANSWER KEY	page 132

INTRODUCTION TO THE COURSE
Welcome to the *Open Mind* Teacher's Book!

Course philosophy

The philosophy that underlies the *Open Mind* series is that language is a life skill – a skill for communicating and connecting with others in our everyday lives. As with other life skills, competence in a foreign language opens up possibilities and enables us constantly to expand our potential and our ability to function effectively within the wider social, cultural and economic worlds.

This course is designed to enable students to interact effectively with others in English in a wide variety of communicative situations: in their learning environment, at work, when travelling, online and so on. The authors recognise that the majority of students studying English in their countries will never live or work in an English-speaking country. Instead, they will be using English in the context of their jobs or studies in their own country. For example, they will probably not need to speak English to a doctor; however, they may have to help a foreign visitor to their country talk to a doctor. The activities in *Open Mind* are designed to reflect the reality of how the majority of students will actually use English in their everyday lives.

The authors are aware that students do not come to the classroom as blank slates. Instead, they bring ideas, opinions, feelings and experiences, all of which enrich the learning process. The course is designed in such a way that the students are given as many opportunities as possible to share these ideas and experiences through pair and group work, and in their writing and communicative work. All this ensures that the students relate to the material and make it their own. They are no longer mere users, but active participants, expressing their own points of view. The progression of tasks in each unit allows the students to relate what they have learned to their own experiences and to express their ideas and opinions in English confidently. Specifically devised unit features ensure this smooth transition.

The course title, *Open Mind*, is a direct reflection of this underlying philosophy. It refers to the way in which mastering a new language enables learners to become acutely aware of the social, cultural and economic activities that take place in that new language. It also reflects the way in which acquiring communicative competence enables learners to engage with those activities, opening doors, both personal and professional, that may otherwise have remained closed. Finally, the title resonates with the fact that learning a new language opens a new channel for meaningful communication, allowing the students to express themselves accurately, creatively and effectively, while maintaining an open mind toward other people's opinions and ideas.

Methodology and unit structure

The creation of *Open Mind* has been a rigorous and carefully researched process. Starting with the overall concept and then underpinning it with specific decisions has ensured that we are presenting you with a course that is meticulously thought-through, market-informed and theoretically solid, and that it works pedagogically to achieve high learning outcomes in a demanding classroom environment.

Each unit in *Open Mind* is written and designed in sections. The sections reinforce each other, but are not interdependent. This adds unrivalled flexibility and allows for variety in the lesson structure. The unit sections can be taught sequentially, or they can be arranged to meet course requirements, e.g. number of hours per term. Of course, you can decide to use any other parameters you deem relevant.

Approaches to teaching language

A Grammar

Most students embarking on a language course expect to find grammar; they see it as the basis of the language they are learning. The teaching of grammar has traditionally involved a deductive approach in which a grammar rule is presented first (either by the teacher or by the textbook) and then practice exercises are given that allow students to apply the rule. In contrast, throughout *Open Mind* an inductive approach is applied, in which the target grammar is first presented in context, thus raising awareness of the structure in use. Students are then encouraged to observe, compare and analyse in order to identify the principles or rules of the new structure. Finally, students are presented with exercises that ensure comprehension of the grammar form in contexts that elicit the target language. To this end, each Grammar section in *Open Mind* follows a dynamic five-step structural approach that activates the students' learning potential, as shown opposite.

In each unit, there are two Grammar sections. The grammar has been selected to 1) reflect the needs of the students at their present level of English and 2) be relevant to the topic of the unit, ensuring that the practice is natural and meaningful. After completing a Grammar section, the students will encounter that grammar again as they work through the remainder of the unit, which reinforces the point and aids retention.

Step 1 – *Language in context*
This stage introduces students to the target grammar in a realistic reading or listening context. A simple comprehension activity ensures that the students have understood the main idea of the text/audio material. Usually this takes the form of a general comprehension question. At this stage, students are not expected to produce the target language, but they are made aware of the structure in a real-life context.

Step 2 – *Notice!*
This feature consists of one or two simple questions to help the students notice something simple about the form or function of the new structure as it appears in the text.

Step 3 – *Analyse*
This stage focuses on a guided inductive presentation that uses examples from the text in the previous step. It usually consists of two subsections: Form and Function. Tasks elicit from the students the rules about the new structure. Having completed the tasks, the students are left with a complete grammar presentation on the page.

What's right?
A feature that inductively draws the students' attention to common learner errors in the use of the new structure.

Step 4 – *Practise*
This stage is a written exercise that enables the students to apply and confirm their inferences from the *Analyse* stage and gives them controlled practice in the use of the target grammar.

Step 5 – *Now you do it*
The final step of each Grammar section is a one-step communicative activity that allows the students to practise the new grammar in a personalised context. The aim of this stage is to give the students the opportunity to employ the new structure in ways meaningful to them, thereby making it both more relevant and more memorable.

Introduction to the course v

B Vocabulary

Language students can make rapid progress in a foreign language if they are able to assimilate and use items of vocabulary quickly and effectively. Traditional methods of teaching vocabulary relied heavily on memorisation of items, which were frequently presented in lists with an accompanying translation. While generations of students learned vocabulary with some degree of success in this way, more recent approaches have focused on the communicative function of vocabulary, and particularly on the way words combine with other words to form chunks of meaningful language, as described in the Lexical Approach. The question of how people store and recall items of vocabulary has also become relevant, and the importance of associating words with a context, an experience, an image or indeed with other words, is seen by practitioners as central to this process. When creating a course, there is the inevitable question of what vocabulary to present and in what order. The seemingly random approach adopted in the past has been quantified with the latest corpus linguistics tools, which in turn has enabled us to identify words that are used most frequently and words that are therefore most useful to students.

In *Open Mind*, the authors have adopted a corpus-based approach to selecting and presenting vocabulary. Information on frequency and collocation patterns has been sourced from the corpus work created for the *Macmillan English Dictionary*. The underlying philosophy to teaching vocabulary is that we should introduce students to the words and phrases that are most frequent and useful in general standard English. To this end, each Vocabulary section focuses on lexical terms that the students can use actively in everyday oral and written communication.

There are no independent vocabulary sections in *Open Mind*. Instead, Vocabulary is integrated into existing skills sections. The rationale behind this is that vocabulary useful to higher levels is more likely to relate to a specific text (such as a listening or reading text) or a productive need and function (such as a Speaking or Writing section). Each unit contains two integrated Vocabulary sections, each consisting of six to eight words which stem from the relevant reading, listening, speaking or writing text. Within each of these sections, there are two vocabulary activities – one to present the language, and a communicative task to put it into practice. The aim is to teach students the words that are most frequent and useful within a given topic and also to highlight collocations wherever possible or relevant. Words are recycled throughout the rest of each unit.

Students at this level often have a good store of words already. To help them boost their vocabulary, you can encourage them to: look at words and phrases that go together (*make a mistake, a decision, a mess*); look at how words and phrases are used in context; make word webs for different word families; look at the connotations of a word (*helpful – positive; poorly made – negative*).

Suggest to the students that they keep a vocabulary notebook to record new items of vocabulary and examples of their use in context.

Step 1 The skills task presents the target vocabulary in context. At this stage, the students are not expected to use the items actively. There are tasks to check students' comprehension before they focus on the language.

Step 2 This step gives the students the opportunity to use the new vocabulary items in a controlled practice activity. They are often asked to compare options, categorise, complete phrases and sentences, and so on.

Step 3 With this last step, the students are encouraged to use the vocabulary items actively in a speaking activity, such as a discussion or roleplay.

C Pronunciation

Accurate pronunciation is a key element of successful communication. Mastering pronunciation requires awareness and practice at three key prosodic levels: sound, word and sentence – all of which are focused on in *Open Mind*.

First of all, there are the individual sounds (phonemes) of English. Here it is important to focus on those sounds that are different from those in the students' mother tongue and that therefore cause the greatest difficulty, both in terms of recognition (listening and understanding) and in terms of production (speaking and being understood). Second, there is the area of word stress, where English, with its numerous word stress patterns, may differ considerably from the students' mother tongues. Finally, there is the question of rhythm and intonation, where English is characterised by a relatively high number of falling tone patterns in comparison with many other languages. Level-appropriate aspects of these three areas of pronunciation are carefully developed and presented.

As with Grammar, Pronunciation in *Open Mind* is taught inductively. Each Pronunciation section in *Open Mind* typically consists of two or three steps. The Pronunciation sections are supported by audio for the presentation and sometimes additionally for the practice steps.

Step 1 Students are given a task which draws their attention to a specific sound or stress pattern. They are always asked to repeat the words or phrases to practise.

PRONUNCIATION: voiced and voiceless consonant sounds

A 🔊 1.08 Listen to each pair of words. 1) Put your hand on your throat and say the first word of each pair. You should feel a vibration. 2) Put the palm of your hand a few centimetres in front of your mouth and say the second word in each pair. You should feel a puff of air after the first letter.
a) vast fast   c) base pace   e) goal coal
b) do too   d) drain train

B 🔊 1.09 Listen to five sentences. Choose the word you hear in Exercise A.

C 🗣 Work in pairs. Take turns saying one word from each pair in Exercise A. Your partner will try to identify which word you are saying.

Step 2 This step provides the students with an opportunity to practise the pattern and to compare and check their grasp of the pronunciation point.

Step 3 This step contextualises the pronunciation point, offering students the opportunity to practise it in real-life speech.

Approaches to teaching the four skills

The four language skills – listening, reading, speaking and writing – are informed by the two modes of communication: spoken and written language. Each of these has a receptive and a productive aspect. To ensure fluency, it is essential that learners of a language get practise in all four skills. However, mere practice alone is not enough. The four skills need to be developed in a planned, coherent way, something that many textbooks have neglected up to now.

Each skill consists of a number of different abilities, or 'sub-skills'. For example, the skill of reading consists of the meaningful use of sub-skills such as scanning, skimming, recognising the main idea, etc. In actual use, we employ a variety of skills and sub-skills simultaneously. Consequently, in order to develop the students' reading and listening skills, it is important to identify and focus on sub-skills in turn. In *Open Mind*, we have devised a skills syllabus that is methodically researched, carefully planned and balanced, and which focuses on sub-skills that are most likely to be of use to learners at their respective level.

All four skills are present in every unit in the *Open Mind* series. However, in order to ensure a balanced development of the four main language skills, we have deployed an alternate pattern of 'on' and 'off' skills: 'on' skills are the ones that are developed through sub-skills, and 'off' skills are the ones that are practised. So every unit includes two types of skills sections:
1) skills development sections for the 'on' skills, and
2) skills practice sections for the 'off' skills. Their pattern is alternate; for example, the two 'on' skills that are developed in Unit 1 are then practised in Unit 2 as 'off' skills, while the two 'off' skills that are practised in Unit 1 are developed in Unit 2 as 'on' skills, and so on.

This alternate pattern of 'on' and 'off' skills sections is clear in the layout of the contents pages, with the two 'on' skills sections in every unit highlighted.

'On' skills.

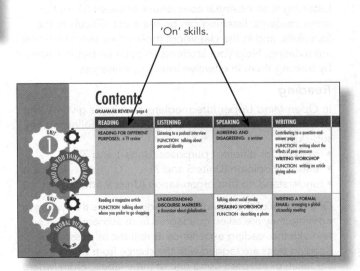

Introduction to the course

1 Teaching sub-skills (skills development sections – 'on' skills)

Each skills development section starts with a skills panel, which informs the students in clear, direct terms what the sub-skill is, why it is important and how to apply it. The sub-skill section builds on the information provided in this feature. The students are always given the opportunity to apply the sub-skill at the end of the section.

'On' skill indicated by cog.

> **SPEAKING: clarifying misunderstandings**
> When you feel you haven't explained something clearly enough, there are phrases you can use to clarify what you mean.

In each level of the course, three sub-skills are covered for reading and listening. Each of these is covered twice, the second time in further detail or in a more challenging context. There are six sub-skills for speaking and writing per level. Further practice of the sub-skills is provided in the Workbook.

Recycled 'on' skill indicated by cog and page reference.

> **LISTENING: understanding discourse markers** page 22
> Discourse markers often act as signposts, giving a listener clues about what they might hear next. They might introduce additional points, contrasting ideas or a conclusion. The correct use of discourse markers in both writing and speaking is one of the things that examiners often look for in academic and proficiency exams.

Listening

In *Open Mind Upper Intermediate*, training is given in the Listening sections in the development of the following key sub-skills:
- understanding discourse markers (Units 2 and 4)
- listening for main ideas (Units 6 and 8)
- rapid speech (Units 10 and 12)

Effective L2 listening is the ability to understand an aural message in another language and respond appropriately. Without the ability to listen effectively, the students will be unable to communicate successfully in the target language. Listening is an essential component of *Open Mind*. For many students, listening can be the most difficult of the four skills, and in the classroom it can often seem the most intimidating. Help your students to become better listeners by training them in effective listening strategies.

Reading

In *Open Mind Upper Intermediate*, training is given in the Reading sections in the development of the following key sub-skills:
- reading for different purposes (Units 1 and 3)
- inferring opinion (Units 5 and 7)
- understanding text organisation (Units 9 and 11)

One feature of the *Open Mind* reading texts is that wherever possible they are taken or adapted from authentic sources, to make the reading experience as realistic as possible. Reading texts are tagged with the source from which they are taken or adapted using one of three labels: *From* (where the text is taken word for word from the source), *Adapted from* (where the text has been adapted from a particular source) or *Information source* (where the text has been written using information from a particular source).

Speaking

In *Open Mind Upper Intermediate*, training is given in the Speaking sections in the development of the following key skills:
- agreeing and disagreeing (Unit 1)
- clarifying misunderstandings (Unit 3)
- suggesting alternatives (Unit 5)
- using distancing language (Unit 7)
- paraphrasing (Unit 9)
- making comparisons (Unit 11)

Apart from the skills development sections, which cover speaking, there are constant opportunities for speaking throughout each unit of *Open Mind*: the students are encouraged to give their own opinions, to discuss their own experiences and to communicate with one another on a variety of topics. A specific speaking stage can always be found in the Grammar section (*Now you do it*), in the Vocabulary section and in the LifeSkills section.

Speaking sections in even units contain an Independent Speaking task, which is similar to the extended speaking task required of students taking the TOEFL exam, as well as being an important part of production as outlined in the Common European Framework. In this task, students take turns to participate in an extended speaking turn for about one and a half minutes.

Writing

In *Open Mind Upper Intermediate*, training is given in the Writing sections in the development of the following key skills:
- writing a formal email (Unit 2)
- writing a thank-you note (Unit 4)
- avoiding run-on sentences (Unit 6)
- sentence variety (Unit 8)
- writing a letter requesting action (Unit 10)
- writing a letter of complaint (Unit 12)

Four of the six writing sections in *Open Mind Upper Intermediate* deal with a genre of writing rather than with smaller writing sub-skills such as using connectors or writing a topic sentence. It is considered that Upper Intermediate level students are ready to tackle the broader challenge of genre writing.

2 Integrating and practising skills (skills practice sections – 'off' skills)

These sections (two per unit) provide the students with opportunities to practise skills with a focus on the communicative outcome (e.g. listening to an interview in Unit 5; writing a memo in Unit 11). Each section comprises two to three steps and integrates two or more language skills, with a primary skill as the focus. The sections allow students to focus more on the end product, with fluency in mind, and less on the process they go through in order to achieve it. In the activities here, there is a strong emphasis on personalisation – relating the material to students' own experiences.

The unit opener

The first two pages of every *Open Mind* unit are the unit opener. It is an exciting visual opportunity for students to engage with the unit. The first page sets the overall scene visually by means of a striking combination of two photos and also by providing a comprehensive list of language objectives for the unit. This page always features two cogs which indicate the two 'on' skills being developed in the unit and which, through simple questions or tasks, aim to help the students to familiarise themselves with the unit.

The LifeSkills panel at the bottom introduces the life skill of the unit and here again a question helps the students to start thinking about the nature of the life skill.

The second page of the unit opener features photos and provides a quick warm-up to the unit, or can be extended to a much longer and enriching speaking activity. This activity never expects the students to use any vocabulary or grammar in the unit to come. Its key purpose is to create excitement and boost motivation.

CEF-oriented unit objectives.

Introduction to the course

Speaking and Writing workshops

The Speaking and Writing workshops are each a page long and come at the end of alternate units. These are intended to provide extra practice and support in the productive skills, as well as expose students to the kinds of writing and speaking they might need to do in exams like IELTS, TOEFL, etc. (Note that extra practice and exam-style questions for reading and listening are provided in the Workbook.)

The structure of both the Speaking and Writing workshops is based on a common concept: the students are first presented with a model, next they analyse it, then they work on their own production and finally they self-assess.

For more independent writing consolidation practice, encourage the students to complete the optional final activity on the SkillsStudio spread in each unit of the Workbook. For more extended speaking practice, use the Independent Speaking feature at the end of Speaking sections in even units.

Step 1
Students are presented with a model conversation or model paragraph, email, etc and a task based on the model. The task focuses on comprehension but it is also an opportunity for the students to start working with the language or structure that will be focused on later.

Step 2
This is a task to focus students on the useful language or structure from the model. This is what they will need to employ in the production task later.

Step 3
Here students start thinking about their own production. The task helps them prepare in terms of information to include, language to use, ways of structuring and organising their ideas, etc.

Step 5
This is a self-assessment feature to get students to analyse and reflect on their production.

Step 4 – Speaking
Having prepared for the speaking task, students engage in a conversation, either in groups or with a partner.

Step 4 – Writing
Having prepared for the writing task, students undertake the piece of writing.

Teaching life skills

One of the unique features of *Open Mind* is its focus on life skills. Each unit ends with an inspiring LifeSkills section. This is based on the notion that in today's highly competitive global environment, students of English need other, higher-order skills besides language skills. Life skills include information and research skills, critical thinking and problem-solving skills, self-direction and learning skills, organisation and planning skills, and collaboration skills. These skills are highly valued by employers and are essential to the students' continued success, and yet rarely form a part of the students' formal education. The authors firmly believe that it is our responsibility to help the students develop these life skills and, in particular, to prepare them to employ those life skills in English-speaking situations. All the life skills covered in *Open Mind* require a certain amount of collaboration, so pair and group work is an essential component of this section.

The life skills in *Open Mind* feature as parts of three domains: *Self and Society*, *Study and Learning* and *Work and Career*. It is important to understand that the use of these three domains is not meant to function as an organising principle but rather as a reflection of one of the many ways in which that particular skill can be applied. Life skills are essential in every aspect of our lives and are therefore transferable. In every LifeSkills spread in *Open Mind*, the particular life skill to be applied in one of the three domains was carefully chosen.

Each LifeSkills section is introduced by a three- or four-step summary of the approach that will be applied through the different activities in the section. These steps are applicable to the skill in general and can be applied in other situations, beyond the English classroom.

Each LifeSkills section is linked to the general unit topic in which it appears, and the language and skills presented in the previous pages of the unit help to prepare the students for this section.

A three-step summary of the approach that will be applied through the different activities in the section.

The chosen domain for the spread is highlighted, but all three domains are mentioned as a reminder of the transferability of the skill.

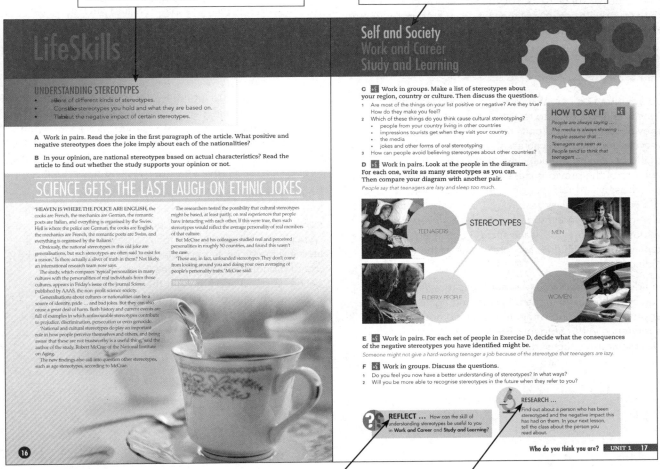

The *Reflect* question gets students to think about how the featured skill can be applied to the other two domains.

The *Research* task encourages students to apply the skill they have learned, or find out more about it, via a short research project.

Introduction to the course

Language wrap-up

Each unit has a Language wrap-up that enables the students to assess their grasp of the new vocabulary and grammar items presented in the unit.

The Language wrap-up exercises can be done in class or assigned as homework. If given as homework, tell the students not to look at the sections of the unit that are being tested in the wrap-up tasks before they do the exercises.

If you use the Language wrap-up in class, you might wish to set a time limit of 10–15 minutes for each task. Again, encourage the students to do the tasks without looking back at the relevant sections of the unit. Motivate them to focus on the tasks individually, as pair or group work could lead to stronger students dominating and would not give accurate feedback on what individual students have learned.

It is a good idea to go over the answers with the whole class. This can lead to some discussion of the answers that might be useful for students.

Make sure the students read the can-do statements in the score boxes and write their score out of 10 or 12 for both the Vocabulary and Grammar sections. If they have a score lower than 8 (out of 10) or 10 (out of 12), encourage them to read the appropriate sections of the unit again for homework, and then do the exercise or exercises again at home.

> **10–12 correct:** I can use verbs with stative and dynamic uses and repeated and double comparatives.
> **0–9 correct:** Look again at the grammar sections on pages 23 and 25. **SCORE:** /12

To aid retention and ensure a long-lasting learning outcome, it is crucial to recycle language points from previous sections and units regularly. For example, to recycle grammar you can ask the students a few questions at the beginning of each class, focusing on the grammar content of the previous class (e.g. for simple past, begin the class by asking *What did you do last weekend? Where did you go after class yesterday?*). Integrated recycling is also emphasised in the way vocabulary is used – the target vocabulary from each section occurs again over the remainder of each unit, reinforcing use of the items and aiding retention.

In addition, to help you plan sub-skills recycling, the cog symbol is used in the unit plan and again in the appropriate heading within the teaching notes, along with a reference in the Student's Book to where that sub-skill was previously practised.

Teaching students at Upper Intermediate Level

Teaching students at Upper Intermediate levels presents the language teacher with certain challenges, often related to gaps in their previous grammatical knowledge and the existence of different levels within a particular group. At this level it is especially important for the students to be independent learners and to expand their vocabulary, in particular, both inside and outside the classroom – by using the internet to research items, through independent reading and listening, and so on.

As at previous levels, it is essential that you use English as the language of the classroom, although there may be instances (where possible and appropriate) when you might encourage learners to compare and contrast a particular structure, item of vocabulary or idiom with the equivalent in their mother tongue. The concept of *false cognates* (words that look or sound similar to words in the students' mother tongue but which have a different meaning in English) can be discussed at this level if applicable and examples highlighted.

Emphasise the advantages of maximising the amount of active use of English during class time in pair and group work activities. The authors have provided the students with model conversations, prompts and phrases in the *How to say it* feature to ensure that the students have a range of functional language at hand to carry out a task confidently. Moreover, the course teaches a variety of useful skills to overcome any obstacles and to promote interaction. When checking answers to exercises, you may at times want to let the students first compare their answers in pairs. This is particularly appropriate in exercises that are more open-ended or where more than one answer is possible for some of the items. The practice of pair checking helps to foment a cooperative learning atmosphere and provides extra speaking opportunities.

When presenting new vocabulary, ensure that the students feel comfortable with the pronunciation and stress of any new words and phrases. Encourage the students to keep a vocabulary notebook and focus on establishing good learning practices. In particular, encourage them to make use of monolingual dictionaries (both hard copies and online versions) and highlight the importance of using these as a means of enhancing independent learning through checking meaning, collocations, pronunciation and word stress.

Open Mind Workbook

The *Open Mind* Workbook is an ideal source of additional activities to engage the students in further practice of the Student's Book material. The Workbook follows a format similar to that of the Student's Book and reflects its section organisation. The dynamic and modern design makes the book appealing and easy to navigate through.

Each Workbook unit can be viewed as consisting of three parts: the first four pages help students to practise and consolidate the unit's grammar, vocabulary and the two target sub-skills.

The last two pages of each Workbook unit contain the *SkillsStudio*. This spread provides students with an extended reading or a listening text as well as tasks similar to the ones they might find in an exam. Comprehension questions follow each text, and the spread ends with an optional free writing task that requires the student to select and synthesise relevant information from the reading or listening.

The Workbook is accompanied by its own audio CD with the tracks for the listening tasks. The listening activities are signposted by an audio icon and the audioscripts appear at the end of the Workbook. The answer key for the Workbook activities (including possible answers) can be found on pp. 132-140 of this Teacher's Book or within the Workbook itself if students have purchased the 'with key' version.

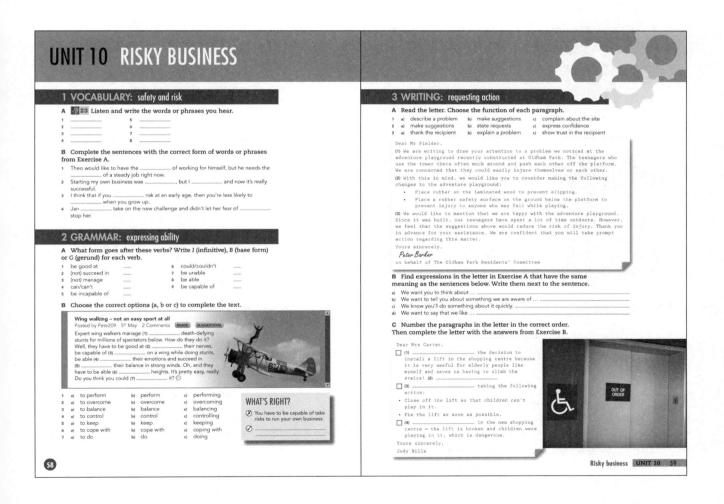

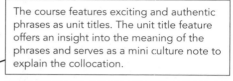
Open Mind Teacher's Book

The Teacher's Book offers carefully planned, well-paced and insightful procedural notes to help you prepare, present and follow up on the unit material in an appropriate way for the students, teaching circumstances and course requirements.

Along with the procedural notes, the Teacher's Book supplies a complete answer key (including possible answers) and includes the audioscripts for the listening tasks in the Student's Book.

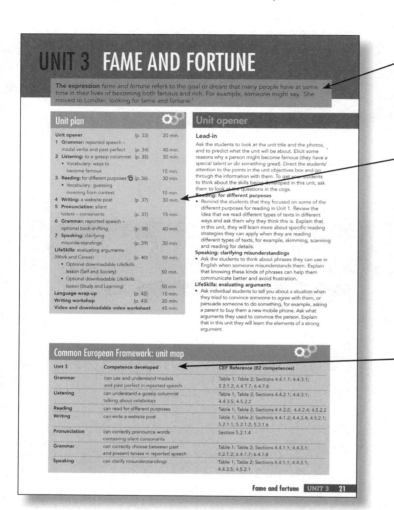

The course features exciting and authentic phrases as unit titles. The unit title feature offers an insight into the meaning of the phrases and serves as a mini culture note to explain the collocation.

The information in the unit plan outlines the target language and objectives by section. It also offers suggested timings.

The Common European Framework of Reference for Languages (CEFR) is an influential document produced by the Council of Europe. Since its publication, it has had a major impact on the work of teachers, teacher trainers, examiners and course designers, both within Europe and in other parts of the world. It describes the linguistic competences language learners possess at different levels of achievement. It does this by describing the things a person with a given language level can do. It covers six main levels of ability: A1, A2, B1, B2, C1 and C2. Students completing *Open Mind Upper Intermediate* should reach the level of ability of B2, as described by the CEFR performance descriptors. The CEFR unit map lists the sections in the unit and, for each section, a can-do statement is provided. These are based on the type of can-do statements found in the CEFR and describe the ability the students should acquire on successfully completing the section. In the map, reference is provided to the relevant sections of the CEFR. These are either the sections where the CEFR specifically mentions the competence being developed in the Student's Book, or sections where the CEFR mentions competences that rely on the competence being developed in the Student's Book. The complete text of the CEFR is available for download from the Council of Europe website (http://www.coe.int/t/dg4/linguistic/source/framework_en.pdf).

Features of the Teacher's Book

The Teacher's Book authors have developed an array of teacher-friendly features that support, build on and/or extend the material in the Student's Book.

Lead-in This feature provides you with optional activities that help you start your lesson or introduce a particular section of the Student's Book. Typically, the Lead-in does not require any additional preparation.

Alternative This instruction presents you with alternative approaches to the Student's Book material. It addresses different learning styles, provides challenging alternatives for high achievers and facilitates the presentation of activities for students who may need more support.

Culture note Here you can find background information that may be of interest to your students and that will help you with the presentation of the section material. It may provide more information about a person, event or place mentioned in the Student's Book. It may also focus on what people in the English-speaking world do or say in a particular situation.

Extra The optional *Extra* activities equip you with ideas for additional classroom practice and homework. The activities always focus on and extend the language point of the section in which they appear. They are ideal for fast finishers. Extra reading comprehension or grammar items are often provided in case you want to exploit a reading text or grammar point further with your class.

Each Workbook unit can be viewed as consisting of three parts: the first four pages practise and consolidate the unit's grammar, vocabulary, and the two target sub-skills; the fifth page is a *Listen and write* or *Read and write* page which consolidates the unit material and offers the student further opportunity for guided, supported and highly personalised writing practice. The language in the *Writing tutor* helps students get started and organise their writing; the last page of each Workbook unit is a *Down time* page which offers fun and engaging activities in the form of quizzes, crosswords, games, riddles, and more. The Workbook is accompanied by its own audio CD with the tracks for the listening tasks. The listening activities are signposted by an audio icon, and the audio scripts appear at the end of the Workbook. The answer key for the Workbook activities (including possible answers) can be found on pp. 128–134 of this Teacher's Book.

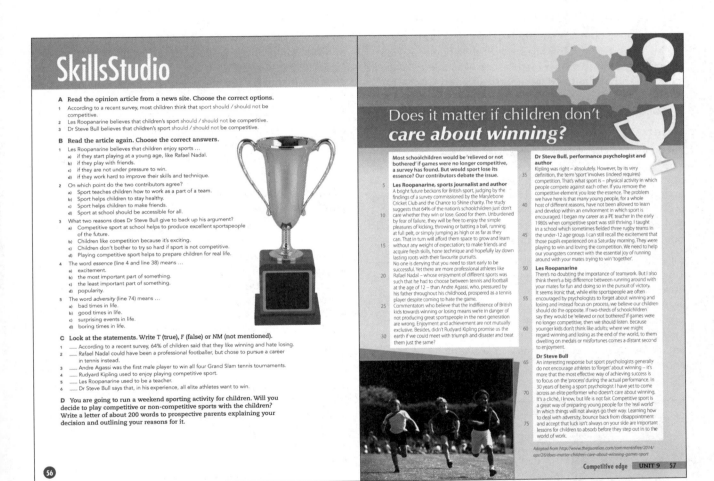

Introduction to the course

Open Mind Digital

Flexible digital resources are a central part of the *Open Mind* approach to language teaching. The range of online and downloadable components and resources can be tailored to each class's needs and facilities, allowing for flipped and blended approaches as well as more traditional teaching styles.

For students, the Online Workbook and self-study video worksheets and video on the Student's Resource Centre consolidate classroom learning and promote autonomy and awareness.

For teachers, *Open Mind*'s digital components provide tools to save you time and add to the class experience, together with a variety of testing options that range from a placement test to customisable unit and mid-course tests and an end-of-course test.

Teacher's and Student's Resource Centres

The online Resource Centre for teachers and students are bursting with materials to support the course, as well as audio and video. Some features are available to both students and teachers, while others can only be accessed through the Teacher's Resource Centre. See the lists at the end of this page for a complete overview.

Video

Each Student's Book unit is accompanied by a new video (see screenshot below) which provides students with engaging material and further language input. Videos feature authentic footage and a range of genres, including reportage, animated presentations and interviews with real people, to provide fascinating lead-ins or jumping-off points for each unit of the course.

All videos are accompanied by downloadable worksheets. These worksheets offer a variety of tasks and activities that build on the students' prior knowledge, generate interest in the topic, check the students' comprehension and practice grammar or vocabulary. Each worksheet presents tasks to be done before, during and after watching, and comes with teacher's notes and answer keys where appropriate.

Example from Open Mind *Upper Intermediate video*

Extra LifeSkills support

The Teacher's Resource Centre includes 24 LifeSkills lesson plans – two for every LifeSkills double-page spread in the Student's Book. Each LifeSkills section in the Student's Book presents a skill (for example, 'Understanding internet search terms') through one domain (for example, *Study and Learning*), while the extra LifeSkills lesson plans will present this same skill through the two other domains (for example, *Self and Society* and *Work and Career*).

Besides offering alternatives to the Student's Book material, the aim of these extra LifeSkills lessons is to show learners how they can apply the same life skill from the Student's Book to other contexts, thereby further developing these competencies and empowering the students.

Tests

All the tests you need for placement, progress and achievement purposes are on the Teacher's Resource Centre. These are available both in ready-to-print PDF versions and customisable Word versions, and comprise:

- *Open Mind* course placement test, with instructions on delivering this
- Unit tests: these test the grammar, vocabulary and skills covered in each unit of the Student's Book
- Mid-course tests: a ready-made review combining items from the unit tests for the first half of the Student's Book
- End-of-course test: a ready-made end-of-course test with completely new test items covering the full *Open Mind 3* language syllabus

Student's Resource Centre – the complete package

The following features are all accessible to your *Open Mind* students:

- Student's Book and Workbook audio files
- *Open Mind* video files
- *Open Mind* video self-study worksheets and answer keys
- CEFR checklists
- Word lists and translated word lists

Teacher's Resource Centre – the complete package

The Teacher's Resource Centre includes everything on the Student's Resource Centre, as well as:

- *Open Mind* video class worksheets, with teacher's notes and answer keys
- Extra unit opener lessons
- Extra LifeSkills lessons
- Communicative wrap-up lessons
- Tests
- Placement test

Online Workbook

The Online Workbook provides extra skills, grammar and vocabulary practice to support the Student's Book. It contains interactive activities, audio for listening practice, video and supporting activities, and automatic marking – so students can instantly check answers and try again as many times as they want.

The Online Workbook is also linked to an LMS (learning management system) gradebook, which means you can see students' marks for each activity, as well as the amount of time (and number of times) it has taken them to complete each task. The Online Workbook is ideal for self-study, but you may wish to consider using it for reviewing students' work in open class via a projector or an interactive whiteboard.

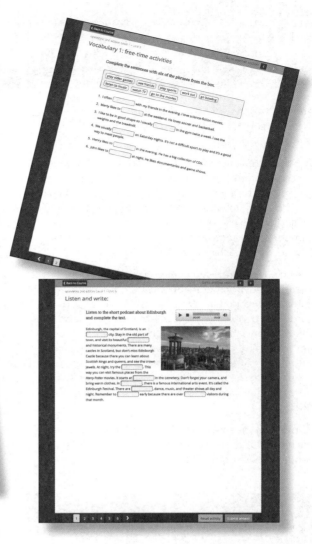

Example from Open Mind *Elementary Online Workbook*

Presentation kit

The Presentation kit is a digital version of the Student's Book designed for enhanced classroom presentation. It features all the content of the print Student's Book with embedded video, class audio, full answer keys and simple interactive whiteboard tools.

Access is easy. The Presentation kit can be downloaded onto your interactive whiteboard or laptop for use with a projector – no disks are required. It's ideal for work in open class as an alternative to 'eyes down' work, as well as for checking and reviewing students' work.

Example from Open Mind *Beginner Presentation kit*

Introduction to the course | xvii

KAGAN STRUCTURES: A MIRACLE OF ACTIVE ENGAGEMENT*

Dr Spencer Kagan and Miguel Kagan
Kagan Publishing & Professional Development
www.KaganOnline.com

Kagan Structures are instructional strategies designed to promote cooperation and communication in the classroom, boost students' confidence and retain their interest in classroom interaction. The Structures work in all teaching contexts – regardless of subject, age group and number of students in class – and are a particularly powerful tool for teaching a foreign language.

In this article, we contrast a conventional classroom lesson and its environment with a classroom where Kagan Structures are brought in. We discuss the benefits of the Structures and explain why this alternative approach to classroom organisation works much better and has a long-term learning effect. Then, we present three of our favourite Kagan Structures that are particularly suitable for the language-learning context, and we offer you an overview and the support to apply them in your daily teaching routines.

For an in-depth presentation of the Structures and our approach to cooperative learning, you can read *Kagan Cooperative Learning* (2009).

Traditional instructional strategies vs. Kagan's cooperative structures

Let's compare a typical, traditional English lesson to an English lesson using Kagan Structures. For example, we might want to teach listening for the main idea or general comprehension.

In a traditional classroom, the teacher may have the class listen to a listening text, then do a whole-class question-and-answer session. During the question-and-answer session, the teacher usually asks questions then has students raise their hands to volunteer answers. Alternatively, the teacher may ask a question and nominate a student to respond. Finally, the teacher may assign a comprehension activity for individual work and have the students complete it individually. Sound familiar?

Traditional learning is either whole-class, with the teacher leading the class, or independent practice work. As we'll see below, traditional learning lacks a high level of active engagement, creates a more intimidating learning environment and often fails to establish an effective communicative context for natural language acquisition.

Cooperative learning offers a powerful alternative for language teaching – interaction! Many teachers believe they are doing cooperative learning by introducing pair and group work. However, unstructured pair and group work lacks the basic principles of effective cooperative learning and therefore does not produce the gains of true cooperative learning. There is a vast difference between Kagan Structures and conventional pair or group work. Kagan Structures carefully engineer student interaction to maximise cooperation, communication and active engagement by all.

The teacher who is fluent with a number of Kagan Structures would teach the same lesson quite differently. She would likely still provide some direct instruction, but skip the whole-class question-and-answer session and not do the individual exercise. Instead, she would choose a Kagan Structure that will involve everyone, and encourage sharing and cooperation. On the subject of listening for the main idea, the teacher might have the students do *RallyRead* – students work in pairs and take turns to read part of a reading text, switching after an assigned amount of text or time. Partner A reads for a specified period while Partner B listens actively. Partner A asks questions to check Partner B's general comprehension of the passage. Or *Timed Pair Share* could be used to practise listening for the main idea. Pairs take turns to talk about a topic for a specified period of time. Their partner must listen attentively.

> *Kagan Structures carefully engineer student interaction to maximise cooperation, communication and active engagement by all.*

Choosing a cooperative learning structure over traditional methods creates a dramatic positive difference in English language learning. We now know that there are many styles of learning and multiple intelligences. What works for some may not work well for everyone. Therefore, we need a variety of strategies to reach and teach our students with different learning styles and intelligences. If we always use lectures and independent exercises, we may inadvertently create barriers to English learning for many students. If, instead, we use a variety of structures as we teach, we engage the different learning styles and students' multiple intelligences. The variety creates greater novelty, increases motivation and maintains attention. Kagan Structures also create greater engagement, lower anxiety and promote natural language acquisition. Let's see how.

---

* The Publishers would like to thank Dr Spencer Kagan and Miguel Kagan of Kagan Publishing & Professional Development for developing this article for the *Open Mind* series. Ownership of the copyright remains with the authors.

Cooperative learning increases engagement for everyone

One attribute that sets cooperative structures apart from traditional instruction is that structures don't call for voluntary participation. In the traditional classroom, the teacher asks students a question, and only those who know the answer, or who are daring enough to respond, raise their hands. The rest of the class can opt out.

When students have the option of non-participation, many don't participate. This is especially true for shy students, lower achievers and early language learners. The result: they don't learn as much or as quickly.

With Kagan Structures, participation is not voluntary. Participation is required by the Structure. In *RallyRead*, students take turns to read a text. With *Timed Pair Share*, students must talk for equal amounts of time. In the traditional classroom, the structure does not require participation from every student. It is the same when *RallyRead* is used for pair work. If pair work is not structured properly, one student can simply do the work, while the other student watches or even tunes out. In contrast, the Structures hold every student individually accountable for participating. There is a direct connection between student participation, engagement, communication and subsequent language learning.

> *There is a direct connection between student participation, engagement, communication and subsequent language learning.*

In the traditional classroom, when one student answers at a time, the ratio of active engagement is quite low. What's more, the rest of the class sits quietly and there is very little involvement. During our cooperative learning practice, the class is divided into pairs, and at least half of the class is generating language at any time and the other half is directly receiving comprehensible input and practising active listening. This radically increases the opportunity to decode and produce language.

Cooperative learning lowers anxiety

Learning and using a foreign language can be stressful. In the traditional English classroom, the teacher quizzes students in front of the entire class. Students may not know the correct answer, may be apprehensive about speaking in public or may be self-conscious about their accent. In global surveys, public speaking ranks as people's greatest fear, beating fear of death, spiders, flying and confined spaces. Whole-class settings for language learning are often perceived as threatening situations. We know from both language learning theory and brain research that stress negatively impacts on attitudes, learning and memory.

With *RallyRead* and *Timed Pair Share*, students are working with just one other student. Most Structures encourage pair work or work in teams of four.

Students who would experience anxiety in a whole-class setting feel more comfortable speaking English in a more intimate setting. Cooperative groups are less intimidating than whole-class settings. This is especially true in cooperative classrooms in which the teacher uses team building to establish trust and encourage support among teammates.

Cooperative learning promotes natural language acquisition

There's a big difference between learning about a language and actually acquiring the language. Too many language courses teach students about the language. Not enough courses allow students to actually use the language in a functional way. In our example of the traditional classroom, students learn about listening for the main idea. They learn to correctly complete a comprehension exercise. But are they really learning effective language use? Results say no.

In the real world, we don't complete exercises on our comprehension of something. But we often do need to understand the main idea of what's being said in many situations.

When the situation of language acquisition (exercise work) is too different from the situation of performance (listening for the main idea), a transference gap is created. *RallyRead* sidesteps the transference gap: the situation of acquisition (listening for the main idea) matches the future situation of performance (listening for the main idea). Many Kagan Structures naturally develop fluency by sidestepping the transference gap.

Too often, language courses fail to build functional fluency. Students learn how to conjugate verbs, memorise vocabulary and learn grammar rules, but too often miss out on the opportunity to use language frequently in a functional way. With the Structures, students not only learn about language, but they actually implement it to accomplish a goal. Natural language acquisition among infants is based on frequent social interaction. Cooperative structures provide the social setting for language use and offer students many more opportunities to receive input, interact in the target language and practise oral production of the language.

Many Structures for many language-teaching objectives

Developing English fluency consists of four major interrelated language objectives: we want to build oral comprehension skills, so students can understand what they hear; we want to build oral fluency skills, so students can communicate with others; we want to build writing skills, so students can express themselves clearly and correctly; we want to build reading skills, so students can read with comprehension and accuracy.

To accomplish these four language goals – reading, writing, speaking and listening – we need an array of teaching tools. That's exactly what Kagan Structures are. Each Structure is a different language-teaching tool designed to develop different skills. Some Structures are more suitable to build listening skills (e.g. *RallyRead*). Others are ideal for practising language skills such as comprehension and fluency (e.g. *Talking Chips*). Many Structures simultaneously address multiple objectives that go beyond the four language objectives outlined above.

> *A wonderful feature of the Kagan Structures is that they are instructional strategies that can be used repeatedly.*

We have developed over 200 Kagan Structures for promoting interaction in the classroom. Because cooperation and communication are two hallmarks of the Kagan Structures, they are particularly well adapted to English learning. A wonderful feature of the Kagan Structures is that they are instructional strategies that can be used repeatedly. They are not limited to one particular exercise, but are designed as shells so you can slot in any activities and target language. Once you learn some basic Structures, you can integrate them easily into your daily English lessons. For example, you may use *RallyRead* today for reading for the main idea, but you can use it again tomorrow for general reading fluency and comprehension work.

Here are three sample Kagan Structures we encourage you to experiment with.

Three Structures for the English language classroom

1 Timed Pair Share

Language functions:
Fluency, Elaboration, Oral comprehension

Advantages:
- Half the class is actively producing language at any time, while the other half is actively listening.
- All students must participate.
- Students listen attentively so they can respond appropriately.
- Students regularly practise producing language on various topics.

Structure summary:
Partners take timed turns listening and sharing.

Description:
Timed Pair Share is one of the simplest cooperative learning Structures – and one of the most powerful. The teacher states a discussion topic, how students are to pair, how long students will have to share and selects who will go first. It is perhaps the easiest way to infuse cooperative interaction into just about any point of the lesson. For example, *What do you predict this text will be about? Work in pairs and share for 30 seconds each. Partners with the darkest clothes begin.*

When you compare *Timed Pair Share* to its traditional counterpart – selecting one student to share with the class – its true power is revealed. With *Timed Pair Share*, half the class is active at any one time, while the other half listens attentively.

In the traditional class, only a single student in the whole class is active at any time; the rest of the class may easily tune out. With *Timed Pair Share*, no students get left behind. Everyone must participate.

Students practise speaking and sharing their thinking and opinions in English. They practise listening attentively. A single *Timed Pair Share* vs. selecting one student in the class probably doesn't add up to much, but when you consider how often teachers ask questions every day, then multiply that by the number of days the course lasts, this simple little Structure has the power to dramatically improve language skills.

Variation:
Progressive Timed Pair Share. In *Progressive Timed Pair Share*, students take turns sharing with different partners on the same topic. Each time they share on the topic, the time limit is increased. This gives students the opportunity to start small and work their way up to more elaborate sentences, phrases and ideas. As they hear ideas and language from their partners, they can incorporate what they've heard into their own turn to speak.

2 RallyRead

Language functions:
Reading, Fluency, Comprehension, Listening

Advantages:
- Students develop language fluency.
- Promotes active engagement as half the class is either actively reading or actively listening.
- Develops reading comprehension because students must respond to frequent comprehension questions.

Structure summary:
Partners (Student A and Student B) take turns reading and checking for comprehension.

Description:
RallyRead is an effective structure for building reading fluency and comprehension. The teacher assigns the reading text. It can be a story, a blog entry, an email, a newspaper article – anything at the appropriate level of difficulty. The teacher informs students how often they need to switch readers. Partners can switch every sentence, every paragraph or every page, depending on the students' ability levels. Partners can also switch roles at timed intervals, such as every minute. Student A reads for his specified reading period. When finished, he asks his partner a comprehension question, for example, *Where did the dog go?* Student B answers. If correct, Student A praises, *Good listening!* If incorrect, Student A offers help, referring the partner to the appropriate reading passage so the partner can find the correct answer.

RallyRead is often preferable to independent reading because students get the opportunity to practise their fluency skills and also get practice in rhythm and intonation. Words often come out differently when pronounced than when read in one's head. *RallyRead* also develops listening skills. Students must listen actively for comprehension to correctly respond to their partners. While the teacher reading aloud is good for modelling correct pronunciation, it lacks the active student participation that *RallyRead* offers.

3 Talking Chips

Language functions:
Communication regulator, Fluency builder

Advantages:
- Every student is held accountable for participating.
- Develops speaking and listening skills.

Structure summary:
Teammates place a 'talking chip' in the centre of the team table each time they talk. When they're out of chips, they may not talk until all teammates have used their chips.

Description:
Each student receives one 'talking chip'. The chips can be any kind of game token, or a pen, pencil, rubber, slip of paper or any other tangible item. It is preferable if each student has a unique colour for his/her chips. The students are given an open-ended discussion topic, such as *Where in the world would you most want to live and why?* In order to speak, a teammate must place his or her chip in the centre of the team table. It is his or her turn to speak. Teammates cannot interrupt and must practise respectful listening. When he or she has finished, another student places his or her chip in the centre of the team table and is free to add to the discussion. When a student uses his or her 'talking chip', he or she cannot speak until all teammates have added to the discussion and placed their chip in the centre of the table. When everyone has had a chance to speak, each student collects his or her chips and continues with the discussion using 'talking chips', or they can start again with a new topic.

Talking Chips regulates discussion, ensuring that everyone participates and everyone contributes. Shy students, low achievers and less fluent students are encouraged by the social norms of the structure to fully participate and develop their language skills too.

About the authors

Dr Spencer Kagan is an internationally acclaimed researcher, public speaker, and author of over 100 books, chapters and journal articles. He is a former clinical psychologist and full professor of psychology and education at the University of California. He is the principal author of the single most comprehensive book for educators in each of four fields: cooperative learning, multiple intelligences, classroom discipline and classroom energisers. Dr Kagan developed the concept of structures; his popular brain-based, cooperative learning and multiple intelligences structures like *Numbered Heads Together* and *Timed Pair Share* are used in teacher-training institutes and classrooms worldwide. He has taught workshops and given keynote speeches in over 20 countries, and his books are translated into many languages. Dr Kagan has been featured in leading educational magazines, including *Educational Leadership, Instructor, Learning Magazine* and *Video Journal*.

Miguel Kagan is Executive Director of Kagan Publishing & Professional Development, an educational organisation that offers publications and workshops on cooperative learning, language learning and active engagement. Miguel, together with Dr Kagan, co-authored a radical revision of the classic book, *Kagan Cooperative Learning*. Miguel has also written, designed and developed a multitude of books, SmartCards, software programs, learning games, and electronic devices for Kagan Publishing. He is the editor of *Kagan Online Magazine*, Kagan's webzine that offers articles, research and tips for educators implementing Kagan Structures.

References

High, Julie (1993). *Second Language Learning Through Cooperative Learning*. San Clemente, CA: Kagan Publishing. This book applies Kagan Cooperative Learning Structures to language learning.

Kagan, Spencer & Kagan, Miguel (2009). *Kagan Cooperative Learning*. San Clemente, CA: Kagan Publishing. This is a recent revision of Dr Kagan's classic book on cooperative learning. It is the most popular and comprehensive book in the field.

Kagan, Miguel (2009). *Match Mine Language Builders*. San Clemente, CA: Kagan Publishing. Based on the Structure *Match Mine*, this book contains 30 ready-made cooperative learning games covering common vocabulary words and concepts.

STUDENT'S BOOK SCOPE AND SEQUENCE

	READING	LISTENING	SPEAKING	WRITING
UNIT 1 **WHO DO YOU THINK YOU ARE?**	READING FOR DIFFERENT PURPOSES: a TV review	Listening to a podcast interview FUNCTION talking about personal identity	AGREEING AND DISAGREEING: a seminar	Contributing to a question-and-answer page FUNCTION writing about the effects of peer pressure WRITING WORKSHOP FUNCTION writing an article giving advice
UNIT 2 **GLOBAL VIEWS**	Reading a magazine article FUNCTION talking about where you prefer to go shopping	UNDERSTANDING DISCOURSE MARKERS: a discussion about globalisation	Talking about social media SPEAKING WORKSHOP FUNCTION describing a photo	WRITING A FORMAL EMAIL: arranging a global citizenship meeting
UNIT 3 **FAME AND FORTUNE**	READING FOR DIFFERENT PURPOSES: an internet article	Listening to a gossip columnist FUNCTION discussing the difference between fame and celebrity	CLARIFYING MISUNDERSTANDINGS: informal conversations	Writing a website post FUNCTION writing about someone you admire WRITING WORKSHOP FUNCTION writing a short essay
UNIT 4 **UPS AND DOWNS**	Reading a magazine article FUNCTION understanding ways to be happier	UNDERSTANDING DISCOURSE MARKERS: a lecture about wealth and happiness	Talking about having a positive attitude SPEAKING WORKSHOP FUNCTION expressing personal preference	WRITING A THANK-YOU NOTE: expressing your thanks in writing
UNIT 5 **SOMETHING IN THE WATER**	INFERRING OPINION: an online article	Listening to an interview FUNCTION discussing a charity	SUGGESTING ALTERNATIVES: a discussion	Contributing to an online debate FUNCTION expressing an opinion on the consumption of bottled water WRITING WORKSHOP FUNCTION interpreting data
UNIT 6 **LIVING TRADITIONS**	Reading a book excerpt FUNCTION understanding traditions	LISTENING FOR MAIN IDEAS: interviews about maintaining traditions	Talking about personal rituals SPEAKING WORKSHOP FUNCTION comparing photos	AVOIDING RUN-ON SENTENCES: writing a comment on a blog

PRONUNCIATION	GRAMMAR	VOCABULARY	LIFESKILLS
WORDS: emphatic *do/did* for contrast	REVIEW OF PAST TENSES FUNCTION talking about a past experience WOULD, USED TO, BE + ALWAYS + -ING FUNCTION talking about family identity	PERSONAL IDENTITY FUNCTION talking about your family background SENSE FUNCTION talking about learning a new language	SELF AND SOCIETY: Understanding stereotypes FUNCTION discussing the consequences of negative stereotypes
SOUNDS: voiced and voiceless consonant sounds	VERBS WITH STATIVE AND DYNAMIC USES FUNCTION talking about the spread of multinational corporations REPEATED AND DOUBLE COMPARATIVES FUNCTION talking about the growth of social media	GLOBALISATION FUNCTION talking about the positive and negative aspects of a global market VERBS FOR TAKING SOCIAL ACTION FUNCTION talking about ways of supporting your local economy	STUDY AND LEARNING: Understanding internet search terms FUNCTION studying the effect of globalisation on your local economy
SOUNDS: silent letters — consonants	REPORTED SPEECH — MODAL VERBS AND PAST PERFECT FUNCTION talking about 15 minutes of fame REPORTED SPEECH — OPTIONAL BACK-SHIFTING FUNCTION talking about lookalikes	WAYS TO BECOME FAMOUS FUNCTION talking about famous people in your country GUESSING MEANING FROM CONTEXT FUNCTION talking about the effects of celebrity	WORK AND CAREER: Evaluating arguments FUNCTION discussing a proposal
WORDS: reduced forms of *would you* and *did you*	NOUN CLAUSES AS OBJECTS FUNCTION talking about laughter therapy REVIEW OF CONDITIONAL FORMS FUNCTION talking about taking a year off before university	LIFE SATISFACTION FUNCTION talking about wealth and happiness MOOD FUNCTION talking about your state of well-being	WORK AND CAREER: Being a positive team member FUNCTION focusing on solutions to problems
SOUNDS: word stress in adjective + compound noun phrases	THE PASSIVE FUNCTION talking about problems caused by the monsoon season EXPRESSIONS OF PURPOSE FUNCTION understanding FAQs about water	MARKETING FUNCTION talking about how packaging can affect your buying decisions ENVIRONMENTAL ISSUES FUNCTION discussing responsibility for solving environmental problems	SELF AND SOCIETY: Developing empathy FUNCTION discussing your water usage
SOUNDS: stress in words with *-tion/-sion*	BE USED TO / GET USED TO FUNCTION describing habits and customs VERB + OBJECT + INFINITIVE FUNCTION comparing traditional and non-traditional jobs	INSTITUTIONAL TRADITIONS FUNCTION discussing customs and rituals PHRASAL VERBS FOR PERSONAL RITUALS FUNCTION discussing why you have rituals	STUDY AND LEARNING: Managing distractions FUNCTION making a plan to change your habits

Student's Book Scope and sequence

	READING	LISTENING	SPEAKING	WRITING
UNIT 7 DESIGNED TO PLEASE	**INFERRING FACTUAL INFORMATION:** an article	Listening to a radio phone-in show **FUNCTION** discussing fashion styles	**DISTANCING LANGUAGE:** a polite conversation	Writing a biography **FUNCTION** writing about a designer **WRITING WORKSHOP** **FUNCTION** writing a review
UNIT 8 A FAIR DEAL?	Reading biographical profiles **FUNCTION** understanding a summary of someone's life	**LISTENING FOR MAIN IDEAS:** a lecture about fair trade	Talking about social justice **SPEAKING WORKSHOP** **FUNCTION** proposing a solution	**SENTENCE VARIETY:** explaining your opinion of international aid
UNIT 9 COMPETITIVE EDGE	**UNDERSTANDING TEXT ORGANISATION:** a scientific article	Listening to experts' opinions **FUNCTION** understanding the main arguments	**PARAPHRASING:** a scientific study	Writing a description **FUNCTION** giving an opinion about reality TV **WRITING WORKSHOP** **FUNCTION** writing a discursive essay
UNIT 10 RISKY BUSINESS	Reading an opinion article **FUNCTION** talking about taking risks	**RAPID SPEECH:** a conversation about a TV stunt	Speculating about events **SPEAKING WORKSHOP** **FUNCTION** responding to a question asking for a choice	**REQUESTING ACTION:** writing clear and concise points
UNIT 11 THROUGH THE LENS	**UNDERSTANDING TEXT ORGANISATION:** an online article	Listening to a podcast **FUNCTION** understanding the description of a photo	**MAKING COMPARISONS:** an informal conversation	Writing a memo **FUNCTION** summarising key points from a phone message **WRITING WORKSHOP** **FUNCTION** writing a report
UNIT 12 BRIGHT LIGHTS, BIG CITY	Reading a guidebook **FUNCTION** talking about a description of a place	**RAPID SPEECH:** a guided tour	Talking about cities of the future **SPEAKING WORKSHOP** **FUNCTION** giving a short presentation	**WRITING A LETTER OF COMPLAINT:** expressing specific details clearly

PRONUNCIATION	GRAMMAR	VOCABULARY	LIFESKILLS
WORDS: 's after names that end in /s/, /ʃ/ or /z/	**POSSESSIVE APOSTROPHE** **FUNCTION** talking about celebrities' clothing sale **PAST PERFECT VS PAST PERFECT CONTINUOUS** **FUNCTION** understanding a biography	**DESIGN** **FUNCTION** talking about revolutionising the design process **PHRASAL VERBS** **FUNCTION** talking about fashion design and trends	**WORK AND CAREER:** Showing initiative **FUNCTION** identifying opportunities to show initiative
WORDS: the contracted form of *would*	***WOULD RATHER* AND *WOULD PREFER*** **FUNCTION** talking about donating to charities **NOUN CLAUSES AS SUBJECTS** **FUNCTION** talking about unemployment	**SOCIAL ISSUES** **FUNCTION** talking about humanitarian causes **SOCIAL JUSTICE** **FUNCTION** talking about a fair society	**SELF AND SOCIETY:** Understanding rights and responsibilities **FUNCTION** sharing your ideas on the rights and responsibilities in your country
WORDS: nouns and verbs with different pronunciation	**GERUNDS AFTER PREPOSITIONS** **FUNCTION** talking about personality types **VERB + GERUND** **FUNCTION** talking about reality shows	**SCIENTIFIC NOUNS AND VERBS** **FUNCTION** talking about psychology and the effects of competition **EXPRESSIONS OF EMOTION** **FUNCTION** talking about feelings and desires	**STUDY AND LEARNING:** Synthesising information **FUNCTION** preparing and presenting a report
WORDS: reduction of *have*	**EXPRESSING ABILITY** **FUNCTION** talking about entrepreneurs **PAST MODALS OF DEDUCTION** **FUNCTION** working out how something happened	**SAFETY AND RISK** **FUNCTION** discussing freedom and security **EXPRESSIONS WITH *RISK*** **FUNCTION** talking about high-risk situations	**SELF AND SOCIETY:** Managing stress **FUNCTION** creating strategies to help you relax
SOUNDS: stress timing	**VERB + GERUND/INFINITIVE WITH A CHANGE IN MEANING** **FUNCTION** talking about a past memory **CONNECTORS OF ADDITION / CAUSE AND EFFECT** **FUNCTION** talking about image manipulation	**DESCRIBING PHOTOS** **FUNCTION** explaining what you like and dislike about photos **MAKING COMPARISONS** **FUNCTION** finding similarities and differences between photos	**WORK AND CAREER:** Giving and receiving feedback **FUNCTION** discussing a campaign to boost local tourism
SOUNDS: connected speech	**CONNECTORS OF CONTRAST** **FUNCTION** talking about a visit to a city **WAYS OF TALKING ABOUT THE FUTURE** **FUNCTION** talking about cities of the future	**FORMAL LETTERS** **FUNCTION** writing a letter of complaint **DESCRIBING PLACES** **FUNCTION** talking about a city that you know	**STUDY AND LEARNING:** Recognising and avoiding plagiarism **FUNCTION** discussing strategies to make your work original

Student's Book Scope and sequence

GRAMMAR REVIEW AND REFERENCE

Grammar review

This Grammar review has been included to help you establish what your students already know before they start *Open Mind Upper Intermediate*. It is designed to be used in the first lesson of the course and has a two-fold aim: firstly, as an introductory activity to help you get to know your students; and second, as a way to establish the general level of the class. It also provides a useful recap of rubrics and classroom language.

The Grammar review can be used in a variety of different ways. It can be completed individually, as a formal diagnostic test, to check that students have been placed at the correct level. A more interactive approach would be to elicit the answer to the first question of each exercise as a class and then have the students complete the rest of the exercise individually.

Answers for the Grammar review can be found on p. 178 of the Student's Book. You can choose to check answers after each exercise or at the end of the review. If you wish, the exercises can be exploited further, and ideas for some of them are given below and on the following pages.

1 (present perfect + *yet/already*, *used to*, definite article *the* / zero article, question tags, past perfect)
- Check that the students understand that they need to delete, add or change one word in each sentence.
- If the students are struggling with item 1, explain that there are two possible answers that have different meanings.

2 (present perfect + *yet/already*, present perfect continuous, *used to*, question tags, past perfect)
- In item 2, the students need to read the second sentence to work out that the missing word is *yet*.

3 (present perfect and present perfect continuous)
- If the students are struggling, tell them that the continuous form gives more emphasis to the duration of the activity. In item 4, both forms are possible, but the use of the continuous form would indicate that this has been an on-going activity.

4 (indirect questions, causative *have* and *get*, *hope* and *wish*)
- If students are struggling with items 3 and 4, point out that they each have two possible answers. The second option for item 3 is to use the passive voice. In item 4, it is possible to get a *haircut* (noun).
- Follow up: Have the students make possible answers for the indirect questions in items 1 and 2.

5 (adjectives ending in -ed/-ing; *so*, *such*, *too*, *enough*)
- Both options are grammatically correct in item 1 so the students need to think about the meaning of the sentences.
- Check that students understand the meaning of *troublemaker* in item 5 (someone who does bad things and causes problems).

6 (reported speech and reported questions)
- Check that the students understand that pronouns, tense, time expressions and place expressions all change when we convert direct speech to reported speech. As a result, there are various possibilities in each of the items. The conjunction *that* is often used, but can be omitted if doing so doesn't change the meaning of the sentence.
- Follow up: Have the students work with a partner and practise converting each other's direct speech into reported speech.

7 (modals of deduction: *must, can't, might/could*)
- Remind the students that *might* and *could* can have the same meaning, and that either of them may be possible answers.

8 (*wish* and *if only* for regrets, third conditional)
- Check that the students understand *turn up* in item 4 (arrive).

9 (verb + gerund/infinitive)
- Follow up: Have the students complete these sentence stems with their own words: *I always avoid … , I usually finish … .*

10 (defining and non-defining relative clauses)
- Draw the students' attention to the example set in item 1, in which the non-defining relative clause is taken from the first sentence, and the object of the main clause is taken from the second sentence. Encourage the students to follow the same pattern in the items that require non-defining relative clauses.

11 (infinitive clauses with impersonal *it*, *should/shouldn't have*)
- Tell the students that one of the words/phrases in the box will need to be used twice.
- Follow up: Have the students discuss with a partner what they would say in each of these situations.

12 (separable and inseparable phrasal verbs)
- If the students are struggling, tell them that in separable phrasal verbs a pronoun cannot go at the end.

Grammar reference

The Grammar reference provides further consolidation of the grammar points covered in each unit. It can be found on pp. 152–165 of the Student's Book, and the answer key on pp. 182–183. For each grammar point, there are clear notes and tables outlining the form and function, as well as two exercises providing further practice. It is designed to be done on a unit-by-unit basis and can either be covered as part of the unit, as a follow-up to each Grammar section, or at the end of the unit in a test format.

UNIT 1 WHO DO YOU THINK YOU ARE?

The expression *Who do you think you are?* refers to our family history and background. Knowing about these things gives us our sense of identity and helps us understand how we relate to other people in society.

Unit plan

Unit opener	(p. 8)	20 min.
1 **Listening:** to a podcast interview	(p. 10)	30 min.
• Vocabulary: personal identity		15 min.
2 **Speaking:** agreeing and disagreeing	(p. 10)	30 min.
3 **Grammar:** review of past tenses	(p. 11)	40 min.
4 **Reading:** for different purposes	(p. 12)	30 min.
• Vocabulary: *sense*		15 min.
5 **Pronunciation:** emphatic *do/did* for contrast	(p. 13)	15 min.
6 **Grammar:** *would, used to, be + always + -ing*	(p. 14)	40 min.
7 **Writing:** contributing to a question-and-answer page	(p. 15)	30 min.
LifeSkills: understanding stereotypes (Self and Society)	(p. 16)	50 min.
• Optional downloadable *LifeSkills* lesson (Work and Career)		50 min.
• Optional downloadable *LifeSkills* lesson (Study and Learning)		50 min.
Language wrap-up	(p. 18)	15 min.
Writing workshop	(p. 19)	20 min.
Video and downloadable video worksheet		45 min.

Unit opener (p. 8)

Lead-in

Ask the students to look at the unit title and the photos, and to predict what the unit will be about. Ask the students to give some examples of factors that determine who we think we are and our sense of identity: nationality, home town, gender, age, family, hobbies, school, job, etc. Direct the students' attention to the points in the unit objectives box and go through the information with them. To get your students to think about the skills being developed in this unit, ask them to look at the questions in the cogs.

Reading: for different purposes

- Ask the students to tell you some of the things they read today. Elicit several different types of texts and write them on the board. Tell them to think about their reason for reading each one and *how* that affects how they read (quickly vs. slowly and carefully, scanning for specific information vs. reading for the overall gist, etc).

Speaking: agreeing and disagreeing

- Ask the students to think about situations in which they would agree or disagree with someone. Elicit a few phrases in English for agreeing and disagreeing. Ask about situations in which they might need to disagree with someone politely, and what they might say.

LifeSkills: understanding stereotypes

- Ask the students what common stereotypes people have about teenagers and elderly people. Discuss whether or not these stereotypes are fair, and why or why not. Extend the discussion by asking what other groups are frequently stereotyped.

Common European Framework: unit map

Unit 1	Competence developed	CEF Reference (B2 competences)
Listening	can understand an interview	Table 1; Table 2; Sections 4.4.2.1; 4.4.3.1; 4.4.3.5; 4.5.2.2
Speaking	can agree and disagree appropriately	Table 1; Table 2; Sections 4.4.1.1; 4.4.3.1; 4.4.3.5; 4.5.2.1; 5.2.3.2
Grammar	can use and understand a variety of past tenses	Table 1; Table 2; Sections 5.2.1.2; 6.4.7.7; 6.4.7.8
Reading	can read for different purposes	Table 1; Table 2; Sections 4.4.2.2; 4.4.2.4; 4.5.2.2
Pronunciation	can appropriately use emphatic *do/did*	Section 5.2.1.4
Grammar	can use and understand *would, used to* and *always* + progressives for habits	Table 1; Table 2; Sections 5.2.1.2; 6.4.7.7; 6.4.7.8
Writing	can contribute to a question-and-answer page	Table 1; Table 2; Sections 4.4.1.2; 4.4.3.2; 4.4.3.4; 4.5.2.1; 5.2.1.1; 5.2.1.2; 5.2.1.6; 5.2.2.2; 5.2.2.4; 5.2.3.2

Who do you think you are? UNIT 1 1

A

- Ask the students to think of different types of identity groups (sports teams, workplace/company, etc). Elicit ideas from the class and list them on the board.
- Put the students in pairs and ask them to look at the photos and identify the groups shown. Point out that one photo may represent more than one identity group. Have pairs make a list of as many groups as they can think of for each photo.
- Combine pairs to form groups of four. Ask the students to share their lists and talk about which similar identity groups they belong to.

B

- Ask the students to think about which identity groups they belong to and how important each of those groups is to their own identity. You may wish to share identity groups of your own and how they influence you. This will facilitate the students' comfort with sharing personal information, as well as helping them get to know you.
- Have the students decide which two groups have the biggest influence on their identity. Ask them to share their ideas in pairs, then ask for volunteers to share something they learned about their partner's identity.

Culture note

Around the world, different cultures place different levels of importance on group identity vs. individual identity. In many western cultures, for example, when making decisions an individual's desires and needs are considered most important, while in some other cultures, particularly those in Asia, it is more important to consider the opinion of, or effects on, the whole group.

Extra: homework

At the beginning of the course, you may wish to have the students create a personalised folder, binder or notebook to use during the course. For homework, have the students create a visual representation of their identity on the cover of the folder or binder. The design should include their name and they could attach photos of friends, family members or pets, colourful drawings, printed images from the internet or anything else they feel represents their personal identity. Have the students bring their folders to class and present them in small groups, saying why the images reflect their identity.

Listening: to a podcast interview (p. 10)

Lead-in

Review the groups that influence identity that the students discussed in the last lesson. Then have the students brainstorm all the factors they can think of that influence identity, e.g. interests, and ask them which ones are most important to their own identity. Elicit some of the factors the students consider important.

A

- Ask the students to read the list of factors that can influence identity and compare them to their own lists. Give the students time to rank the factors in order of importance to their own identity.
- Take a class poll to find out the top three factors the students selected.

B 1.01

- See p. 121 for the **audioscript**.
- Tell the students they are going to listen to a podcast interview with a man from Scotland who now lives in Japan talking about what was important to his identity in the past. Elicit a few predictions about which factors he will mention from the list in Ex. A.
- Play the audio and have the students choose the factors Dylan mentions. Tell them that they should also write down any other factors he mentions that are not on the list.

Answer

Students should circle: friends, clothes, interests, job.

C 1.02

- See p. 121 for the **audioscript**.
- Ask the students to read the two questions silently. Elicit a few predictions.
- Play the audio. As the students listen, they should take notes on the factors that have changed in Dylan's sense of identity.
- Put the students in pairs to compare answers. Then elicit the answers from the class.

Answers

1 He is more aware of other people's opinions (of what he does).
2 Music is no longer so important, because the same music tradition doesn't exist where he is now. It has been replaced by new hobbies. Family and family values have become much more important to him now because of his experience of his wife's family and their idea of family.

D

- Give the students time to match the vocabulary items with their definitions. Have them compare answers in pairs before checking the answers with the class.

Answers

1 c 2 f 3 d 4 a 5 b 6 e

E

- Direct attention to the questions. Give the students time to think about their answers and make notes in preparation for the group discussion.
- Put the students in groups. Circulate and help as needed during the discussions.
- To conclude, discuss the questions with the whole class.

 Workbook p. 5, Section 2

Speaking: agreeing and disagreeing (p. 10)

Lead-in
Write the following saying on the board and elicit or explain its meaning: *Blood is thicker than water.* (Family members are more important than friends.) Ask the students to say whether they agree or disagree. Elicit several reactions and write any expressions the students use for agreeing/disagreeing on the board. Ask the students to read the information in the skills panel. Ask them to identify an example of agreement, partial agreement and disagreement from the list on the board.

A
- Have the students work in pairs to make a list of expressions, beginning with the ones on the board.

B 1.03
- See p. 121 for the **audioscript**.
- Tell the students they will be listening to part of a university seminar on identity.
- Play the audio and elicit the answer to the question.

Answer
Sean thinks it's important to keep a strong sense of personal identity and to respect family members as individuals. He would not take a job where he couldn't be himself.

C
- Give the students time to read the partial expressions. Have them listen again and write the missing words in the blanks.
- Have each pair compare answers with another pair and identify which phrases are used for agreement, partial agreement and disagreement. Then check the answers with the class.

Answers
1 certain 2 Yes 3 sorry 4 afraid
5 way 6 couldn't

D
- Put the students in groups to discuss the question. Remind them to try to use the target phrases for agreement, partial agreement and disagreement.

▶ Workbook p. 6, Section 3

Grammar: review of past tenses (p. 11)

A
- Direct the students' attention to the blog title and subtitle. Ask what they think the phrases *identity crisis* and *living in two worlds* mean. Elicit ideas from the class.
- Ask the students to scan the text for another phrase that includes the word *identity* (*losing my identity*). Based on this phrase and the title/subtitle, ask the students to predict what the blog entry will be about.
- Give the students time to read the blog entry. Elicit the answer to the question.

Answer
Akna may have had a hard time adjusting to the crowded city, making new friends or with others not understanding her background or culture.

NOTICE!
- Direct the students' attention to the **Notice!** box.
- Have them find and underline all the verbs in the blog entry that are in a past tense.
- Put the students in pairs to compare answers and make a list of the past tenses used.
- After checking answers as a class, ask the students what auxiliary verb is sometimes used for emphasis.

Answers
<u>grew</u>, <u>spent</u>, <u>changed</u>, <u>met</u>, <u>had arrived</u>, <u>met</u>, <u>was studying</u>, <u>fell</u>, <u>got</u>, <u>moved</u>, <u>did try</u>, <u>suffered</u>, <u>felt</u>, <u>was</u>, <u>didn't</u>, <u>was</u>, <u>realised</u>, <u>had made</u>. The past tenses in the text are past simple, past continuous and past perfect. The auxiliary verb *did* is sometimes used for emphasis.

B

Form
- Briefly review the three past tenses used in the text. Have the students read the blog again, focusing on the use of the past tense verbs.
- Give the students time to complete the table individually with examples from the text. Then check the answers with the class.
- **Highlight** the phrase *was scared* in the text and point out that the verb *be* + feeling adjective does not exist in the continuous form (*being*) without the verb *feel*. Write on the board: ✓*was scared* ✓*was feeling scared* ✗ *was being scared*.

Answers
1 grew 2 changed 3 did try 4 was studying
5 had made

Who do you think you are? UNIT 1

Extra: thinking/feeling/perceiving verbs

Point out the phrase *I finally realised …* in the text. Explain that there are three categories of verbs – thinking, feeling and perceiving verbs – that are not generally used in the continuous form. List examples for each category on the board and elicit more verbs for each category from the class, e.g. feeling: *love, hate, enjoy, want, need*; thinking: *believe, realise, suppose, decide*; perceiving: *hear, taste, smell, see*, etc.

Extra: pronunciation preview

Preview the stress and intonation of the emphatic *did* introduced later in the unit. Have the students repeat several phrases or sentences stressing the word *did* (*I did study last night, He did call me to say he'd be late*).

Function

- Give the students time to read the explanations and write the correct tense for each one. Have them compare answers in pairs.
- Direct the students' attention to the **What's right?** box.
- Have students work in pairs to discuss which sentence is correct.
- Elicit that the first sentence is correct and the second sentence is incorrect because the past simple should be used to describe a completed action or state in the past, not the past continuous. Point out that *fishing* is a gerund and not the continuous tense.

Answers

1 past perfect   2 past simple   3 past continuous

C

- Have the students work individually to complete the paragraph with the past tense verbs. Point out that there is more than one possible answer for some blanks. Then check answers with the class. Ask the students to support and explain their reasons for choosing a particular tense using the descriptions of the functions.

Answers

1 happened
2 moved / had moved
3 was snowing
4 was blowing
5 had been
6 missed / was missing
7 had frozen
8 decided / had decided
9 were fishing
10 looked / were looking
11 started
12 noticed
13 had caught / was catching
14 applauded / were applauding
15 was laughing
16 helped

D

- Have the students read the instructions. Explain or elicit the meaning of *feel out of place* (to feel like you don't belong). You may wish to provide a model for the task by telling a story about a time when you felt out of place.
- Give the students time to make notes on the topic before forming groups for their discussion.

Extra: idioms and expressions

Introduce additional phrases to describe the feeling of being out of place: *to feel like a fish out of water, to stick out like a sore thumb, to feel like an oddball*. Put the students in groups for their discussions. Encourage them to ask follow-up questions to find out more about their group members' experiences. To conclude, ask for volunteers who are comfortable sharing their experiences with the class to do so. Ask them to share their feelings about the experiences and what helped them to feel better about the situation. Some students may feel sensitive about sharing this information, so only work with volunteers.

 Workbook p. 6, Section 4

Reading: for different purposes (p. 12)

Lead-in

Before the lesson, collect some samples of different types of reading texts, for example, a dictionary entry, a newspaper article, a blog post, a bus/train schedule, a textbook excerpt, a travel website, a novel. Ask the students to read the information in the skills panel. Show them the different reading texts you have brought and ask them why they would read each one, for example, to get information, to study for a test, etc. Explain that the idea is to think about the different purposes we have for reading and their effects on how we read.

Alternative

Put the students in small groups. Ask them to work together to write a list of all the different types of things they read in an average week. Then have the students discuss their purpose for reading a specific type of text. For example, you might read a travel website to find interesting places to visit, things to do near a place you plan to visit or places to stay and/or eat in a specific town or city. As a class, have one group name a type of text and share their purposes for reading it. Ask other groups to name additional purposes for reading that type of text.

A

- Put the students in pairs and ask them to read the purposes for reading. Give the students time to think of types of texts for each one. Ask them to think of at least three text types for each purpose.
- Elicit answers from the class. Ask the students if they can think of any other purposes we have for reading.

Possible answers

1 a novel, a story, a poem
2 an advertisement, a brochure, a catalogue, a (review) website
3 a newspaper, a website, a magazine
4 a textbook, an encyclopaedia, a website
5 a recipe book, a set of instructions, a manual

B

- Ask the students to look at the photo. Ask what they can guess about the woman and her situation.
- Ask the students to look at the text and identify what type of text it is. Ask them to choose the reasons why someone would read a text like this and point out that more than one reason is possible. Elicit the answers from the class.

Answers

1 review of a TV show   2 c, d

Extra: ways of reading

Preview the skill introduced in Unit 3, which introduces reading strategies (skimming, scanning, etc) for different types of texts. Ask the students to think about different types of texts and how, depending on their purpose for reading, they might approach the text differently, i.e. whether they would read a text more slowly to get a general understanding or quickly for specific points of information, how much attention they would pay to details, etc. Ask the students to describe how they might read a newspaper article, a reading assignment for a history class, a restaurant menu, a train timetable, etc.

Culture note

Reading habits among British adults have changed since the introduction of electronic books. According to a 2013 study:
Nearly a fifth (18%) never read physical books, and 71% never read e-books. A fifth (20%) never buy physical books at all (either in a shop or online). Over half (56%) of the people who took part in the survey think that the internet and e-readers will replace books in the next 20 years; the proportion with this view rises to 64% of 18 to 30 year-olds. Twenty-seven per cent prefer the internet and social media to reading books, rising to 56% among 18 to 30 year-olds. Forty-five per cent prefer television and DVDs to reading.
http://www.booktrust.org.uk/usr/library/documents/main/1576-booktrust-reading-habits-report-final.pdf

Extra: class discussion

Ask the class how they think the internet has changed the way people read. Elicit ideas such as shorter attention spans, more distractions, easier to find information. Draw a two-column table on the board with a plus and minus heading, then write their ideas in the correct column according to whether they are positive or negative. Ask how they think the way people read in the future will change.

C

- Give the students time to read the article and then work individually to answer the questions.
- Have the students compare answers in pairs. Finally, ask them to point out to each other the information in the text that gave them the answer.

Answers

1 b   2 b   3 a   4 a

Extra: vocabulary expansion

Highlight some of the challenging vocabulary from the reading text: *clash of cultures* (communication problems between people from different cultures), *nomadic* (moving from place to place), *clumsy* (said in a way that isn't well thought-out and might upset someone), *anonymous* (when someone's name is not known), *conservative* (not willing to accept change), *insight* (a chance to understand something or learn more about it). Write the words on the board before the students read. Encourage them to try to guess the meanings from the context.

Extra: past tense review

Have the students work in pairs to find and underline the examples of the past tense verbs they learned in the grammar section and discuss why they might have been used.

▶ Workbook pp. 4–5, Section 1

D

- Ask the students to brainstorm words with the root *sens-* or *sense*. Write their ideas on the board.
- Ask the students to read the list on the board and try to elicit a general meaning for the root. Ask what underlying meanings the words have in common (related to feeling or feelings, or having a clear meaning). If the students are unable to deduce the meaning yet, do not tell them as they should be able to do so after they complete the exercise.
- Give the students time to underline the words in the text and complete the exercise.
- Have the students compare answers in pairs. Then check the answers with the class.

Answers

1 make sense of 2 sense 3 sense of humour
4 sensitive 5 sensible 6 sensitive
7 common sense

Extra: word family table

Introduce the concept of word families – different word forms (and parts of speech) that are based on the same root. Draw a word family table on the board. Have the students copy the table and complete it with as many *sense* words as they can.

Noun	Verb	Adjective	Adverb
sense	sense	sensitive	sensitively
sensitivity	resent	insensitive	sensibly
nonsense		sensory	
resentment		sensible	

E
- Give the students time to read the questions and make notes for their discussion.
- Put the students in groups to discuss the questions.
- Have the groups choose a facilitator to make sure all members participate equally and that everyone answers each of the questions.

 Workbook p. 7, Section 5

Pronunciation: emphatic *do/did* for contrast (p. 13)

A 🎧 1.04
- See the Student's Book for the **audioscript**.
- Have the students read the two conversations. Point out the words in italics and ask them why they think these words are stressed.
- Play the audio once and have the students listen. Then play it a second time and have the students repeat the second line of each conversation.
- Elicit or explain the reason behind the use of emphatic *do/did* (to emphasise specific or correct information).

B 🎧 1.05
- See the Student's Book for the **audioscript**.
- Play the audio and have the students listen and notice the emphatic *do/did*.
- Put the students in pairs to practise the conversation. Then have them practise the conversations in Ex. A. If they are finding the word stress difficult, encourage them to exaggerate, saying the *do/did* louder and longer until they feel more at ease.

Grammar: *would, used to, be + always, + -ing* (p. 14)

A
- Tell the students they are going to read an excerpt from a magazine article about family memories.
- Ask the students to read the magazine article silently and then elicit responses to the questions.

Answers
Louise. Her sister used to try on her clothes without permission and leave them on the floor.

NOTICE!
- Direct the students' attention to the **Notice!** box.
- Have them find and underline all the examples of *always* and *never* in the text.
- After checking answers as a class, ask the students to tell you the purpose of the structure with *always* and *never* (to describe past habits or routine activities).

Answer
They are used with *used to*, *would*, the past continuous and the present continuous.

B
Form
- Ask the students to read the article again, paying attention to the use of *always* and *never*.
- Have the students work individually to complete the table with examples of each form in the text.
- Call on students to write the examples on the board.
- **Highlight** the placement of *always* and *never*. Elicit that the adverb follows *would* and *be* in the continuous; however, it precedes the phrase *used to*.

Answers
1 He would never say he was too tired. / … she would leave my nice clothes all over the floor
2 My dad always used to throw a cricket ball for me … / I used to get annoyed with her …
3 My little sister was always sneaking into my room …
4 … we're always borrowing each other's clothes!

Function
- Give the students time to read the statements and write the correct structures.
- Check the answers with the class.
- **Highlight** the fact that both *would* and *used to* can be used for repeated events in the past. However, only *used to* can be used for non-repeated events in the past.
- Direct the students' attention to the information in the **What's right?** box. Have students work in pairs to discuss which sentence is correct.
- Elicit that the first sentence is correct and that adverbs of frequency (*always, often, sometimes, never*) come between the auxiliary and the main verb.

6

> **Answers**
> 1 a, b 2 c

C
- Give the students time to complete the activity individually. Point out that more than one answer is possible in some cases.
- Have the students compare answers in pairs before checking the answers with the class.

> **Answers**
> 1 used to / would ask / was always asking
> 2 was, making / would, make / used to, make
> 3 would, get
> 4 used to / would carry
> 5 used to / would hide
> 6 used to / would cry
> 7 used to / would feel
> 8 asking

> ### Extra: grammar practice
> Have the students imagine themselves at the age of ten. What things did they do that were annoying to others? In pairs, have students tell each other how they were annoying to their brothers, sisters, etc. (*I would always take my sister's favourite book without asking her. She was always yelling at me to give it back!*) Invite volunteers to share their ideas with the class, in a lighthearted and fun way.

D
- Give the students time to read the instructions. Have the class brainstorm some typical habits that annoy other family members. Write their ideas on the board.
- To help the students get started, you may wish to provide a model by sharing a story of your own about a family member's annoying habits.
- Give the students time to think about the topic and make notes about their own experience.
- Put the students in groups for their discussion.
- When the groups have finished, call on individual students to share their responses with the class.

Alternative
Instead of a group discussion, have the students work individually to write a paragraph about a family memory or a family member's annoying habits. This can be done in class or as homework.

 Workbook p. 7, Section 6

Writing: contributing to a question-and-answer page (p. 15)

Lead-in
Ask the students if they are familiar with any question-and-answer websites. If possible, use class computers or the students' tablets to show a few examples, like Ask.com or Yahoo Answers. Ask the students to share if/how they have used question-and-answer sites in the past, what kinds of questions they have asked or what answers they have submitted.

A
- Write the words *peer* (someone who is of the same age or social class as another person) and *pressure* (an attempt to persuade or make someone do something) on the board separately. Elicit a definition for each word. Then ask the students what they think the phrase *peer pressure* means. Ask them to think about this as they read the website posts.
- Have the students read the website posts silently. Then elicit the answer to the question.

> **Answer**
> *Peer pressure* is the influence that other people of your own age or social class have on the way you behave or dress.

> ### Extra: discussion
> Put the students in pairs to summarise the people's interaction on the website. Write questions on the board to guide their discussion.
> *What problem is Gina expressing? How is she feeling?*
> *What helps her feel better?*
> *Does Maura share Gina's opinion?*
> *What experience does Len have with peer pressure?*
> *What opinion does Gary give about peer pressure?*
> *What does Aran want to know?*

B
- Ask the students to reread Aran's post and summarise his comment (peer pressure in his culture is sometimes positive, not always negative). With the whole class, brainstorm different contexts or situations when people might experience peer pressure, for example, in one's family, with a group of friends, at school, at work, in an organised social group like a sports team, etc.
- Give the students time individually to brainstorm examples of different types of peer pressure, both positive and negative, that they are familiar with.
- Direct the students' attention to the examples in the **How to say it** box, and encourage them to use the expressions in their discussion.
- Put the students in groups to share their ideas. Have groups choose a person to write down the group's examples of peer pressure in two columns: positive and negative.
- Ask for a volunteer from each group to present the group's lists.

Who do you think you are? UNIT 1

- Lead a whole-class discussion about the general effects of peer pressure. Invite the students who are comfortable doing so to share their own experiences of peer pressure. Decide as a class whether peer pressure has more positive or negative effects.

C

- Have the students stay in their groups from Ex. B. Give them time individually to think of some ideas and make notes for how to respond to Aran.
- Give the groups time to write their responses. Remind them that it's OK to write in the casual style of a question-and-answer website.

D

- Have the students post their responses around the classroom on the wall. Alternatively, if they have access to an online discussion board, such as Moodle or Blackboard, they can post their responses there.
- Have the groups read one another's responses. Then discuss the similarities and differences between the various groups' responses.

Extra: homework

Have the students go to real online question-and-answer sites and find examples of people writing about experiences related to peer pressure and identity. Have them report on any interesting or surprising posts they read.

LifeSkills: understanding stereotypes (p. 16)

Step 1: Be aware of different kinds of stereotypes. (Ex. A, Ex. B)
Step 2: Consider the stereotypes you hold and what they are based on. (Ex. C)
Step 3: Think about the negative impact of certain stereotypes. (Ex. D, Ex. E)

Lead-in

Read the target skill aloud and invite the students to tell you why understanding stereotypes is important. Then **highlight** the three-step strategy to develop the skill of *understanding stereotypes*.

Elicit a definition for *stereotype* (an idea about what a person or group of people is like). Give or elicit stereotypical characteristics of a male secondary school / university student: doesn't like to wake up in the morning, sends a lot of text messages, wears jeans and a T-shirt, has a skateboard, etc. If possible, draw this stereotype on the board as you describe it, or have the students draw as you describe it.

Ask the students to think about examples of stereotypes they may have seen in films, on TV, etc. Ask the class to give you some social identity factors that are often stereotyped, for example, gender, age, nationality, region, occupation, etc.

A

- Give the students time to read the joke in the first paragraph silently. Answer any questions about unfamiliar vocabulary (*heaven*: a wonderful place you go to after you die; *hell*: a terrible place you go to after you die; *mechanic*: someone who works on cars).
- Have the students think about their response to the question. Then have them share their ideas in pairs.
- Finally, discuss the positive and negative nationality stereotypes with the class. Ask what the joke implies that each nationality is good and bad at. Ask the students what they think about the stereotypes mentioned in the article and where these ideas might have come from.

Answer

The joke implies that all English people are good police officers, that French people are good cooks, that Germans are good mechanics and Italians are good romantic poets. It also implies that English people are bad cooks, that French people are bad mechanics, that Germans make bad police officers and Swiss people are bad romantic poets.

B

- Take a class vote to find out how many students feel that nationality stereotypes are based on true characteristics and how many do not. Tally the numbers on the board. Ask for a few volunteers from each opinion to give reasons to support their opinion.
- Have the students read the title of the article. Explain the expression *to get the last laugh* (to be correct in the end).
- Give the students time to read the article silently. Then put them in pairs to summarise the main points of the article.
- Elicit the overall idea of the article (a study proved that national stereotypes are not based on true characteristics). Point out the number of 'winning' votes on the board.

C

- Put the students in groups to list stereotypes they have heard of about their culture.
- Write the following topic areas on the board to help them: *appearance, personality traits, occupations, behaviours*. Encourage the students to think about how members of their culture are commonly depicted on TV and in films, as these images are often stereotypical.
- Have the groups discuss questions 1 and 2 and report their ideas to the class.
- Discuss question 3 with the whole class. Ask the students why people should avoid believing in stereotypes.

Possible answer

3 People can learn as much as they can about other cultures, remembering to keep an open mind and to avoid adopting ideas about people or cultures based on what they see on TV or in films.

D
- Have the students look at the photos in the diagram and the example sentence.
- Put the students in pairs and have them write as many stereotypes as they can for each group.
- Point out the language in the **How to say it** box and encourage the students to use the phrases as they work with their partner.
- Combine pairs to form groups of four and have the students share their lists. Tell them to notice whether any traits are the same and where they think these ideas came from.

E
- Read the instructions aloud and have the students read the example silently.
- Put the students in pairs and have them first identify the negative stereotypes on their list. Then have them brainstorm the negative consequences.
- Elicit ideas from the class. Ask the students whether they feel they have encountered any consequences – positive or negative – based on their nationality.

F
- Ask the students to discuss the questions in groups.
- Ask the students to share their ideas as a class. Then lead a class discussion about what they have learned and whether they might feel they are better able to recognise and understand stereotypes in the domain of **Self and Society**.

Alternative
Have the students write a journal entry about what they have learned about stereotypes in this unit, and how they feel the skill might be useful to them in the future, including examples of situations when they might apply the skill.

REFLECT
- Discuss the question with the whole class. Ask the students to say what they feel are the most useful points they learned from this lesson, and how the skill of *understanding stereotypes* might be useful in the domains of **Work and Career** and **Study and Learning**, either now or in the future.
- Elicit the following ideas: *helping them understand others' (and their own) opinions and attitudes, helping them communicate with co-workers and classmates, helping them with intercultural experiences, etc.*

RESEARCH
- Go through the task and check that the students are clear about what they have to do.
- Suggest that the students research celebrities or famous people, such as film stars, pop singers or sportsmen and women. Depending on class time and availability of computers, this could be done in class rather than outside of class.
- Have them share their findings in class. Lead a class discussion about the stereotypes they researched.

Language wrap-up (p. 18)

There are several approaches that you can use for the Language wrap-up exercises:
- in class as a test
- in class as a review
- as homework

Class test
- Ask the students to do the exercises in test conditions and give a time limit (e.g. 20 minutes).
- Check answers with the class and deal with typical errors or problems.

Class review
- If you decide to do the exercises in class, you can approach the Language wrap-up as a two-step review. First, ask the students to do the Vocabulary section individually. When they finish, ask them to check their answers carefully. Then put them in pairs to compare answers and discuss any differences.
- You can then apply the same procedure to the Grammar section.
- Self- and peer-correction are two excellent ways of developing learner independence and creating a cooperative learning environment.

Homework
- If you give the exercises for homework, you can ask the students to do them in test conditions, i.e. without referring to the language they covered in the unit, their notes, the Grammar reference section, dictionaries, etc.
- Give them a time limit (e.g. 20 minutes).
- Check answers with the class in the next lesson and deal with typical errors or problems.
- The scoring system has been designed to give the students an idea of the progress they are making. Each section has a total score of 10 or 12, depending on the complexity of the language covered and the nature of the exercises. Whichever approach you take to the Language wrap-up, after checking the answers to each section ask the students to write their score. If they have a score lower than 8 (out of 10) or 10 (out of 12), direct them to the appropriate sections of the unit and encourage them to read them again for homework. After that, ask the students to complete the exercise(s) again at home.

Alternatives
- With any of the approaches above, you can assist the students by looking at the exercises with them before they start and discussing how they should go about them. For example, if they have to fill in the blanks in a text, encourage them to read through the whole text first to get an idea of the general meaning of it. If they have to choose the correct option to complete a sentence, encourage them to make sure they read the whole sentence first to understand the context.
- You can also use the Language wrap-up to review the material in the unit with the class and work on the exercises together as a class activity. In this case, you can ask the

students, for example, to look back at the appropriate Grammar section in the unit and review the main points to clarify any misunderstandings before they begin an exercise. Similarly, you can ask the students to first work in pairs to check the meanings of words to be used in fill-in-the-blanks exercises in the Vocabulary section.
- Note that the more assistance you give the students, the higher the score you should expect them to get when they do the exercises.

1 Vocabulary

A
- Ask the students to read the conversation for general understanding and to gain an idea of the context before filling in the blanks with the words from the box. Remind them that each blank is worth one point.
- Check the answers with the class by calling on individual students to read the lines of the conversation aloud.

B
- Remind the students to use the context of each sentence and the whole conversation to help them choose the correct words.
- Give them time to complete the task individually. Then have them compare answers in pairs.
- Check the answers by calling on pairs to read lines of the conversation, saying the correct answers.

2 Grammar
- Check that the students understand the task: point out that they will choose the correct verb form to complete the text.
- Ask the students to read the whole text through first before completing the exercise. Encourage them to say each sentence silently to themselves before deciding on their answers.

Writing workshop: writing an article (p. 19)

A
- Have the students read the title of the article. Elicit the meaning of *culture shock* (the nervous or confused feeling that people sometimes get when they arrive in a place that has a very different culture from their own). Then ask the students to predict what kind of advice the writer will give.
- Give the students time to read the article. Answer any questions about unfamiliar vocabulary.
- Have the students write a few sentences in their own words to explain what the article is about.

Answer
The writer says that you should not take things seriously and realise that when you come across stereotypes, it's actually your opportunity to correct those stereotypes. The writer also says that you should be prepared to ask questions and not be scared of making mistakes. You should be open and try not to worry about taking on a new identity.

Extra: Discussion
Before the individual writing, lead the class in a group discussion about the article. Ask students questions to elicit specific information and write their answers on the board. Have volunteers summarise orally each of the suggestions that the author makes.

B
- Give the students time to read the styles/devices.
- Have the students complete the task individually and then compare answers in pairs. Encourage them to give specific examples from the article to illustrate the use of the devices.
- Lead a whole-class discussion about the possible reasons why the writer chose to apply each of the devices, e.g. to appeal to a young audience (university students), to get the reader's attention and generate interest in the article, etc.

Answers
1 T 2 T 3 T

C
- Have the students read the instructions. Explain that they are going to write an article like the one in Ex. A, giving advice to people who are going to study or work overseas. But first they will make notes.
- Elicit contexts or situations in which a newcomer to a country might experience culture shock, for example, with their host family, at school or work, with housing, transportation, eating, shopping, meeting people, etc. Encourage the students to think of their own experiences, if applicable.
- Give the students time to make notes. Remind them to provide advice for each problem.

D
- Give the students time to write their article in class or for homework. Remind them to write about 200 words and to follow their notes.
- Encourage the students to use new language and structures from the unit in their writing. Award an extra mark or marks for including the verb tenses or vocabulary from the unit.

Extra: grammar practice
Have the students write sentences using past tense verbs. Encourage them to use the context of culture shock to write four sentences using the simple past tense, the past tense with *did* for emphasis, the past continuous and the past perfect.

How are you doing?
- Ask the students to read the statements and tick the ones they believe are true.
- Ask them to discuss their article with another student in the class and identify things they could improve on next time.

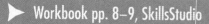 Workbook pp. 8–9, SkillsStudio

UNIT 2 GLOBAL VIEWS

The expression *to have a global view of something* means that you consider all aspects of it in order to formulate that view. In the title of this unit, *global views* can either refer to this meaning or to more literal meanings, namely *opinions of the world* or *opinions from around the world*.

Unit plan

Unit opener	(p. 20)	20 min.
1 **Listening:** understanding discourse markers (fillers)	(p. 22)	30 min.
• Vocabulary: globalisation		15 min.
2 **Grammar:** verbs with stative and dynamic uses	(p. 23)	40 min.
3 **Speaking:** talking about social media	(p. 24)	30 min.
4 **Pronunciation:** voiced and voiceless consonant sounds	(p. 24)	15 min.
5 **Grammar:** repeated and double comparatives	(p. 25)	40 min.
6 **Reading:** a magazine article	(p. 26)	30 min.
• Vocabulary: verbs for taking social action		15 min.
7 **Writing:** a formal email	(p. 27)	30 min.
LifeSkills: understanding internet search terms (Study and Learning)	(p. 28)	50 min.
• Optional downloadable *LifeSkills* lesson (Work and Career)		50 min.
• Optional downloadable *LifeSkills* lesson (Self and Society)		50 min.
Language wrap-up	(p. 30)	20 min.
Speaking workshop	(p. 31)	30 min.
Video and downloadable video worksheet		45 min.

Unit opener (p. 20)

Lead-in

Ask the students to look at the unit title and the photos and to predict what the unit will be about. Ask what the term *globalisation* means (that the world is becoming more integrated since products, ideas and cultures are being shared more easily due to improvements in transportation, technology and communication methods). Direct the students' attention to the points in the unit objectives box and go through the information with them. To get your students to think about the skills being developed in this unit, ask them to look at the questions in the cogs.

Listening: discourse markers

- Ask the students the questions and give them time to talk with a partner. Extend the discussion by asking the students for examples that they have noticed when listening to people speak English.

Writing: a formal email

- Survey the class to see how many students use email and how frequently. Ask the questions and give the students time to talk with a partner. Elicit answers from the students and create a list on the board.

LifeSkills: understanding internet search terms

- Ask the students if they agree that the internet provides huge amounts of information on every topic. Ask volunteers to share topics they have searched for on the internet. Put the students in small groups to list effective ways they have found to search for information.

Common European Framework: unit map

Unit 2	Competence developed	CEF Reference (B2 competences)
Listening	can understand informal discourse markers	Table 1; Table 2; Sections 4.4.2.1; 4.4.3.1; 4.4.3.5; 4.5.2.2; 5.2.3.1
Grammar	can use and understand verbs with stative and dynamic uses	Table 1; Table 2; Sections 5.2.1.2; 6.4.7.7; 6.4.7.8
Speaking	can talk about social media	Table 1; Table 2; Sections 4.4.1.1; 4.4.3.1; 4.4.3.5; 4.5.2.1; 5.2.1.1; 5.2.1.2; 5.2.3.2
Pronunciation	can correctly pronounce voiced and voiceless consonants	Section 5.2.1.4
Grammar	can use and understand repeated and double comparatives	Table 1; Table 2; Sections 5.2.1.2; 6.4.7.7; 6.4.7.8 Section 5.2.1.2
Reading	can understand a magazine article	Table 1; Table 2; Sections 4.4.2.2; 4.4.2.4; 4.5.2.2
Writing	can write a formal email	Table 1; Table 2; Sections 4.4.1.2; 4.4.3.2; 4.4.3.4; 4.5.2.1; 5.2.1.1; 5.2.1.2; 5.2.1.6; 5.2.2.2; 5.2.2.4; 5.2.3.2

Global views UNIT 2

A

- Put the students in pairs. Ask them to look at the photos and captions. Check that the students understand the difference between *migration* (the process of going to another place or country, often in order to find work) and *immigration* (the process in which people enter a country in order to live there permanently). Ask the students if they have any personal experience of any of the activities pictured (stock markets, border control, online communication). Give them time to discuss the questions.
- Listen to the students' ideas as a class. Then ask them if they are familiar with the effects of globalisation on any other countries. Accept any reasonable answers. Remind them that everyone may have different opinions.

Alternative

If the students find it difficult to answer the questions, write some or all of these other questions on the board to help them.

What companies do you think people invest in? Are they companies in your own country or in another country?

Are there a lot of tourists that visit your country? Are there many international people who relocate to live in your country? Where do they come from? What country would you like to visit or live in?

How do you communicate with your friends who live in other cities and countries? What language do you use?

Culture note

Stock exchanges, where stocks are listed and traded, are located in many countries around the world. Some of the major stock exchanges include the New York Stock Exchange, the London Stock Exchange and the Nikkei in Tokyo.

Culture note

Skype enables its users to communicate in a variety of ways using audio, video and instant messaging. At peak times, there are more than 40 million Skype users online.
Research shows that worldwide Skype usage is now equivalent to over one-third of all international phone traffic, with users spending approximately two billion minutes a day connecting over the network.

B

- Have the students work in groups. Ask them to list as many aspects and consequences of globalisation as they can and to offer reasons for their answers.
- Listen to their ideas as a class. Note that there is no single answer to the questions. The aim is to encourage critical thinking and for the students to have the opportunity to express and explain their ideas.

Possible answers

Other aspects of globalisation might include business relocation, call centres located in other countries, waste disposal (especially technology) and cheaper products sold on global markets.
Positive and negative consequences might include:
positive: increased employment and job opportunities in poor countries, more opportunities to learn about other cultures, increased media coverage of world events, more rapid responses to natural disasters;
negative: increased unemployment in developed countries, exploitation of workers in developing countries, less job security, multinational companies taking over local industries, the spread of fast-food chains leading to increased consumption of fast food.

Listening: understanding discourse markers (p. 22)

Lead-in

Ask the students if it is ever difficult for them to think of what words to say when they speak in their native language and in English. Continue the discussion by asking them what they do when they need to think before they speak.

Ask the students to read the information in the skills panel. Mention that fillers like these are common in English. Point out that discourse markers are words or phrases that do not change the meaning of the sentence. Ask them to list any others they can think of. Write their answers on the board. Elicit answers such as *oh, now, then, I know what you mean, but* and *I mean*.

A 1.06

- See the Student's Book for a partial **audioscript** and p. 122 for a complete version.
- Give the students time to read the five sentences. Tell them that they will hear five speakers give their opinions about globalisation. Ask them to write the missing discourse markers that they hear.
- Play the audio once and check progress. If necessary, play the audio one more time but not more than that.
- When you check the answers, you may want to remind the students of the fact that although these phrases do not really mean very much, they are used as follows: *kind of* – to make an opinion less strong (e.g. *It's kind of sad that …*); *you know what I mean* – to check that the listener is following; *you know* and *like* – to create time to think; *I mean* – to add information or explain something we've said.

Answers

1 I mean   2 like   3 You know   4 kind of   5 well

B

- Draw attention to the illustration and make sure the students understand that it represents globalisation. Check that the students understand the task. Play the audio again and then ask them if they have matched all the answers. If not, play the audio one more time.
- When you check the answers, ask if they can determine which speakers are broadly positive (1, 5) and which are negative (2, 3, 4).

Answers

1 a 2 e 3 c 4 b 5 d

Extra: agreeing and disagreeing

Extend Ex. B by asking the students if they agree or disagree with the speakers. Ask them to support their answers by explaining why they agree or disagree.

 Workbook p. 10, Section 1

C

- Have the students read the sentences silently and notice the words in bold. Ask them to match each word or phrase with the correct definition, a or b.
- Check the answers as a class.

Answers

1 a 2 a 3 b 4 a 5 b 6 a

Extra: parts of speech

Ask the students to identify the part of speech of each of the vocabulary words or phrases in Ex. C (*economic growth*: noun; *profits*: noun; *multinational*: adjective; *regional*: adjective; *dominate*: verb; *facilitates*: verb). Ask them to use each word in another sentence. You could also elicit other related parts of speech, e.g. *profits – profitable* (adjective) and ask the students for example sentences using these.

D

- Put the students in pairs to discuss how much they agree or disagree with each of the statements in Ex. C. Encourage them to explain their answers.
- If time allows, ask each pair to share their answers for one of the six statements in Ex. C with the class and explain why they agreed or disagreed.

Extra: homework

Ask the students to choose one of the statements from Ex. C and write a paragraph giving their own opinion. Explain that they should include at least two reasons with examples.

 Workbook pp. 10–11, Section 2

Grammar: verbs with stative and dynamic uses (p. 23)

Lead-in

Ask the students if they know any of the multinational companies in the photo, e.g. 7-Eleven, KFC. Ask them to work in pairs and think of examples of other multinational companies. Listen to their ideas as a class (e.g. McDonald's, Sony, IBM, Dell, American Express, etc).

A

- Have the students read the question first. Then ask them to read the text and identify the positive aspects of multinational companies.
- Ask them if the article mentions only positive aspects. (No, it also mentions that some people think that multinationals take money out of developing countries, and it implies that they hurt smaller, local companies.)
- Ask the students if they agree with the opinions expressed in the article.

Answer

Multinationals can offer varied job opportunities, especially for young people.

NOTICE!

- Direct the students' attention to the *Notice!* box.
- Explain that there are examples of both simple and continuous verb forms in the article. Give the students time to underline all the simple forms, circle the continuous forms of the some verbs and then answer the question.
- After checking the answers as a class, explain that simple verb forms are often used to describe unchanging or repeated actions; they are permanent or general truths. Explain that continuous verb forms often describe people's behaviour or actions; they are continuous or ongoing.

Answers

Simple: see; have; offer, showed; think; take; looks, are
Continuous: are having; are thinking
Progressive form is dynamic (refers to action/activity), simple form is stative (refers to state or condition)

B

Form & Function

- Direct the students' attention to the language box. After they have read the information, check that they understand the difference between stative and dynamic verbs. Elicit other examples of stative verbs, e.g. *believe, seem*. Then check that the students understand that the verbs they circled in the text and the other verbs in the table can be both stative and dynamic, with different meanings, and can therefore be used in the continuous form.
- Point out the examples for the verb *be* in the table and make sure they understand the difference in meaning (as explained in the parentheses).

Global views | **UNIT 2** | **13**

- Ask the students to read the text again and complete the table using examples from the text.
- Check the answers with the class. Explain the fact that *think* as a stative verb means *have an opinion* (e.g. *I think that's true*), while *think* as a dynamic verb means either *plan* (e.g. *I'm thinking about getting a haircut*) or *consider facts carefully* (e.g. *Be quiet! I'm thinking*).
- Point out that the dynamic use of *have* is often in set phrases, e.g. *I'm having a good time; This is having a major effect on the economy.*
- Explain that *seeing someone* in the dynamic example means *dating*.

Answers

1 They often have branches in many countries …
2 These companies are having a major effect on emerging economies …
3 you see signs …
4 some people think that …
5 more young people than ever are thinking of applying for jobs …

C

- Direct the students' attention to the **What's right?** box. Elicit that the first sentence is incorrect because *be* is used in its stative sense, and so it needs to be in the simple form, not the continuous.
- Ask the students to complete the exercise individually.
- Check the answers with the class. Ask the students to explain why each verb is stative or dynamic.

Answers

1 am thinking   2 don't have   3 are being
4 see   5 do you think 6 are
7 Are they seeing

D

- Put the students in pairs and ask them to choose one of the roles.
- Ask them to read the information from the box for their role. Give them two or three minutes to work individually, thinking of some ideas and making some notes.
- Remind them to try to use the four verbs at least once in their discussion. Tell them to pay attention to whether the verbs should be stative or dynamic.
- Ask a few pairs to perform their roleplays for the class.

Extra: homework

Ask the students to write a short paragraph about the advantages and disadvantages of multinational corporations. Ask them to use some of the verbs *be*, *have*, *see* and *think* in their paragraph and to use the stative and dynamic form correctly.

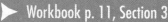 Workbook p. 11, Section 3

Speaking: talking about social media (p. 24)

Lead-in

Before the students open their books, survey them to see how they feel when they read or hear a word they do not know and what they do to try to find the definition. Ask the students how they can find definitions of a word (e.g. *blog*) on the internet. Elicit different possibilities, e.g. *using an online dictionary; typing the question 'What does blog mean?' into a search engine; typing the words 'definition of blog' into a search engine*, etc.

A

- Ask the students to read the definition of *social media*.
- Elicit different examples of social media, e.g. Facebook, Twitter, LinkedIn, Flickr, YouTube, Foursquare, etc. and write them on the board. Ask the students to identify which social media they use from the list on the board. Tally the answers.

B 1.07

- See p. 122 for the **audioscript**.
- Tell the students they will hear three people talking about their use of social media.
- Make sure the students understand the task (to fill in the social media, if any, that the people use and to write the advantages/disadvantages they mention).
- Play the audio once. The students may find this challenging. If necessary, play the audio again before checking the answers with the class.

Answers

Speaker 1: Twitter
<u>Advantage</u>/Disadvantage: can send and receive lots of short messages
Speaker 2: Flickr
<u>Advantage</u>/Disadvantage: can share photos and information with friends
Speaker 3: doesn't use social media
Advantage/<u>Disadvantage</u>: people/companies can get hold of your personal information

C

- Refer to the list of social media on the board and ask the students to choose one to use in Ex. C. Tell the students that if they don't use any of them, they can talk about any media they use (email, texting, etc). Ask them to use the headings in the table to help them make notes about the type of media they use. Give them time to make notes.

D

- Put the students in pairs. Tell them to take turns being Student A and Student B. Explain that the students should talk about the form of social media they made notes about for about one and a half minutes. While one student talks, the other should listen and take notes but should not interrupt or ask questions.

- Ask the students to use their notes to tell the whole class about their partner's use of one type of social media.

Pronunciation: voiced and voiceless consonant sounds (p. 24)

A 🎧 1.08

- See the Student's Book for the **audioscript** – the words in the list.
- Ask the students to listen to the audio and repeat each pair of words with one hand on their throat and the other a few inches in front of their mouth. Explain that the vibration happens when the vocal cords move, and the puff of air happens when they do not. Point out that this puff of air is called *aspiration*.
- Elicit the difference between a voiced consonant and a voiceless one, e.g. *vast* and *fast*. With a voiced consonant, the vocal chords vibrate and with a voiceless consonant they do not vibrate, so the sound is heard through aspiration only.

B 🎧 1.09

- See p. 122 for the **audioscript**.
- Make sure the students understand the task (to choose the word they hear in each pair in Ex. A).
- Play the audio once. Repeat only if necessary. Check the answers with the class.

> **Answers**
> 1 vast 2 do 3 pace 4 drain 5 coal

C

- Put the students in pairs to take turns saying one word from each pair of words. Ask them to pronounce it correctly so that their partner can identify the word correctly.
- Circulate to help as needed.

> **Extra: voiced and voiceless consonant sounds**
>
> In pairs, challenge the students to add to the list of words in Ex. A. Then have Student A say a word from one column and Student B say the matching pair (e.g. Student A: *fine*; Student B: *vine*). Have the students take turns. Monitor, listening for correct pronunciation.

> **Extra: homework**
>
> For homework, ask the students to write one sentence using each of the words in Ex. A. In class the following day, have the students take turns reading a sentence. Their partner identifies the word from Ex. A and tells whether it has a voiced or voiceless consonant sound.

Grammar: repeated and double comparatives (p. 25)

Lead-in

Ask the students which communication methods they consider to be fast (e.g. instant messaging) and which they think are slow (e.g. post). Continue the discussion by asking which they prefer and encourage them to give a reason. Explain that this section is about comparing things, such as fast methods of communication with slow methods, and that they will learn the grammatical way to do this.

A

- Ask the students to read the question first. Then ask them to read the two opinions and decide which person they agree with more. Ask them to support their answer with reasons.
- Encourage them to discuss their opinions and reasons as a class.

> **NOTICE!**
>
> - Direct the students' attention to the **Notice!** box.
> - Ask the students to look at the underlined phrase and think about why the word *faster* is repeated. Ask them if the action is finished or if it is continuing.
>
> **Answer**
>
> *Faster and faster* indicates that change is continuing to happen. *Faster* is repeated for emphasis.

B

Form & Function

- Ask the students to read the text in Ex. A again, paying attention to the comparative forms.
- Present the information in the table. Ensure that the students understand the uses and examples. You could give them another example or two (not from Ex. A), such as *This class is getting more and more exciting*; *The less we litter, the less polluted the world will be*. Then ask them to complete the table individually using examples from the text.
- Check the answers. Remind the students that short adjectives (usually one syllable but sometimes two, e.g. *funny*) form their comparatives by adding *-er*, while multi-syllable adjectives use *more* and do not add *-er*.
- Point out the form of double comparatives and in particular the word order, e.g. *The closer people become, the more peaceful the world is*. Draw the students' attention to *the* and explain that it comes before the comparative.
- Ask the students to look at the language box. Point out that *more* and *less* can be used with nouns, with nouns + a verb phrase or used on their own. **Highlight** the use of the definite article *the*.
- Show the students that different combinations are possible, e.g. *The more exercise you do, the healthier you will be*; *The more I study, the more I learn*; *The less I watch TV, the more I miss it*.

Global views **UNIT 2** **15**

- Direct the students' attention to the **What's right?** box. Explain that it is easy to make mistakes when using comparatives and elicit the reason why the second sentence is incorrect (the adjective cannot be used in the first instance with *more and more*).

Answers
1 faster and faster
2 more and more popular
3 The more, the more peaceful
4 the faster, the less interesting

C
- Point out that the students need to decide if they need a double comparative or a repeated comparative to complete the sentences.
- Ask them to work individually and then to compare their answers in pairs. Tell them to check each other's spelling as well as the forms of the comparative.
- When you check the answers with the class, note that more than one answer may be possible in some cases, depending on your opinion.

Answers
1 more and more sympathetic
2 smaller and smaller
3 The more, more interested
4 The more, the funnier
5 The more, the confusing
6 The faster, the easier

D
- Give the students two or three minutes to work individually and complete the sentences. Tell them to write their sentences about globalisation and social media.
- Put them in pairs and ask them to compare their ideas.
- Listen to some of their ideas with the whole class. Correct any errors in the use of repeated and double comparatives.

Extra: repeated and double comparatives
Ask the students to use the sentence beginnings in Ex. D to write more sentences. Tell them that this time, they can use different topics and write about anything they choose.

▶ Workbook p. 12, Section 4

Reading: a magazine article (p. 26)

Lead-in
Write the phrase *going local* on the board. Ask the students if they know what this means. Elicit answers such as *using products and companies that are located in the community rather than from outside the local area*. Ask the students to name any businesses or markets that are specific to the local area. Draw a table with three columns on the board. Title the columns as 'Small local shop', 'Large department store' and 'Online'. Ask the students to brainstorm a list of retailers for each category. Accept any reasonable answers. Continue the discussion by asking the students where they shop most often and which retailers they like best.

A
- Put the students in pairs to share their answers about where they prefer to go shopping and why. If time allows, make a list on the board of all the answers. Poll the class and tally how many students raise their hands for each answer. Ask the students to share the reasons for their preferences.
- Ask the students to read the article. Ask them to notice if any of their ideas are mentioned in the article.
- When the students have finished reading, ask them if any of their ideas were mentioned.

Culture note
A farmer's market is a place where farmers sell their produce directly to the buyers. There is a rich tradition of farmers markets in the UK and many have been happening over hundreds of years. They are usually held weekly or monthly in an outdoor location. The aim of the market is to allow people to purchase products such as fruit, vegetables, dairy products and meat direct from their local farms. Some markets also include livestock (live animals) and traditional craft products.

B
- Remind the students that reading for information is an important part of studying. Explain that they can scan the text for the answers. Remind them or point out that scanning is reading something in order to find particular information. Give them time to work on the comprehension questions individually.
- Put the students in pairs to compare their answers before checking the answers as a class.

Possible answers
1 customers can support local farmers and meet local growers/producers; customers feel part of the community; farm food is fresher; it supports local businesses; customers can learn more about the products they buy; it's a more enjoyable experience
2 the prices are lower; there's a greater variety/choice
3 The writer is for 'going local'. Most of the article is about why you should shop locally, and there is only one sentence about shopping in larger supermarkets.

C
- Show the students the list of vocabulary words. Explain that these are all social action verbs, but they can also be used in other contexts as well.
- Define *synonym* (a word that has the same meaning as another word). Give the students time to find the synonyms for the verbs in the article.

- Put the students in pairs to compare their answers and then check the answers as a class.

Answers
1 support 2 value 3 generate 4 campaign
5 participate 6 sustain 7 boost 8 generate

D
- Give the students time to complete each question individually.
- Put the students in pairs to discuss the questions. Ask the pairs to share their answers with the class.
- Extend the discussion by asking them to think of three ways to help support the local economy. Ask groups to share their answers with the class.

Answers
1 sustain 2 generate 3 support 4 value

Extra: homework
Ask the students to choose one of the questions in Ex. D and write a short paragraph to answer it.

 Workbook p. 13, Section 5

Writing: a formal email (p. 27)

Lead-in
Give the students time to read the information in the skills panel. Ask the students how often they use email and who they usually use email with. Generate a discussion about topics people may write about in email.

A
- Explain that sometimes formal letters are still sent by regular post, but now many letters are sent via email. The form of these emails is different from normal, everyday email messages that are more informal. Point out that sometimes email may need to be formal, such as email from a bank or via inter-office communication. Remind the students they should check emails carefully before sending them to make sure they're clear and contain all the necessary information.
- Put the students in pairs to brainstorm a list of situations in which they would need to send a formal email. Elicit answers such as *to pass along information* or *to request information from someone they don't know*. Ask each pair to share their list with the class. Create a list on the board.

B
Ask the students to read the instructions and check that they understand the task. Give them time to read the emails. Then ask the students to decide individually which email is more formal and why. Elicit answers from the class.

Answers
The email from Kathy to Mr Scott is more formal.
The elements that give email a formal tone are: the use of complete sentences, the division into paragraphs and the use of correct punctuation.
The language that identifies the formal tone: *Could you please let us know which one you prefer*, as well as more formal words and phrases and indirect questions used to make polite requests.

C
- Put the students in pairs and ask them to first identify which of the greetings and closing expressions are formal, and then which are informal.
- When you check the answers, ask the students which of these greetings they have used and under what circumstances.

Answers
1 Formal 2 Informal 3 Informal 4 Informal
5 Informal 6 Formal

D
- Ask the students to read the information in the note and decide if the email should be formal or informal (formal). Have them work individually to write the email. Point out that we usually use Ms (pronounced /mɪz/) to address a woman, so they should begin with *Dear Ms Sinclair*.
- Ask them to read the formal email in Ex. B again to help them. Encourage them to use some of the expressions from that email in their own.
- Invite volunteers to read their email aloud to the whole class. Make sure they have used formal expressions as well as complete sentences.

Culture note
The use of the title Ms for women was introduced in the 1970s when women began to object to the distinction between married women (Mrs) and unmarried women (Miss) when the title for men (Mr) had no such distinction. Nowadays, though Mrs and Miss are still used, in business correspondence the most commonly accepted form of address is Ms.

In the UK, the title Dr is used for men or women who have a PhD in any subject, or who are medical doctors, dentists or veterinarians.

Extra: homework
Ask the students to reply to the formal email in Ex. B, indicating which of the dates they would prefer and whether they could bring some photos with them or not. Tell them to write the email in a formal style using complete sentences, paragraph divisions and correct punctuation.

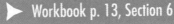 Workbook p. 13, Section 6

LifeSkills: understanding internet search terms (p. 28)

Step 1: Determine what information you need to find. (Ex. A, Ex. F)
Step 2: Choose effective search terms. (Ex. B, Ex. E, Ex. F)
Step 3: Evaluate search results and refine your search if necessary. (Ex. B, Ex. C, Ex. D, Ex. G)

Lead-in

Read the target skill aloud and invite the students to tell you what they think *understanding internet search terms* means (knowing the right words to type in to get the best results). Remind the students that writing essays is common in academic studies and that conducting research online can be useful. Ask the students what kinds of things they typically conduct internet searches for. Ask them as a whole class to brainstorm ideas about how to do searches efficiently and accurately.

Then **highlight** the three-step strategy to develop the skill of *understanding internet search terms*.

A

- Give the students time to read the essay topic.
- Brainstorm international fast-food chains if you feel the students need help with ideas.
- Have the students work individually to complete the task. You may want to let them discuss their answers in pairs before eliciting the answers from the class.

Possible answers

dates when the two chains were first set up in India; figures for the local economy (especially from cafés and restaurants) before and after the set-up of these chains

Culture note

India is one of the fastest growing economies in the world. The acronym BRICS is often used to refer to the five current major emerging economies – Brazil, Russia, India, China, South Africa.

B

- Put the students in pairs and ask them to discuss the advantages and disadvantages of these five search terms for finding the type of information they will need for the essay.
- Direct the students' attention to the examples in the **How to say it** box and encourage them to use the expressions when they discuss the search terms.
- When they have finished their discussion, listen to their ideas as a class.

Possible answers

fast food: Many search engines can handle this kind of natural English search. However, this search term may be too general and would probably return too many links, which are unlikely to contain specific information students will need to write the essay.
top fast-food companies in India: This may return useful results. The use of 'top fast-food companies' rather than specific names may help to avoid corporate websites.
non-Indian fast-food companies: This search term might generate too many results because it could lead to sites about any fast-food company in the world outside India. It would probably return links to corporate websites, which are unlikely to contain the information students are looking for.
fast-food effects in India: This would probably return results that discussed the effects of fast food generally in India and it could be a useful starting point.
effects on Indian economy of fast-food chains: This is probably the best search because it is likely to produce information that students could use for their essays.

C

- Have the students read the instructions and explain that search engines allow users to customise their searches. Customised searches usually generate better results with information that can be used for essays or other assignments.
- Put the students in pairs. Give them time to discuss what each of the searches means.
- Check the answers as a class.

Possible answers

fast-food restaurants in India: If you put in specific key words, without any refining elements, the search engine will look for each of the key terms in the phrase, so the results will be reasonably accurate. However, to produce even more relevant and specific results, you could put this whole phrase in quotation marks, which forces the search engine to look for the exact phrase.
India AND food AND industry: The search engine would search for all pages that contain all of these search terms. (Note: Many search engines do this automatically.)
McDonald's OR KFC India: This would return pages that contain the word *India* and contain either the word *McDonald's* or the word *KFC*.
India culture -celebrity: This would return all pages that contain the word *India* and the word *culture*, but would exclude all pages that contain the word *celebrity*.
India * industry: This would search for all phrases that have any word in the middle of the phrase, so it would return results such as India movie industry, India food industry, etc.

Alternative

Schedule time in the computer lab to let the students conduct the searches from Ex. B and Ex. C and discuss what they find. Alternatively, ask them to do this at home and report back.

D

- Put the students in groups to discuss the questions. Share ideas from your own experience. Then ask volunteers to share their stories with the class.

E

- Ask the students to look at the search-engine results and read the instructions.
- Remind them that search engines can provide many results in response to a keyword search, and that it is necessary to evaluate the results to determine which will provide the most useful information.
- Review the essay topic. Ask the students to read the results for this search of 'India globalisation'. Put them in pairs to discuss which ones they think will be most useful when writing the essay.
- Check the answers as a class.

Answers

Influence of globalisation on developing countries: This mentions globalisation, India and local culture. It looks as if it would be a useful, trustworthy site. However, it is possible that www.globalmonitor.com is not an independent, unbiased source, so some care would be necessary.
American fast food? No thanks!
This clearly links to a blog (www.blogmasterglobal.com/vijay). Although it is possible that the blog contains links to other, more useful material, this blog on its own is likely to be one person's opinion and should not be treated as a reliable source unless the information is checked against other websites.
IBC NEWS Fire strikes fast-food outlet, Delhi, India: This page looks as if it would be irrelevant to the search. It should probably be ignored.
India fast-food industry statistics:
This looks like the most useful result as it contains statistics and mentions international companies. Although www.india-food.in looks like a trustworthy site, care should still be taken and the source of the information should be checked.

F

- Explain that the students are now going to create a research plan to investigate the effects of globalisation on the economy of their own country. Ask them to choose one area of the local economy to focus on as their topic for research. If they are having problems thinking of a topic area, give them some suggestions (e.g. *tourism, the car industry, travel and infrastructure, finance,* etc).
- Elicit some common international search engines (e.g. *Google, Yahoo!*) and search engines commonly used in their country.
- Model the activity by filling out a sample plan on the board. Put the students in small groups and ask them to complete a research plan for their group.

G

- Ask each group to present their plan to the class. Encourage the students to make notes on any interesting ideas, and then give them some time to amend their plans if necessary.

H

- Ask the students to work in pairs to discuss the questions. Encourage them to think about the questions in relation to the domain of **Study and Learning** in particular.
- Combine the pairs to form groups of four and share their ideas. Then ask for feedback as a class and remind the students to give reasons and examples.

 REFLECT

- Discuss the question with the whole class. Ask the students to say what they feel are the most useful points they learned from this lesson, and how the skill of *understanding internet search terms* might be useful in the domains of **Work and Career** and **Self and Society**, either now or in the future.
- Elicit the following ideas: *finding a job, helping them advance in their career, finding, a place to live, learning more about their local area, finding places to shop locally,* etc.

 RESEARCH

- Go through the task and check that the students are clear about what they have to do.
- Encourage the students to complete an internet research plan for the essay topic given and bring it to the next lesson.
- Have them share their findings in class. Lead a class discussion about the idea that creating a research plan will be an effective tool when they have academic writing tasks.

Language wrap-up (p. 30)

For notes on how to approach the exercises in the Language wrap-up section, please see page 9.

1 Vocabulary

- Ask the students to read the whole paragraph for general understanding and to gain an idea of the context before filling in the blanks with the words or phrases from the box. Remind them that each blank is worth one point.

2 Grammar

- Check that the students understand the question: point out that they will be choosing the correct option to complete the conversation.
- Ask the students to read the whole conversation through first before completing the exercise. Encourage them to say each sentence silently to themselves before deciding on their answers.
- When checking the answers with the students, remind them that stative verbs refer to states or conditions that continue over a period of time, and that some are frequently used in the continuous or dynamic forms when they have certain meanings. Remind them of the form and function of repeated and double comparatives, and give examples such as *more and more connected, faster and faster* and *the more we understand, the more peaceful the world will be*.

Speaking workshop: describing a photo (p. 31)

Lead-in
Ask the students if they like to take photos, and extend the conversation by asking what they usually take photos of.

> **Alternative**
> Ask the students to bring in their favourite photo. Put the students in small groups to share their favourite photo and to explain to their group why it is their favourite.

A 🎧 1.10
- See p. 122 for the **audioscript**.
- Explain that description is an important concept in academic studies. Give examples of assignments such as writing a descriptive essay or giving a presentation describing an object.
- Tell the students they will listen to someone describing a photo. Ask them to take notes about the main points the speaker makes, using the given headings.
- Play the audio once and give the students time to write. Then play the audio again.
- Put the students in pairs to compare notes and then check the answers as a class.

> **Answers**
> Where is it? A café.
> Who are they? They are three young women. There are other people in the background.
> What are they doing? One woman is looking at her laptop. One is looking at her tablet. The other is on her mobile phone and looking at her tablet.
> What is unusual or interesting? They're sitting close together so they probably know each other, but they are very involved in their electronic devices and aren't looking at each other at all.

B
- Have the students read the list of points. Then play the audio again and ask the students to check the points the speaker mentions.
- Repeat the audio only if necessary.
- Check the answers as a class.

> **Answers**
> The speaker …
> describes the background
> describes the foreground
> describes the people and what they are doing
> describes the general setting and context
> makes an inference about the relationship between the people

C
- Explain that the students will now give their own descriptions. Encourage them to follow the same process as in Ex. A by first writing their own notes to answer the questions about the photo provided.
- Put the students in pairs to share their notes and ideas.

D
- Put the students in small groups. Have each student present a description of the photo to the members of their group. Each student should talk for about one minute.
- Remind the students that they should describe all the details, speak clearly and vary their tone of voice.

> **Extra: describing photos**
> Ask the students to choose one of the photos on p. 21 to describe. Have them use the notes in Ex. A to identify the main points they want to talk about. Then they take notes about the setting, the context, the people, and what the people are doing. When they are ready, the students describe the photo to a partner. The partner should look at p. 21, identify the photo and add any other details to complete the description.

> **Extra: group writing**
> Ask the students to look at the photo on p. 26. Point out that this photo contains a lot of people and details. In small groups, have the students take turns describing the setting, the context, the people and what the people are doing. Have the students choose a scribe to write down the ideas. Give the groups a few minutes to organise their ideas and write their descriptions. Then the groups take turns reading their descriptions to the rest of the class.

How are you doing?
- Ask the students to read the statements and tick the ones they believe are true.
- Ask them to discuss their description with a member of their group and identify things they could improve on next time.

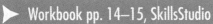 Workbook pp. 14–15, SkillsStudio

UNIT 3 FAME AND FORTUNE

The expression *fame and fortune* refers to the goal or dream that many people have at some time in their lives of becoming both famous and rich. For example, someone might say, 'She moved to London, looking for fame and fortune.'

Unit plan

Unit opener	(p. 32)	20 min.
1 **Grammar:** reported speech – modal verbs and past perfect	(p. 34)	40 min.
2 **Listening:** to a gossip columnist	(p. 35)	30 min.
• Vocabulary: ways to become famous		15 min.
3 **Reading:** for different purposes	(p. 36)	30 min.
• Vocabulary: guessing meaning from context		15 min.
4 **Writing:** a website post	(p. 37)	30 min.
5 **Pronunciation:** silent letters – consonants	(p. 37)	15 min.
6 **Grammar:** reported speech – optional back-shifting	(p. 38)	40 min.
7 **Speaking:** clarifying misunderstandings	(p. 39)	30 min.
LifeSkills: evaluating arguments (Work and Career)	(p. 40)	50 min.
• Optional downloadable *LifeSkills* lesson (Self and Society)		50 min.
• Optional downloadable *LifeSkills* lesson (Study and Learning)		50 min.
Language wrap-up	(p. 42)	15 min.
Writing workshop	(p. 43)	20 min.
Video and downloadable video worksheet		45 min.

Unit opener (p. 32)

Lead-in

Ask the students to look at the unit title and the photos, and to predict what the unit will be about. Elicit some reasons why a person might become famous (*they have a special talent or do something great*). Direct the students' attention to the points in the unit objectives box and go through the information with them. To get your students to think about the skills being developed in this unit, ask them to look at the questions in the cogs.

Reading: for different purposes
- Remind the students that they focused on some of the different purposes for reading in Unit 1. Review the idea that we read different types of texts in different ways and ask them why they think this is. Explain that in this unit, they will learn more about specific reading strategies they can apply when they are reading different types of texts, for example, skimming, scanning and reading for details.

Speaking: clarifying misunderstandings
- Ask the students to think about phrases they can use in English when someone misunderstands them. Explain that knowing these kinds of phrases can help them communicate better and avoid frustration.

LifeSkills: evaluating arguments
- Ask individual students to tell you about a situation when they tried to convince someone to agree with them, or persuade someone to do something, for example, asking a parent to buy them a new mobile phone. Ask what arguments they used to convince the person. Explain that in this unit they will learn the elements of a strong argument.

Common European Framework: unit map

Unit 3	Competence developed	CEF Reference (B2 competences)
Grammar	can use and understand modals and past perfect in reported speech	Table 1; Table 2; Sections 4.4.1.1; 4.4.3.1; 5.2.1.2; 6.4.7.7; 6.4.7.8
Listening	can understand a gossip columnist talking about celebrities	Table 1; Table 2; Sections 4.2.2.1; 4.4.3.1; 4.4.3.5; 4.5.2.2
Reading	can read for different purposes	Table 1; Table 2; Sections 4.4.2.2; 4.4.2.4; 4.5.2.2
Writing	can write a website post	Table 1; Table 2; Sections 4.4.1.2; 4.4.3.4; 4.5.2.1; 5.2.1.1; 5.2.1.2; 5.2.1.6
Pronunciation	can correctly pronounce words containing silent consonants	Section 5.2.1.4
Grammar	can correctly choose between past and present tenses in reported speech	Table 1; Table 2; Sections 4.4.1.1; 4.4.3.1; 5.2.1.2; 6.4.7.7; 6.4.7.8
Speaking	can clarify misunderstandings	Table 1; Table 2; Sections 4.4.1.1; 4.4.3.1; 4.4.3.5; 4.5.2.1

A

- Draw the students' attention to the photos and elicit what they think each person's profession is (writer, athlete, scientist, celebrity, politician, king/queen/president). Have the class think of a famous person to represent each photo. Elicit other categories of famous people not represented in the photos (artists, discoverers, military leaders, etc).
- Put the students in pairs and ask them to list five of the most famous people in the world. Stress that they should be people whose names everyone around the world would know. You may wish to allow the students to include both living and dead people, or limit them to only the living or only the dead.
- Encourage partners to discuss their choices and say why they think each person belongs on the list.
- Have the pairs share their lists with the class, explaining why they think the people are among the most famous people in the world. Note that this is an opportunity to preview the elements of a strong argument, presented in the *LifeSkills* section. Remind the students to support their arguments with evidence and examples.

Alternative

Ask the students to name the professions of the people in the photos or represented by the photos. Ask them to brainstorm other professions that famous people have. Write the professions on the board. Encourage the students to name four or five famous writers and write their names beneath their profession. Repeat this with the other categories. Then put the students in pairs to review the list of famous people and choose the top five. Ask the students to discuss their reasons for each of their choices. Ask them to discuss what the top five people on their list do. Do they have five different professions or are more than one of them in the same profession?

Culture note

Buckingham Palace (bottom photo) has been the official residence of the British royal family since 1837. It has 775 rooms, which include 19 staterooms, 240 bedrooms, 92 offices and 78 bathrooms! The majority of employees at the Palace support day-to-day activities and duties of The Queen and The Duke of Edinburgh and their immediate family.

Extra: class poll

Take a class poll to find out who the students think is the single most famous person of all time. Distribute slips of paper to be used as ballots and have the students write the name of one famous person and the reason why the person is the most famous. If the students are all from one country, this can be limited to the most famous person from their country. Tally the votes and have a class discussion about what the students know about the person.

Extra: celebrity game

Give each student five small slips of paper and tell them to write the name of a famous person on each one. Explain that it should be a person all the students in the class will know. Put the students in groups and tell them to put their slips of paper face down in the middle. Divide each group in half to form two teams. Then choose one student on each team as a 'clue-giver'. The clue-giver has one minute to pick up slips of paper and give clues to their team members about who the famous people are (their profession, appearance, what they are famous for, etc). Team members guess as many famous people as they can in one minute. When a name on a slip is guessed, the clue-giver keeps the slip and moves on to the next slip. If team members are taking too long to guess, the clue-giver may pass, put the slip back and go on to the next slip. After one minute, the other team has a chance. The team should select a new clue-giver for each new round. The team with the most slips after all names have been guessed wins. For an added challenge, limit the students to three-word clues, or have them use only gestures as in charades.

B

- Put the students in groups by combining two or three pairs from Ex. A. Have the students brainstorm how famous people's lives are different from ordinary people's lives, for example, *they are always in the spotlight, have no privacy, have to travel a lot*, etc. Have the class categorise these differences as positive or negative. Elicit a few real-life examples of problems famous people have had as a result of being in the public eye too much (*Miley Cyrus had to grow up too fast because she became famous when she was so young*, etc).
- Have them decide together if the famous people they chose in Ex. A are different or special compared to ordinary people, and if so how. Circulate and monitor, helping with ideas as necessary.
- You could give the students time to make notes in preparation for their discussion.
- Have the students share their opinions with the class.

Grammar: reported speech – modal verbs and past perfect (p. 34)

A

- Draw the students' attention to the photo of Andy Warhol and ask them to share any information they know about him.

Culture note

Andy Warhol was an influential American artist and filmmaker in the 1960s. He is well known for his pop-art painting series of Campbell's Soup cans and Marilyn Monroe. He once famously said, 'In the future, everyone will be world-famous for 15 minutes.'

- Give the students time to scan the article and ask any questions they may have about unfamiliar vocabulary.
- Have the students read the articles. When they have finished, ask them whether the two people's experiences of fame were positive or negative and why.

Answer
They were both negative. They both found it hard to deal with sudden wealth/fame.

Extra: comprehension questions
Ask the students the following questions.
1 How did Steve Jennings become famous?
2 Why does he say he 'had to get help'?
3 What happened to Tom Reynolds?
4 What does he advise for people in a similar situation?

Answers
1 He appeared as Des in a popular TV series.
2 to deal with the pressures of being famous
3 He inherited a fortune.
4 They should get advice on handling and investing their money.

NOTICE!
- Direct the students' attention to the **Notice!** box.
- Check that the students understand what a reporting verb is/does. Elicit that reporting verbs are used to report what a person has said.
- Have the students scan the article and underline the five reporting verbs. Elicit the answers and list them on the board. Then ask the class to think of additional reporting verbs

Answers
said, admitted, confessed, commented, suggested (other examples: ask, deny, insist, promise, reply, respond, tell, etc)

B
Form
- Have the students read the article again.
- To focus on the comparison between direct speech and reported speech, call on the students to read aloud the sentences that use reported speech. Then elicit the direct speech quotation for each one and write both versions on the board, for example:
Steve said no one had told him what to expect →
'No one told me what to expect.'
- Have the students answer the questions and then complete the sentences in the table, changing each direct quote into reported speech. Then check the answers with the class.

Answers
1 It usually shifts to a past tense. Yes 2 No
3 hadn't thought 4 might 5 would

- Ask the students to articulate the rules about reported speech with past perfect and modals in their own words, for example, *In reported speech, verbs in the past perfect tense do not change; present modals change to past modals; past modals do not change.*
- Direct the students' attention to the **What's right?** box and ask what is wrong in the incorrect sentence. Elicit that in reported speech where there is a tense shift, the modal *must* changes to *had to*.

C
- Ask the students to read the quotes and identify the main verb or modal in each. Ask them to consider whether that verb or modal changes in reported speech. Refer the students to the examples in the table if they have trouble remembering.
- Have the students work individually to rewrite the sentences using reported speech. Explain that in reported speech it's not always necessary to include *that*: *He said (that) everyone would be famous for 15 minutes.*
- Check the answers with the class.

Answers
1 Andrew said (that) he would like to see Lily Allen in concert.
2 *Entertainment Weekly* reported (that) Pharrell Williams might perform at the new stadium.
3 Clare asked whether/if she would see some celebrities during her holiday in Los Angeles.
4 The security guard told us (that) we had to leave our cameras at the door.
5 Dylan said (that) he had never used Twitter before he went to university.

D
- Ask the students to think about the challenges and disadvantages of becoming famous.
- Give them time to think about their own opinions and to complete the statements.
- Put the students in pairs to share their responses. Remind them to take notes of their partner's ideas.
- Combine pairs to form groups of four and have the students take turns sharing their partner's opinions using reported speech. Encourage them to use the reporting verbs from Ex. A.
- To assess whether the students can use reported speech correctly, call on the students from each group to share a few of the opinions expressed.

 Workbook p. 16, Section 1

Listening: to a gossip columnist (p. 35)

Lead-in
Explain that a gossip columnist writes about celebrities' personal lives for websites and magazines. Ask the students whether they enjoy reading celebrity gossip and elicit the names of some gossip magazines or websites the students know of (*OK!*, *Hello*, *TMZ.com*).

Fame and fortune UNIT 3

A

- Put the students in pairs to discuss the questions.
- Elicit responses from the class. Ask the students what they think makes someone a celebrity. **Highlight** the fact that there is no clear-cut definition of the difference between being famous and being a celebrity, but a general rule is that all celebrities are famous but not all famous people are celebrities. Some people would say that celebrities are people who are in the media a lot or who work particularly in the field of entertainment, for example, film stars, television actors, musical artists, professional athletes, etc. On the other hand, people who are famous, but not celebrities, might be people who are well known but who are not constantly in the spotlight, like authors, scientists, film directors, etc.

B

- Put the students in pairs to identify the people in the photos and discuss any information they know about them. Elicit responses from a few volunteers.
- Ask the students to discuss in pairs which people pictured qualify as celebrities and the reasons why they think they do.

Answers

1 the Duchess of Cambridge, Catherine (Kate) Middleton is married to Prince William, future king of the UK 2 Usain Bolt: Jamaican sprinter; holds world record for 100-metre and 200-metre sprints (at time of printing). 3 Psy: holds the record for the most-viewed YouTube music video – famous for introducing Gangnam-style dancing to the world, 4 Victoria Beckham: former Spice Girl, fashion designer, wife of ex-footballer David Beckham 5 Stephen Hawking: physicist and author

C 🎧 1.11

- See p. 122 for the **audioscript**.
- Give the students time to read the questions. Then play the audio.
- Before discussing the questions, ask the class to explain what the 'Ulmer Scale' is (a system for ranking how famous celebrities are).
- Discuss the questions with the class.

Answer

1 A-list: people who have been famous for a long time or are the hottest celebrities of the moment
B-list: people who are famous in their own country or profession but aren't as well known to the general public
C-list: people who don't have special talents, but have done something like being on a reality show or are just rich and attractive

D

- Have the students read the verbs in the box and the list of phrases and think about which verb best matches each phrase.
- Go over any unfamiliar vocabulary. Then play the audio again and have the students complete the phrases.
- Check the answers with the class.

- Brainstorm other ways to become famous, for example, record a great album, star in a Hollywood film, etc and make a list on the board.

Answers

1 break 2 run 3 inherit 4 write 5 discover 6 cause
7 come up with

E

- Put the students in pairs. Tell them to think of three celebrities who became famous in the ways listed in Ex. D or on the board, and to write sentences about them.
- Point out the model sentence. Remind them to discuss whether they think each person is an A-, B- or C-list celebrity, or even a celebrity at all.

F

- Combine pairs to form groups of four and have the students share their sentences. Encourage them to discuss any differences in their opinions about whether each celebrity belongs on the A, B or C list. Point out the example and remind the students to use reported speech.

▶ Workbook p. 16, Section 2

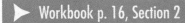

Reading: for different purposes (p. 36, p. 12)

Lead-in

Ask the students to read the information in the skills panel. Remind them that they discussed different types of reading texts, and different purposes for reading them, on p. 12. Elicit a few examples. Write the four ways of reading on the board: *skimming, scanning, reading in detail* and *general reading*. Tell the students that this lesson will focus on these four ways of reading and the best way to read a text based on its purpose.

A

- Give the students time to read the list of text types and the descriptions of the four ways of reading. Do a quick check to make sure the students recognise the terms for the ways of reading. Ask them to close their books. Then read aloud the definition for each way of reading and ask the students to identify it (skimming, scanning, etc).
- Have the students complete the matching exercise individually and then compare answers in pairs.
- Check the answers with the class.

Possible answers

a 1,4 b 4 c 2,3 d 1,4 e 1 f 2,3 g 1,4
h 2 i 3 j 2

B

- Tell the students they are going to read an article about the trend of young people wanting to become famous. Ask if any of them dreamed about becoming famous when they were younger and how they hoped this

would happen. Go over the questions with the class and explain any unfamiliar vocabulary. Encourage the students to think about how they will read the text in order to find out the answer to each question.
- Give the students time to read the text and answer the questions.
- Put the students in pairs to discuss how they read the text differently for each question.
- Elicit responses to the questions from the class. Ask the students to explain why they chose to read the text differently for each question.

Possible answers

1 Skimming: The text is about what children say they want to be when they grow up, and whether they aspire to realistic careers or want to be rich and famous. By skimming the title, students get an idea of the topic of the article, and this is reinforced if they skim the first paragraph.
2 Scanning: Twenty-five years ago, children wanted to be teachers, doctors or work in finance. Now they want to be sports stars, singers or actors. Students can get the answer by scanning paragraph 2 for key words.
3 General reading: These changes have happened because of society's fascination with celebrities and the great number of TV talent competitions. The author thinks this is a negative change because for most people becoming rich and famous is an unrealistic goal, and this leads to failure and disappointment. In addition, even if you do become famous, sometimes this is not as good as you thought it might be.
Students have to read the whole article to get the general idea of what has caused the changes and how the author feels about them.
4 Reading in detail: According to the author, TV talent competitions have made people believe that it's easy to become famous and wealthy. Students have to read paragraph 4 in detail to find the answers.
5 Reading in detail: Fame and fortune can have negative effects on people because their careers are often short, and when their careers end, they lose self-esteem and also often run out of money. It can be difficult for them to adapt to normal life. Students have to read paragraph 5 in detail to find the specific reasons why the author says that fame and fortune can have negative effects.

Extra: homework

Have the students write their answers to the questions based on the text, but write them in paragraph format. Encourage them to include their own opinions about the negative consequences of fame when it comes to children and young people.

C

- Direct the students' attention to the emboldened words and phrases in the text. Ask them to read the text again and guess the meaning of the emboldened words and phrases from the context of the sentence they are in.
- Have the students complete the activity individually and then compare answers in pairs.
- Then check the answers with the class.

Answers
1 similar   2 mind   3 successful   4 fame
5 a decrease   6 negative   7 negative   8 negative

D
- Give the students time to complete the sentences with words and phrases from Ex. C.
- Put the students in pairs to compare answers. Then check the answers with the class.
- Have the pairs discuss the questions. Ask the students to use as many of the new vocabulary items from Ex. C as they can.

Answers
1 aspirations   2 traumatic, in the spotlight   3 dwindle

Extra: homework

Have the students choose one of the questions from Ex. D and expand their answer by writing a few paragraphs.

Extra: modern fame

Lead a class discussion, or have the students do a journal entry, about the reasons why young people are obsessed with fame today. Discuss what has changed in our society to bring about this phenomenon, for example, reality TV shows and talent contests, the popularity of social, public content-sharing sites such as YouTube.

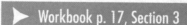 Workbook p. 17, Section 3

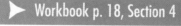 Workbook p. 18, Section 4

Writing: a website post (p. 37)

A
- Draw the students' attention to the photo of Dany Cotton.
- Elicit any information the students know or can guess about Cotton.
- Tell the students they are going to read a website post about Cotton and find out why she is the writer's hero.
- To review the reading skill (reading for different purposes), ask the students the ways they might choose to read the text in order to find that information quickly (general reading, skimming, scanning for the word *hero*).
- Have the students compare their answer in pairs and then elicit the answer from the class.

Answer
She is the writer's hero because she has excelled in a dangerous and demanding profession that is usually more associated with men.

Fame and fortune UNIT 3   25

B

- Encourage the students to brainstorm a list of people whom they admire and then choose one to write about. You may wish to limit them to famous people, or allow them to choose someone they admire who is not famous, such as a teacher or a family member.
- When the students have chosen the person they wish to write about, show them how to make a word web / mind map to gather and organise their thoughts. Draw a sample on the board, for example:

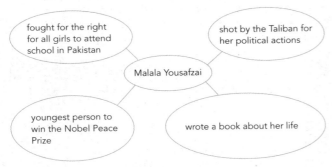

- Ask the students to write their posts and remind them to give reasons why they admire the person they chose.

C

- Have the students share information about their heroes in pairs.
- To conclude, ask for a few volunteers to share with the class their heroes and their reasons for choosing them.

Pronunciation: silent letters – consonants (p. 37)

A 1.12

- See the Student's Book for the **audioscript** – the list of words.
- Play the audio once and have the students listen. Ask them to tell you what happens to the underlined consonant sounds (they are silent). Then play the audio a second time and have the students repeat each word.
- Ask the students if they can think of any other words in which the same consonants are silent (e.g. clim<u>b</u>, <u>p</u>neumonia, <u>k</u>nowledge, <u>h</u>onour, assi<u>g</u>n, ca<u>l</u>m).

B 1.13

- See the Student's Book for the **audioscript** – the words in the box.
- Give the students time to read the list of words and think about which consonant is silent.
- Play the audio and have the students underline the silent letter in each word.
- Have the students compare answers in pairs and then practise saying the words in both Ex. A and Ex. B.

Answer

com<u>b</u>, <u>d</u>esigner, <u>g</u>host, <u>h</u>onest, <u>k</u>nee, <u>k</u>nife, <u>k</u>nock, resi<u>g</u>n

Grammar: reported speech – optional back-shifting (p. 38)

A

- Write the term *celebrity lookalike* on the board and ask the students to tell you what they think it means. Tell them that the man in the photo on the left is an Indonesian man named Ilham Anas. Elicit that Anas is a lookalike for President Barack Obama.
- Have the students read the article and think about the question. Elicit answers from the class.

Answer

Mr Anas is a shy person, but he thinks looking like Mr Obama is a blessing (a good thing).

NOTICE!

- Direct the students' attention to the **Notice!** box.
- Have the students find and underline the reporting verbs in the article. Remind them that they can use their scanning reading strategy to locate the verbs.
- Elicit the five verbs and the tense after each one.

Answer

said: past, revealed: present, explained: present, said: future, told: present

Extra: reported speech

Say the sentences from the text as quotes. Call on the students to change them to the reported speech form without looking at the text.

B

Form

- Have the students read the text again, paying attention to the reported speech.
- Ask the students to read the information in the language box. Check that they understand *optional* (possible but not necessary).
- Present the table to the students, reading from left to right. Ask them to complete the table with examples from the text using the grammar rules they already know for reported speech. Then have them answer the question.
- Check the answers with the class.
- Check understanding by asking the students to tell you in their own words when back-shifting is necessary.

Answers

1 He told reporters (that) he wasn't getting much 'Obama work' anymore.
2 He told reporters (that) he isn't getting much 'Obama work' anymore.
3 He said (that) he would keep taking all the opportunities that come along.
4 He said (that) he'll keep taking all the opportunities that come along.
5 At first, he claimed (that) he couldn't see a strong likeness.
6 No
7 i both, ii b

- Direct the students' attention to the **What's right?** box. Elicit that since 'he' is famous now, he is reporting something that is no longer true. As a result, back-shifting is necessary, i.e. *would* has to be used, not *will*.

Extra: homework

Ask the students to choose a celebrity and find an interview with them online or in a magazine. Tell them to look through the article, find six to eight quotes from the celebrity's interview responses and write them down. They should then rewrite the quotes in reported speech, using back-shifting when necessary.

C

- Give the students time to read the instructions and the prompts. Point out that where possible they should write the reported speech versions both with and without back-shifting. Elicit which item requires back-shifting (item 2 requires back-shifting because the statement was about an event that happened yesterday and is no longer true).
- Have the students work individually to complete the sentences and then compare answers in pairs.
- Check the answers with the class.

Answers

1 John announced (that) they were holding an Oscars party.
John announced (that) they are holding an Oscars party.
2 Nadia told us (that) she was really excited about the concert that evening.
3 The lecturer declared (that) technological advances would change the way we watch films.
The lecturer declared (that) technological advances will change the way we watch films.
4 Julia stated (that) you didn't have to be 18 to get a backstage pass.
Julia stated (that) you don't have to be 18 to get a backstage pass.

D

- Check that the students understand the instructions. Give them time to think about how and why they have become famous and what kind of celebrity they are. They should make some notes of their experiences of being a celebrity.

- Put the students in pairs. Have them take turns talking about their experiences. When they are listening, the students should take notes on what their partner says.
- Then have them change partners and report on what their previous partner said using the notes they made.
- To conclude and assess the students' grasp of the target grammar, ask for a few volunteers to report to the class what their partner said.

▶ Workbook pp. 18–19, Section 5

Speaking: clarifying misunderstandings (p. 39)

Lead-in

Ask the students to tell you what they think the advantages of being a famous person are. Elicit ideas from the class and write them on the board, e.g. *having a lot of money, travelling a lot*. Ask the students to read the information in the skills panel. Elicit examples of phrases they sometimes use to clarify what they mean, such as *I mean …, Sorry, I meant to say …, Let me say that again*, etc.

A

- Direct the students' attention to the photo and the quote. Explain that *image*, in this case, means the way others view you and the opinion they have of you.
- Ask the students what they know about Elvis Presley and to explain the meaning of his quote in their own words.
- Put the students in pairs to discuss their opinions of the quote and the disadvantages of fame.

B 1.14

- See the Student's Book for a partial **audioscript** and p. 123 for a complete version.
- Give the students time to read the partial expressions and ask them to listen for these in the audio. Play the audio once. Encourage the students to listen for the point when the listener misunderstands or questions something, and then focus on the speaker's response or explanation.
- Play the audio again and have the students complete the phrases.
- Check the answers with the class.

Answers

1 meant 2 say 3 making 4 rephrase 5 Actually
6 Put

C

- Have the students work individually to complete the sentences. Remind them that more than one answer is possible for some sentences.
- Have the students compare answers in pairs. Then check the answers with the class.

Fame and fortune   **UNIT 3**   **27**

Answers

1 What I meant was / What I'm trying to say is
2 Maybe I'm not making myself clear. / Maybe I should rephrase that. / Actually, that's not what I meant.
3 put it that way
4 Maybe I'm not making myself clear. / Maybe I should rephrase that. / Actually, that's not what I meant.

D

- Encourage the students to practise using phrases for clarifying information as they discuss their opinions about fame.
- Have the students read the model conversation and notice how A rephrases to clarify a point.
- Give the students time to think of a few opinion statements about fame.
- Put the students in pairs for their discussion. Encourage them to disagree with each other, express misunderstanding or question something in order to give their partner a chance to use the target phrases.

 Workbook p. 19, Section 6

LifeSkills: evaluating arguments (p. 40)

Step 1: Identify claims made and evidence for those claims. (Ex. A)
Step 2: Understand strong and weak points. (Ex. C, Ex. D)
Step 3: Evaluate the argument based on the strength of the points. (Ex. E)

Lead-in

Read the target skill aloud and invite the students to tell you what they think *evaluating arguments* means. Then **highlight** the three-step strategy to develop the skill of evaluating arguments.

Elicit a definition for this usage of the word *argument* (reason(s) used to persuade someone to believe a particular idea or to take a particular action). Give or elicit examples of situations relating to **Work and Career** in which people might need to make a strong (convincing) argument for something (*suggesting a change in company policy, requesting a budget increase, presenting an idea for a new product, describing a product or service to a customer,* etc).

Highlight that this skill is highly useful in the business world, especially in the fields of sales and marketing, when one needs to convince others to buy a product. Ask the students to think about what makes an argument strong. Elicit that a good argument has enough support (evidence) or reasons why someone should be persuaded.

Highlight the importance of being able to evaluate an argument in terms of how strong it is and how well it is supported.

A

- Give the students time to read the instructions and the definition silently. Check the difference between *a claim* and *evidence* and make sure the students understand it clearly.

Alternative

To preview the reading, take a quick class poll to find out how often the students read newspapers and which sections they read most often. Go over the common sections of a newspaper and what kind of information is included in each.

- Have the students read the proposal once without underlining or circling their answers. Remind them to think about the purpose of the bold sentences as they read.
- Ask the students to summarise the reasons for the proposed change to the newspaper, some of the options suggested and what the writer proposes as the best solution.
- Check that the students understand the task. If necessary, clarify by eliciting one example of a claim and one example of evidence in the proposal.
- Have the students read the proposal again, underlining the claims and circling the evidence.
- Check the answers with the class and list the claims and evidence in two columns on the board.

Answers

1 evidence 2 claim 3 claim 4 evidence 5 claim

Extra: supporting evidence

After checking the answers, ask the students to explain how they know that the evidence is in fact evidence, for example, words like *survey, research,* use of statistics, etc. Ask them to tell you which claim a piece of evidence supports.

Answer

2 supports 1.

B

- See p. 123 for the **audioscript**.
- Tell the students they are going to listen to a board meeting in which newspaper editors are discussing the proposal to change the newspaper's content. Elicit some opinions from the class about what they think should be done about the problem. Go over the abbreviation 'L&E' (lifestyle and entertainment) used in the audio.
- **Highlight** that the students should listen specifically for the action the board decides to take.
- Play the audio and elicit the answer. Ask the students whether they agree with the decision, and why or why not.

Answer

They decide to do a survey of their subscribers to find out who reads their paper and what sections they read.

C

- Put the students in pairs to discuss the definitions of a strong point and a weak point and match the two halves of the sentences. Encourage them to discuss the reasons for their choices.
- When pairs finish, have them join another pair and compare answers, discussing any differences.

> **Answers**
> 1 b 2 a

D

- Tell the students they are going to evaluate the claims from the board meeting in Ex. B and decide whether they are strong or weak based on how well they are supported. Have the students stay in their pairs from Ex. C. Tell them to read the claims in the table. Point out that the claims in the left column are points against cutting the L&E section, while the claims on the right support cutting it. To provide a model, ask the students whether claim 1 in the Against column is a strong or a weak point (strong) and why (it includes evidence that can be verified – *50 letters related to that section* – to support it).
- Have pairs complete the task. Then elicit the answers from the class. Ask the students to support their answer choices.

> **Answers**
> Against cutting the L&E section:
> 1 S 2 W 3 W 4 S 5 W
> For cutting the L&E section:
> 1 W 2 W 3 S 4 W 5 S 6 W

E

- Tell the students they are going to work in groups and discuss their opinions about whether the newspaper should cut the Lifestyle and Entertainment section.
- Before they begin their discussions, give the students time to look back at the proposal and if necessary listen to the audio again. Tell them to think about their opinions and make some notes. They should each decide which side of the argument they support and why. Point out the language in the **How to say it** box and encourage the students to use the phrases in their discussion.
- Have groups choose one person to begin the discussion by sharing their opinion and supporting it. Encourage the students to use all the information on the spread to inform their discussion.
- Group members should then agree or disagree and offer additional support for their own opinions. Encourage them to try to persuade others to agree with their side of the argument.

> **Extra: discussion expansion**
>
> When all group members have had a chance to contribute, have groups reflect on their discussions and discuss which side offered the strongest argument, which points were especially convincing, which group members presented the strongest argument and what made their argument convincing.

F

- Lead a class discussion on what the students have learned about the skill of *evaluating arguments* and how it can be useful to them in the domain of **Work and Career**.
- Put the students in pairs to discuss the questions, and encourage them to think about the factors that make an argument weak or strong.

- Then have the pairs report back to the class and see if they all agree about strong and weak arguments.

REFLECT

- Discuss the question with the whole class. Ask the students to say what they feel are the most useful points they learned from this lesson, and how the skill of *evaluating arguments* might be useful in their lives in the domains of **Study and Learning** and **Self and Society**, either now or in the future.
- Elicit the following ideas: *contributing to online forums that relate to issues they care about, writing letters to the local newspaper about issues, joining the debate team or a community activism group, etc.*

RESEARCH

- Go through the task and check that the students are clear about what they have to do.
- Suggest some possible newspapers with accompanying websites. Have the students compare the print and online versions and make notes on the answers to the questions.
- Have them share their findings in class. Lead a class discussion about the advantages of print vs. online newspapers and ask for the students' opinions on whether print newspapers, as many believe, will eventually be obsolete.

> **Extra: debate an issue**
>
> Provide the students with regular opportunities to express and support their opinions in class. Elicit some issues or problems the students would like to discuss, for example, a school policy or a problem in the local community. Have the students debate the best way to address the issue, either in the form of a spoken discussion or via the use of an online discussion board.

Language wrap-up (p. 42)

For notes on how to approach the exercises in the Language wrap-up section, please see page 9.

1 Vocabulary

A

- Ask the students to read the sentences for general understanding and to gain an idea of the context before filling in the blanks with the correct form of the verbs from the box. Remind them that each blank is worth one point.
- Check the answers with the class by calling on individual students to read the completed sentences aloud.

B

- Remind the students to use the context of the sentences to help them choose the correct words.
- Give them time to complete the task individually. Then have them compare answers in pairs.

Fame and fortune UNIT 3 **29**

- Check the answers by calling on individual students to read the completed sentences aloud.

2 Grammar

- Encourage the students to read through the sentences first before rewriting them. Elicit that the two ways the sentences can be rewritten are with and without back-shifting, that is, with and without changing the verb tense.
- Call on individual students to read the rewritten sentences aloud. Ask the rest of the class to say whether the sentence is correct or not.

Writing workshop: writing a short essay (p. 43)

A

- Direct the students' attention to the essay question. Elicit the meaning of *positive influence* (having the power to make positive changes in the world). Draw the students' attention to the photo of Gisele Bündchen and ask them what they know about her.

Culture note

Gisele Bündchen is a Brazilian fashion model and actress. As well as donating money to different charities, she does volunteer work for the United Nations as a Goodwill Ambassador. Goodwill Ambassadors are usually famous athletes, actors, musicians, etc who care about making the world a better place and volunteer to help different United Nations agencies to achieve their goals.
Bono is the lead singer of the Irish rock band, U2. In recent years, he has been playing the role of diplomat, meeting with world leaders and contributing money to causes he is passionate about, such as world poverty and hunger.

- Ask the students to predict what kinds of information the writer will give.
- Give the students time to read the true/false questions and then read the essay. Check that they understand the meaning of *charity* (an organisation to which you give money so that it can give money and help to people who are poor or sick, or who need advice and support). Point out that *good causes* in the essay means *charities*.
- Have the students compare answers in pairs. Then check the answers with the class.

Answers
1 T 2 T 3 F

Extra: in your own words

Have the students write a few sentences in their own words to explain what the essay is about.

B

- Have the students look back at the essay, complete the task individually and then compare answers in pairs.

Answers
1 a 2 a 3 b 4 c

C

- Have the students read the instructions. Ask them to read the essay question in Ex. A again and decide what their own opinion is.
- Elicit the opinion expressed by the writer in the article in Ex. A. Ask the students to think about whether they agree or disagree with this opinion.
- Give the students time to make notes on their opinions and list evidence and examples to support their ideas.
- Have the students use their notes to come up with an introductory topic sentence, two reasons for their opinion, one or two supporting details or examples for each reason and a concluding sentence.

D

- Give the students time to write their article in class or for homework. Remind them to write about 200 words. Encourage them to use new language and structures from the unit in their writing.
- **Highlight** the importance of using paragraphs to organise their article, and draw the students' attention to the paragraphs in the essay in Ex. A and to questions 1–3 in Ex. B. Award an extra mark or marks for including reported speech or new vocabulary from the unit.

How are you doing?

- Ask the students to read the statements and tick the ones they believe are true.
- Ask them to discuss their essay with another student in the class and identify things they could improve on next time.

Extra: debating

Organise a debate about whether celebrities are a positive or negative influence on people. Put the students in two groups according to their opinion. Give each group a few minutes to prepare their arguments. Each group chooses a representative to debate their ideas. Group members should raise their hand during the debate if they want to provide their representative with additional facts or a supporting argument.

 Workbook pp. 20–21, SkillsStudio

UNIT 4 UPS AND DOWNS

The expression *ups and downs* is used to describe a variety of situations and experiences that are both good and bad at different times. For example, someone might say, 'My brother has had his share of ups and downs, but he is happy now.' People may describe life as having its *ups and downs*.

Unit plan

Unit opener	(p. 44)	20 min.
1 **Listening:** understanding discourse markers	(p. 46)	30 min.
• Vocabulary: life satisfaction		15 min.
2 **Grammar:** noun clauses as objects	(p. 47)	40 min.
3 **Reading:** a magazine article	(p. 48)	30 min.
• Vocabulary: mood		15 min.
4 **Grammar:** review of conditional forms	(p. 49)	40 min.
5 **Writing:** a thank-you note	(p. 50)	30 min.
6 **Pronunciation:** reduced forms of *would you* and *did you*	(p. 50)	15 min.
7 **Speaking:** talking about having a positive attitude	(p. 51)	30 min.
LifeSkills: being a positive team member (Work and Career)	(p. 52)	50 min.
• Optional downloadable *LifeSkills* lesson (Self and Society)		50 min.
• Optional downloadable *LifeSkills* lesson (Study and Learning)		50 min.
Language wrap-up	(p. 54)	15 min.
Speaking workshop	(p. 55)	20 min.
Video and downloadable video worksheet		45 min.

Unit opener (p. 44)

Lead-in
Ask the students to look at the unit title and the photos and to predict what the unit will be about. Write *paradise* and *utopia* on the board and ask the students what they mean. Explain that the words have similar meanings (*paradise*: a beautiful and peaceful place or a state of total happiness; *utopia*: an imaginary place in which all conditions are perfect). Direct the students' attention to the points in the unit objectives box and go through the information with them. To get your students to think about the skills being developed in this unit, ask them to look at the questions in the cogs.

Listening: discourse markers
- Ask the students the question and give them time to talk with a partner. Extend the discussion by asking the students for examples they have noticed when listening to people speak English. Make a list on the board.

Writing: a thank-you note
- Read the questions and have the students discuss with a partner. Elicit answers and create a list on the board.

LifeSkills: being a positive team member
- Ask the students if they have ever worked on a team. Expect answers such as playing on sports teams, participating in academic projects or working on community service activities. Ask if they agree that it is important to be positive when working on a team. Put the students in small groups to list characteristics of a positive team member. Ask the groups to share their lists with the class.

Common European Framework: unit map

Unit 4	Competence developed	CEF Reference (B2 competences)
Listening	can understand formal discourse markers	Table 1; Table 2; Sections 4.4.2.1; 4.4.3.1; 4.4.3.5; 4.5.2.2; 5.2.3.1
Grammar	can use and understand noun clauses as objects	Table 1; Table 2; Sections 5.2.1.2; 6.4.7.7; 6.4.7.8
Reading	can understand a magazine article	Table 1; Table 2; Sections 4.4.2.2; 4.4.2.4; 4.5.2.2
Grammar	can use and understand a variety of conditional forms	Table 1; Table 2; Sections 5.2.1.2; 6.4.7.7; 6.4.7.8
Writing	can write a thank-you note	Table 1; Table 2; Sections 4.4.1.2; 4.4.3.2; 4.4.3.4; 4.5.2.1; 5.2.1.1; 5.2.1.2; 5.2.1.6; 5.2.2.2; 5.2.2.4; 5.2.3.2
Pronunciation	can correctly pronounce reduced forms of *would you* and *did you*	Section 5.2.1.4
Speaking	can talk about having a positive attitude	Table 1; Table 2; Sections 4.4.1.1; 4.4.3.1; 4.4.3.5; 4.5.2.1; 5.2.3.2

A

- Ask the students to read the six definitions of happiness. Give them a few minutes to work in pairs and to make a few notes about why they agree or disagree with the definitions.
- Write each definition on the board and poll the class. Make a tally of how many students agree with each definition. Discuss which one is most popular and which is least popular. Ask the students to state why the most popular one won. Remind them there is no one right answer.

Alternative

Ask the students to work individually and rank the definitions from 1 (the best) to 6 (the worst). Ask them to think of reasons for their rankings. Let the students compare their rankings with a partner. Listen to some of their ideas as a class.

B

- Remind the students that everyone's definition of happiness is different. Ask the students to complete their own definition of happiness. Tell them they can make use of the ideas on this page and/or use ideas of their own. Encourage them to write as much as they want; the definitions do not need to be restricted to one sentence. Get them started by asking what their idea of paradise is. Review the definition of this from the Lead-in work on p. 44. Ask what qualities or activities make them happy.
- Put the students in pairs and ask them to share their definitions with their partners. Give them time to explain why they chose their definitions. Ask all the pairs to read their definitions to the whole class. Take a class vote on which definition they like best. Extend the activity by voting on other types of definition, such as most surprising or most unique.

Alternative

Ask the students to bring in a picture of an item or activity that makes them happy. The picture can be from a magazine or the internet or it can be a personal photo. If the students choose to bring a personal photo, ask them to make sure there is no identifying information linking the student to the photo. Collect all the pictures and then show each picture individually. Have the students guess who the picture belongs to. When they get an answer right, ask the student who the picture belongs to to say why this item or activity makes them happy.

Extra: group project

Let the students create a class poster using all of the pictures.

Extra: speaking

Extend the exercise by asking the students to work individually and write a definition for unhappiness, beginning *Unhappiness is …* . Put them in pairs and ask them to explain their definition to their partner. Listen to their suggestions as a class.

Extra: homework

Review the meanings of the words *paradise* and *utopia* (see the Lead-in on p. 44). For homework, ask the students to write two short paragraphs. One paragraph should describe what they think paradise would be. The other should describe a utopia. Ask volunteers to read one of the paragraphs to the class in the next lesson. Classmates determine whether the paragraph describes paradise or utopia.

Listening: understanding discourse markers (p. 46, p. 22)

Lead-in

Write the word *lecture* on the board. Elicit what features make up a lecture and write the students' ideas on the board. Survey the class to see how many students find lectures challenging. Ask them what makes listening to lectures difficult. Ask the students to read the information in the skills panel. Explain that discourse markers can make listening to lectures easier. Remind them that they studied discourse markers (fillers) on p. 22 and encourage them to name the ones they remember.

A 1.16

- See p. 123 for the **audioscript**.
- Explain to the students that they are going to listen to the introduction to a lecture in order to find out what it is going to be about.
- Play the audio and then check the answer with the class.

Answer

The relationship between wealth and happiness

B 1.17

- See p. 124 for the **audioscript**.
- Point out the four partial phrases. Explain that the full phrases are used in the lecture. Ask the students to listen to the full lecture and fill in the missing words.
- Play the audio and check progress. If necessary, play the audio one more time. After checking answers, ask the students to put the phrases in the correct section of the table. Explain that each phrase has a specific function.

- **Highlight** the functions of the phrases and give examples. Point out, for example, that people use *As a result*, *As a consequence* and *Consequently* to talk about the result of something, e.g. *People need companionship. As a consequence, married people tend to be happier.*

Answers
In general
On the other hand
In addition
As a result
1 In general
2 On the other hand
3 As a result
4 In addition

C
- Explain that a common task in academic settings is to listen to a lecture and then answer questions about the content. Draw attention to the four questions. Tell the students you will play the lecture again and they should listen for those answers.
- Play the audio more than once if necessary. Put the students in pairs to discuss their answers.

Answers
1 People with higher incomes feel more satisfied with their lives.
2 People with higher incomes are not necessarily happier than those who earn less.
3 Satisfaction is an element of happiness.
4 Student's own answers, but will likely be based on this sentence in the lecture: People with lots of money can purchase lots of positive life experiences, like exotic holidays and expensive meals, and as a result, they may enjoy everyday pleasures less.

 Workbook p. 22, Section 1

D
- Remind the students that words can have more than one part of speech, and that knowing other forms of words can help them expand their vocabulary.
- Ask the students to complete the word form tables individually. Then check the answers with the class.

Answers

Adjective	Noun
happy	happiness
wealthy	wealth
pleased/pleasing	pleasure
content	contentment

Verb	Noun
appreciate	appreciation
enjoy	enjoyment
satisfy	satisfaction

E
- Ask the students to work with a partner. Make sure they understand that they need to complete the sentences individually with the correct form of the word in parentheses and their own ideas, and then discuss them with their partner.

Answers
1 satisfied   2 appreciate   3 content
4 wealth   5 Enjoyment

 Workbook pp. 22–23, Section 2

Grammar: noun clauses as objects (p. 47)

Lead-in
Write the word *laugh* on the board. Put the students in pairs and ask them to tell their partner what makes them laugh. Listen to their suggestions as a class. Elicit responses such as funny jokes, television sitcoms (situation comedies), friends, comedians and so on.

A 🎧 1.18
- See the Student's Book for the **audioscript**.
- Draw attention to the photo. Ask the students where they think these people are and what they are doing (they are laughing during a laughter therapy workshop).
- Ask them to read the poster, then check their answers. Ask for opinions as to whether the students agree or disagree that laughter can change their lives.
- Ask the students to read the question and say how they think laughter therapy works. Then tell them to listen and read the conversation, and find out what Michelle says about it. Play the audio once and elicit the answer from the class.

Answer
Laughter helps you deal with a problem. You learn techniques to see the positive side of a situation.

Alternative
Ask the students to close their books. Write the question from Ex. A on the board. Play the audio once and ask the students to answer the question. Then ask them to open their books and read the conversation to check their answer.

Culture note

When people laugh, their body relaxes. When that happens, the body releases natural painkillers called endorphins. The endorphins enter the bloodstream. The point of laughter therapy is to help people laugh more easily. In laughter therapy sessions, there are a range of activities designed to get people laughing, but luckily the body can't actually distinguish between real and fake laughter. In other words, pretending to laugh has the same beneficial effect.

NOTICE!

- Direct the students' attention to the **Notice!** box.
- Ask the students to underline all the examples of *what*, *where*, *when*, *why* and *how* in the conversation.
- Ask the students what they notice about the word order following each question word.

Answer

Do you know **what** it involves?
I think they explain **how** laughter could help …
I wonder **when** they're holding the workshop.
Does it say **where** we can get more …
We might need to explain **why** we want …

The word order is subject + verb (i.e. it is not inverted after the question word).

B
Form

- Ask the students to read the conversation again, paying attention to the question words.
- Present the table. Explain that noun clauses can function as nouns, and that like nouns they can be the object of verbs and they can follow prepositions.
- **Highlight** that a noun clause contains a verb but it is not a complete sentence by itself. Point out that the clauses in the table all function as objects.
- Ask the students to complete the table with examples from the conversation.
- Check the answers with the class.
- Direct the students' attention to the **What's right?** box. Point out or elicit that the second sentence is incorrect because it is necessary to use the affirmative form, not the question form, in this type of clause. Elicit other examples and write them on the board.

Answers
1 what   2 how   3 when   4 where   5 why

C

- Ask the students to complete the exercise individually. Remind them that there may be more than one possible answer. Encourage them to refer to the table if they need help.
- When you check the answers, ask different students to read the complete sentence aloud in each case.

Answers
1 what   2 how   3 how   4 why   5 where   6 when

D

- Give the students a few minutes to work individually to complete the sentences with their own ideas.
- Then put them in pairs and ask them to compare and contrast their views.

Extra: homework

Give the students some more sentence beginnings and ask them to complete them. For example, *A good holiday is when …*, *An embarrassing situation is when …*, *A nice place to relax is where …*, *A good job is when …*, *I like talking to friends when …*, *We should all live where …*, *School teaches you what …* .

 Workbook p. 23, Section 3

Reading: a magazine article (p. 48)

Lead-in
Ask the students if they ever read magazines. Invite volunteers to share the titles of their favourite magazines. Continue the discussion by asking if the students read magazine articles online, on e-readers or in printed versions. Ask them to share the topic of an interesting magazine article they have read recently.

A

- Ask the students to close their books. On the board, write the question *What are some ways to be happier?* Elicit ideas from the class and write them on the board. Explain that that they will read a magazine article on this topic and see if their ideas match what the research mentions in the article.
- Ask the students to read the article, keeping the question in mind.
- Allow enough time for them to read the article silently. Then elicit answers to the question. See if any of their original ideas were the same as the two ways mentioned in the article.

Answer
Deciding to be optimistic about life and practising positive emotions are two ways to be happier.

Extra: reading practice

Write these questions on the board to check the students' comprehension.
1 How do psychologists define happiness?
2 Why is happiness subjective?
3 What are some basic components of happiness?
4 What is the greatest influence on happiness?
5 Why do scientists research happiness?

Answers
1 'a state of well-being'
2 Because it can mean different things to different people.
3 physical condition, genetics and choice about how we feel and think
4 our choice about how we feel and think
5 It is useful and we can learn more about developing social or psychological traits that can help us lead fuller lives.

B

- Remind the students that understanding when something is accurate is important to succeeding in school. Give the students time to answer the true/false questions individually. Point out that they have a third option for each question: *NM* (not mentioned).
- Put the students in pairs to compare their answers before checking the answers as a class.

Answers
1 F 2 NM 3 T 4 T 5 F 6 T

Extra: reading practice

Ask the students to read the article again and to find the reasons or explanations for the statements.

Answers
1 Happiness is a very subjective state and can mean different things to different people.
2 NM
3 One component of happiness is genetic.
4 Some research has found that practising positive emotions can have a positive effect on our general state of well-being.
5 A recent study found that using an app to find out how happy people are feeling was reliable.
6 A study found that people who are less focused are less happy.

Extra: discussion

Put the students in pairs or small groups to discuss if they agree or disagree with the statements in Ex. B.

C

- Ask the students to notice the words in bold in the article. Explain that these are all mood words. Define the word *mood* if necessary (the way that someone is feeling, for example, whether they are happy, sad or angry).
- Give the students time to match each mood word with its definition. Have them work individually for this activity.
- Put the students in pairs to compare their answers before checking the answers as a class.

Answers
a optimistic b distracted c state of well-being
d pessimistic e emotions f depressed
g focused h in a good mood

D

- Put the students in pairs to discuss answers to the questions. Encourage them to give reasons for their answers.
- Ask the pairs to share their answers with the class. Extend the discussion by asking the students what may cause states of well-being or moods to change. Ask them if they think it is possible to change a mood easily (either their own or someone else's).

Extra: homework

Ask the students to choose a mood word from Ex. C and write a paragraph describing a time they felt this mood or emotion. Encourage them to answer questions such as who or what made them feel this way, where they were, why they felt this, when it was and how they changed (or stayed the same).

▶ Workbook p. 24, Section 4

Grammar: review of conditional forms (p. 49)

Lead-in

Ask the students to look at the photo. Ask them who they think these people are, how old they are and what their relationship is. Listen to their ideas as a class. Eventually reveal that they are an uncle and nephew. Explain that the nephew, Tom, is getting advice from his uncle. Encourage them to talk about who they talk to when they need advice. Ask them what kinds of things they need advice about.

A 1.19

- See the Student's Book for the **audioscript**.
- Ask the students to read the question first. Then ask them to listen and read the conversation and find the answer. Play the audio once.
- Elicit the answer and encourage the class to discuss whether they agree or disagree with the advice.

Ups and downs UNIT 4

Answer

Tom's uncle advises him to take a year off before going to university.

Extra: speaking

Put the students in pairs to rewrite the conversation and change the advice the uncle gives. Encourage them to be creative. Plan time for the students to perform their conversations in front of the class.

NOTICE!

- Direct the students' attention to the *Notice!* box.
- Review the conditional forms if necessary. Ask the students how many types of conditionals there are in one conversation.

Answers

If people take a year off, they're more mature when they start university… (zero conditional)

If I had taken a year off, I would have travelled around the world. (third conditional)

I think it can be a very good idea if you plan it properly and do something useful with it. (zero conditional)

But Mum thinks that if I travel for a year, I won't want to go to uni when I return. (first conditional)

… but if I were you, I'd go for it. (second conditional)

B

Form & Function

- Ask the students to read the conversation again, paying attention to the conditional forms.
- Review the forms and functions in the table. Give the students time to write the statements from the conversation that they underlined earlier in the correct place in the table.
- Check the answers. Remind the students that apart from *would*, they can also use *could* and *might* in third conditionals. Explain that this introduces an element of possibility into the sentence. Compare the meaning of *I would have got a much better job* (definite) and *I could have got a much better job* (possible).
- Direct the students' attention to the *What's right?* box. Point out that *would have* never goes in the clause beginning with *if*, but in the main clause, so the second sentence is incorrect. You could write some other incorrect sentences on the board for the students to correct.

Answers

1. If I had taken a year off, I would have travelled around the world.
2. If I were you, I'd go for it.
3. if I travel for a year, I won't want to go to uni when I return.
4. if people take a year off, they're more mature when they start university
5. It can be a very good idea if you plan it properly.

C

- Go over the instructions. Make sure the students understand that the first column contains the first parts of the sentences and the second column contains the second parts of the sentences.
- Ask them to work individually. Tell them to pay special attention to the verb forms to help them find the right answers. Encourage them to look at the table if they need help as they work.
- Check the answers with the class.

Answers

1 b 2 d 3 c 4 a

D

- Give the students time to work individually and complete the sentences.
- Put them in pairs to share their ideas. Encourage the partners to ask questions to get more information.
- Ask them to find three things they have in common.
- Listen to some of their ideas with the whole class. Correct any errors in the use of the conditionals.

Extra: grammar practice

Ask the students to use the sentence beginnings in Ex. D to write more sentences. Tell them that this time they can use different topics and write about anything they choose.

 Workbook pp. 24–25, Section 5

Writing: a thank-you note (p. 50)

Lead-in

Define *favour* (a nice or helpful thing you do for someone else). Put the students in small groups to talk about favours that they've asked for and favours that they've done for someone else. Ask a member of each group to summarise the discussion for the rest of the class.

Ask the students to read the information in the skills panel. Point out that thank-you notes include two elements: what you are thanking the person for and the effect it has had on you. Provide an example: *Thank you for the flowers you sent me when I was sick. They made me feel a lot better!* Hold a whole-class discussion about how the students feel when they receive a thank-you note and how they feel if they don't receive one when they've done someone a favour or given someone a gift.

A

- Put the students in pairs to brainstorm a list of situations in which they would need to send a formal thank-you note. Elicit answers such as *a gift from a grandparent* or *information from a teacher*. Ask each pair to share their list with the class. Create a list on the board.

- Give the students time to read the thank-you note. Then ask them to read the questions and read the note again to find the answers. Point out that the first letter is given for each word in item 4.
- Check the answers with the class.

Answers

1 giving an inspiring workshop and explaining how the work environment affects mood
2 The workers are all smiling more and the workplace is more attractive and pleasant.
3 formal; students should note the use of complete sentences, division into paragraphs, use of correct punctuation, formal language and tone formal ending
4 a) inspiring b) fascinating c) beneficial

B

- Tell the students that they are going to write a thank-you note and ask them to choose one of the situations.
- Present the starting expressions that the students can use in their letters.
- Encourage the students to write a beneficial effect and ending expression, based on the letter they choose to write. Provide some common ending expressions, such as *Take care, Keep in touch, See you soon, Love, Thanks again*.
- Remind them to think about what they are thanking the person for and the effect this has had: how their actions helped and/or how things might have been different if they hadn't helped. Suggest some common phrases (*If you hadn't given me ..., If I hadn't got that ...*) and review conditionals if necessary.

C

- Put the students in pairs for a peer-review session. Ask the students to suggest ways to improve each other's notes.

Extra: homework

Ask the students to take the advice from the peer-review session into consideration and to rewrite their thank-you note for homework.

▶ Workbook p. 25, Section 6

Pronunciation: reduced forms of *would you* and *did you* (p. 50)

A 1.20

- See the Student's Book for the **audioscript**.
- Explain that native English speakers often use reduced forms. Remind the students that reduced forms are never written; they are only spoken. Tell the students it is important not only to be able to pronounce these, but also to understand them when they are listening to native speakers.
- Write *would you* and *did you* on the board. Briefly pronounce the reduced forms and tell the students that the audio you are about to play has more examples.
- Play the audio. Ask the students to notice the reduced forms of *would you* (/wʊdʒə/) and *did you* (/dɪdʒə/) in each pair.
- Play the audio again and pause after each question. Ask the students to repeat the question using the reduced form.

B 1.21

- See the Student's Book for the **audioscript** – one question in each pair in Ex. A.
- Make sure the students understand the task (to choose the question they hear from each pair in Ex. A).
- Play the audio once. Repeat only if necessary. Check the answers.

Answers

1 a) What would you do?
2 b) Why did you go?
3 b) When did you leave?
4 a) How would you find out?

C

- Put the students in pairs to take turns saying one question from each pair in Ex. A. Ask them to pronounce it clearly so that their partner can identify it.
- Circulate to help as needed.

Speaking: talking about having a positive attitude (p. 51)

Lead-in

On the board, write the phrases *I never promised you a rose garden; Every day may not be good, but there's something good in every day; April showers bring May flowers;* and *Life isn't a bowl of cherries*. Ask the students if they know what the phrases mean (*I never said that life would be perfect; Even bad days have some positive aspects; A negative situation can lead to a positive outcome; Life isn't always happy or easy.*). Ask the students if these are positive or negative (negative, positive, positive, negative). Continue the discussion by asking the students if they know of equivalent sayings in their own languages.

A

- Ask the students to read the sayings. Explain that they are additional common sayings, or proverbs, in English. Put the students in small groups to discuss what the sayings mean and whether they express a positive or negative attitude. Ask them to explain why.
- Listen to their ideas as a class before giving the answers.

Ups and downs UNIT 4 37

Answers

Every cloud has a silver lining. = A negative situation always brings some positive result. (positive)

Think of the glass as half full, not half empty. = Focus on the positive aspects of a situation, not the negative aspects. (positive)

Always expect the worst and then you're never disappointed. = Expect very little, in order to avoid unhappiness. (negative)

Alternative

Put the students in pairs to discuss what the sayings mean and whether they are positive or negative. Have the pairs combine to form groups of four to discuss their answers. Then have the groups take turns contributing their ideas to a class discussion.

Extra: proverbs

Ask the students if any of these proverbs translate into their language. Do they know any other proverbs in their language?

B 1.22

- See p. 124 for the **audioscript**.
- Tell the students they are going to listen to a person talking about a workshop. Explain the task to the class, making sure they all understand the instructions.
- Play the audio once and check progress. If necessary, play the audio again before checking the answer.

Answer

Students should tick: talking about a problem, thinking positively

C

- Explain the task. Make sure that the students have read and understood the questions. Point out that this task is in preparation for an independent speaking exercise. You could model the task by making notes on the board and completing a sample table.
- Give the students plenty of time to think of a situation and write notes for each question.

D

- Direct the students' attention to the examples in the **How to say it** box and encourage them to begin their story with the first expression (*I'd like to tell you about what happened when …*). Encourage them to use the third conditional in their story as well as any sayings. Review conditionals if necessary.
- Put the students in pairs. Ask them to talk to their partner about the situation they made notes on and to speak for about one and a half minutes. Their partner should listen without interrupting, but partners can ask questions when they have finished. Ask the partners to tell the problem back to the speaker and to offer advice and suggestions. Then ask them to change roles and repeat the exercise.
- When the students have finished, have each pair join with another pair to share stories and get more advice.
- Ask volunteers to share what they learned with the whole class. When a student has finished speaking, point out any sayings from Ex. A or any conditionals or phrases from the **How to say it** box that were included.

LifeSkills: being a positive team member (p. 52)

Step 1: Focus on finding solutions rather than blaming people for problems. (Ex. B, Ex. C)
Step 2: Listen to other team members with a positive attitude. (Ex. D)
Step 3: Present your point of view in a positive way. (Ex. D, Ex. E)

Lead-in

Read the target skill aloud and invite the students to tell you what they think *being a positive team member* means. Continue the discussion by asking the students what kind of business they might like to work in and if there is any business or job where being a positive team member is important. Ask them to look at the photo and say what kind of business would use this type of equipment (an athletic company that produces sports and fitness equipment). Extend the discussion by asking them if they have used any of this type of equipment and if they like exercise and how it makes them feel. Ask them to support their answers.

Remind the students that group work and team projects are an important part of academic work as well as of careers and society. Ask the students in what kinds of situations people have to function as team members. Remind them that having a positive attitude is important. Ask them to share any personal experiences they have had with positive or negative attitudes when working in a group or team.

Then **highlight** the three-step strategy to develop the skill of *being a positive team member*.

A

- Ask the students to read the memo about Sportsense. Explain that this company is fictional but the situation is similar to real-life situations people can face in their work. Ask the students what is happening in the photo at the bottom of the page (a business meeting).
- Address any vocabulary questions before asking the students to answer the question and underline the company's issues.
- Check the answer with the class.

Answer

The problem is that the company's new project is facing a number of difficulties, including: it's behind schedule, costs seem to be increasing, there seem to be personal problems between team members.

B

- Point out that positive thinking focuses on solutions, while negative thinking only focuses on problems. Explain that each pair of sentences contains one statement that focuses on a problem and one that focuses on a solution. Ask the students to work individually, read the sentences and mark them with either *P* (for problem) or *S* (for solution).
- Have the students compare their answers in pairs before checking the answers with the class. Check that they understand *challenge* (something that requires a lot of skill, energy and determination to deal with) and *supplier* (a company that supplies products or services).

Answers

1 a) P b) S   2 a) S b) P   3 a) P b) S   4 a) S b) P

C

- Draw attention to the photo and ask the students to contrast this with the photo on p. 52. Make sure they notice that this is another business meeting, but in this meeting the team members are working well together, are listening to each other and seem to feel positively.
- Explain that the students are going to work in groups of four and that each person will have a role to play. Explain the setting (an office) and the situation (having a meeting to solve the company's problems that are putting the project at risk – being behind schedule, facing increasing costs, struggling with personal problems among members of the team). Tell them that they will have time to think of ideas for solving the problems from the point of view of their position in the company. Remind them that their goal is to think of positive ways to present their problems together with possible solutions.
- Put the students in groups of four and ask them to decide together which role each group member will take. Ask them to read their role and not to read the others.
- Give the students time to prepare what they will say.

D

- Present the **How to say it** box. Explain that this language is used to give positive feedback to other members of a team. Encourage them to use these phrases in the roleplay. Remind them to make positive statements as often as they can. Reiterate that using positive language and praise when working as a team motivates team members.
- Explain the roleplay instructions. Remind them that the overall goal is to create one action plan to make the project more successful. Explain that there is likely to be conflict depending on their role, so approaching problems positively is the best option. Review the positive phrases in Ex. B and tell them that some of these phrases can be used. For example, the project leader might use the solution-focused phrase from item 3 as part of the discussion.
- Have the students roleplay their meeting in their groups from Ex. C. Check that they are using positive language and giving praise where appropriate.
- Make sure that they have a clear action plan at the end of the meeting.

E

- Leave time for each group to present their final action plan to the rest of the class. Ask them to give reasons for their choices.
- Ask the class to decide which action plan is the most effective.

Extra: homework

Ask the students to use the action plan to write a short report outlining the problems and solutions that their group presented.

F

- Ask the students to discuss to the questions in groups.
- Focus the students on what they still need to work on in order to improve the skill of *being a positive team member* in the domain of **Work and Career**.
- Elicit some suggestions from the class for how the students might continue to practise and develop those skills, for example, by *participating in school projects, pair and group work in classes, working with peers on homework, going to study groups, displaying school spirit*.

 REFLECT

- Discuss the question with the whole class. Ask the students to say what they feel are the most useful points they learned from this lesson and how the skill of *being a positive team member* might be useful in the domains of **Study and Learning** and **Self and Society,** either now or in the future.
- Elicit the following ideas: *joining team sports, participating in family activities, making big decisions, helping friends or family with tasks*, etc.

RESEARCH

- Go through the task and check that the students are clear about what they have to do.
- Suggest that the students search for information related to business. Depending on class time and availability of computers, this could be done in class rather than outside of class.
- Have them share their findings (in class). Lead a class discussion about the information and any differences in the opinions given.

Language wrap-up (p. 54)

For notes on how to approach the exercises in the Language wrap-up section, please see page 9.

1 Vocabulary

- Ask the students to read the sentences for general understanding and to gain an idea of the context before filling in the blanks with the words from the box.
- Check the answers with the class by calling on individual students to read the completed sentences aloud.

Ups and downs   **UNIT 4**   **39**

2 Grammar

A

- Remind the students of the importance of word order in sentences with noun clauses as objects.

B

- Ask the students to read the whole text through first before completing the exercise. Encourage them to say each sentence silently to themselves before deciding on their answers.

Speaking workshop: expressing personal preference (p. 55)

Lead-in

Survey the class. Ask them which they prefer: milk or juice, fruits or vegetables, pizza or spaghetti, dogs or cats, ginger biscuits or chocolate chip biscuits. Create as many choices as you like to get the students focused on expressing personal preferences.

A 1.23

- See p. 124 for the **audioscript**.
- Ask the students if they have taken a standardised test in which they had to speak or write an answer expressing a personal preference and supporting their answer. Invite volunteers to share their experiences and discuss what makes these questions challenging.
- Draw attention to the question in the box. Point out that this is similar to the types of questions they'll see on standardised tests or that they will have to answer in academic studies.
- Ask the students what their answer would be.
- Explain that they will hear a response to this question.
- Play the audio and have the students take notes on the speaker's main points on the notepad provided. Put the students in pairs to discuss what the sayings mean and whether they are positive or negative. Have the pairs combine to form groups of four to discuss their answers. Then have the groups take turns contributing their ideas to a class discussion.
- Put the students in pairs to compare their notes. Then discuss answers as a class.

Answers

Which option does the speaker select? family and friends are more important than money

Reason 1: You can still be unhappy if you have lots of money.

Example: His friend's grandfather was rich and lonely.

Reason 2: Money is (very) temporary.

Example: His neighbour's house burnt down and she lost everything very suddenly.

Conclusion: Money by itself can't make you happy. Your relationships make you happy in the long run.

B

- Explain that English has collocations (words that often go together). It is important to remember these word combinations. Tell the students they will practise listening for some common word combinations.
- Play the audio again and ask the students to match the words in the first column with the words that go with them in the second column.
- Repeat the audio only if necessary.
- Check the answers with the class.

Answers

1 e **2** d **3** a **4** b **5** c

Extra: speaking

Ask the students to choose two or three of the discourse markers and use each one in a sentence. Then put the students in pairs and have them take turns saying their sentences to their partner.

C

- Explain that the students will now give their own answer to a new question. Encourage them to follow the same process by reading the question in the box and then writing their own ideas for their answer on the notepad provided.
- Give the students time to make notes and prepare a response. Point out that they will present their answer to a partner.

D

- Put the students in pairs. Schedule enough time for each pair of students to present their answer to the question to each other. Each student should talk for about one minute.
- Remind the students that they should cover all the points in their outline and should try to use the discourse markers from Ex. B in their answers.

How are you doing?

- Ask the students to read the statements and tick the ones they believe are true.
- Ask them to discuss their answer with their partner and identify things they could improve on next time.

 Workbook pp. 26–27, SkillsStudio

UNIT 5 SOMETHING IN THE WATER

The expression *it must be something in the water* is used to describe something that can't be easily explained, e.g. why everyone in a group is in a good or bad mood for no obvious reason (because they have all drunk the same water). This unit is about the effects of water on society in general.

Unit plan

Unit opener	(p. 56)	20 min.
1 Grammar: the passive	(p. 58)	40 min.
2 Reading: inferring opinion	(p. 59)	30 min.
• Vocabulary: marketing		15 min.
3 Writing: contributing to an online debate	(p. 60)	30 min.
4 Pronunciation: word stress in adjective + compound noun phrases	(p. 60)	15 min.
5 Grammar: expressions of purpose	(p. 61)	40 min.
6 Listening: to an interview	(p. 62)	30 min.
• Vocabulary: environmental issues		15 min.
7 Speaking: suggesting alternatives	(p. 63)	30 min.
LifeSkills: developing empathy (Self and Society)	(p. 64)	50 min.
• Optional downloadable *LifeSkills* lesson (Work and Career)		50 min.
• Optional downloadable *LifeSkills* lesson (Study and Learning)		50 min.
Language wrap-up	(p. 66)	15 min.
Writing workshop	(p. 67)	20 min.
Video and downloadable video worksheet		45 min.

Unit opener (p. 56)

Lead-in
Ask the students to look at the unit title and the photos and to predict what the unit will be about. Ask them what role they think water has in our society and what needs and uses humans have for water. Direct the students' attention to the points in the unit objectives box and go through the information with them. To get your students to think about the skills being developed in this unit, ask them to look at the questions in the cogs.

Reading: inferring opinion
- Ask the students what *read between the lines* means (to get information from a text that is not directly stated by the writer). We can combine the information given in a text with our own knowledge and experiences in order to infer many things, such as the writer's attitude toward the topic and people's backgrounds and relationships.

Speaking: suggesting alternatives
- Ask the students to think about the last time they helped someone make a decision and the language they used to suggest alternatives. Ask them what they can say in English when they want to offer several options or choices. Explain that knowing these kinds of phrases can help them in situations when they want to be helpful to others.

LifeSkills: developing empathy
- Ask the students how they feel when they see a person less fortunate than themselves. Explain that the ability to understand others' feelings is called *empathising*. Elicit several reasons why empathising is a useful skill.

Common European Framework: unit map

Unit 5	Competence developed	CEF Reference (B2 competences)
Grammar	can use and understand the passive in a variety of tenses	Table 1; Table 2; Sections 5.2.1.2; 6.4.7.7; 6.4.7.8
Reading	can infer a writer's opinion	Table 1; Table 2; Sections 4.4.2.2; 4.4.2.4; 4.5.2.2
Writing	can contribute to an online debate	Table 1; Table 2; Sections 4.4.1.2; 4.4.3.2; 4.4.3.4; 4.5.2.1; 5.2.1.1; 5.2.1.2; 5.2.1.6; 5.2.2.2; 5.2.2.4; 5.2.3.2
Pronunciation	can correctly apply word stress in adjective + compound noun phrases	Section 5.2.1.4
Grammar	can use and understand expressions of purpose	Table 1; Table 2; Sections 5.2.1.2; 6.4.7.7; 6.4.7.8
Listening	can understand an interview	Table 1; Table 2; Sections 4.4.2.1; 4.4.3.1; 4.4.3.5; 4.5.2.2
Speaking	can suggest alternatives	Table 1; Table 2; Sections 4.4.1.1; 4.4.3.1; 4.4.3.5; 4.5.2.1; 5.2.3.2

Something in the water UNIT 5 41

Lead-in
Ask the students why people collect water (for drinking, bathing, watering the garden, etc). Have a discussion about what the water people collect might be used for. As a class, brainstorm ways that they know of to collect water. Make a list of their ideas on the board. Ask if they have ever had a situation when they have needed to collect water and why.

Culture note
Over 70% of the Earth's surface is covered with water. Approximately 95% of that is ocean water. Only around 2.5% of the Earth's water is fresh water that is safe to drink. Safe drinking water is essential to human life. Nearly one billion people worldwide have no, or limited, access to safe drinking water. Scientists are exploring many new ways to increase the amount of available drinking water. They include desalination, filtration, building reservoirs and collecting rain water and groundwater.

A
- Draw the students' attention to the photos, the captions and the explanations.
- Put the students in groups to discuss the photos and answer the questions.
- When the groups have finished their discussions, elicit their responses. Ask the students which systems they are familiar with and to give specific examples of any that can be found in their local region, in their country or in other countries they have visited or studied in.

Extra: research
For any of the water collection systems that the students are unfamiliar with, give them time to do some research online to find examples of places where they are used and why they work well in those areas.

B
- Have the students stay in the same groups as in Ex. A.
- Have the students read the questions silently. Give them time to think about their answers and make notes for their discussions.
- Give the groups time to complete their discussions. Circulate during the discussions and ask follow-up questions to encourage more detailed responses.

Extra: clarifying language review
During their discussions, encourage the students to use the phrases and expressions they learned for clarifying in Unit 3 (p. 39).

- Call on a student from each group to share their group's answers with the class.
- Extend the discussion by asking about water-related problems in the students' region or country, the cause of these problems, the consequences and what the local and national governments have done or could do about them.

Extra: the power of water
Have the class brainstorm the positive and negative powers of water. Write them on the board. Elicit the fact that water is one of the most important and powerful forces in nature. Most of nature cannot survive without water. It is renewing and life-giving; yet water also has great destructive power, not only in the form of floods and erosion but also because it is scarce in many places in the world, and it even causes war.

Grammar: the passive (p. 58)

A
- Draw the students' attention to the photo and ask them what is happening (animals are looking for dry ground).
- Give the students time to scan the article for unfamiliar vocabulary and ask any questions they may have (*suffered*: to experience something very unpleasant or painful; *canal*: an artificial river; *lack of funding*: not enough money to reach a goal).
- Have the students read the article. When they have finished, ask them what a monsoon season is and what problems it can create.

Answer
Monsoons are big rainstorms with wind and sometimes floods, usually occurring at a particular time of year, which can cause heavy damage to buildings, homes and crops. They often result in loss of human life.

NOTICE!
- Direct the students' attention to the **Notice!** box.
- Have them examine the three underlined examples of the passive in the text. Ask them to tell you which one is present (*is estimated*) and which ones are simple past (*were caused, were killed*), and to explain how each is formed.

Answer
We form the passive using the present/past form of *be* + past participle.
We use passive forms to focus on the person or thing affected by the verb.

B

Function
- Have the students read the article again, paying attention to the passive forms.
- Ask them to work individually to determine when the passive is used and to tick the appropriate phrases.
- Check the answers with the class.

> **Answers**
> Students tick the following items:
> when the action is more important than the person doing the action
> when we do not know the person doing the action

Form

- Have the students complete the table. Then check the answers with the class.
- Ask the students to scan the text for the following additional examples of the passive: *crops were damaged or destroyed*; *1.5 million people were affected*; *people are being advised*.

> **Answers**
> 1 is/are + being 2 have/has + been 3 had + been

C

- Direct the students' attention to the **What's right?** box. Elicit that a past participle is needed with *be* to form the passive. The second sentence uses a continuous form with *be* instead, and is therefore incorrect.
- Give the students time to read the partial sentences silently and think about which form of the passive best fits each one. Remind them that more than one form may be possible in some sentences.
- Have the students work individually to complete the sentences, and then compare answers in pairs.
- Check the answers with the class.

> **Answers**
> 1 is hit 2 have been killed 3 were evacuated
> 4 were destroyed/have been destroyed 5 had (already) been damaged / were (already) damaged 6 have been reopened 7 is being rebuilt 8 is being constructed / will be constructed / has been constructed

D

- Tell the students they are going to have a chance to practise the forms of the passive as they talk about a water disaster they have either experienced or heard about.
- Elicit and list on the board different types of water-related disasters (or those that relate to a lack of water) to give the students additional ideas, for example, flood, monsoon, hurricane, typhoon, landslide, tsunami, flash flood, drought.
- Put the students in pairs to think of a water-related disaster. Tell them that it could be a major one in their own country or one they heard about on the news, or it could be a minor one that occurred in their own home or community.
- Have the pairs make notes using the prompts provided. Remind them to use the passive where possible.
- When the pairs have finished making notes, have them combine to form groups of four and share their descriptions. Encourage the students to ask follow-up questions to find out more information.

▶ Workbook p. 28, Section 1

Reading: inferring opinion (p. 59)

Lead-in

Ask the students to read the information in the skills panel. Tell them we frequently infer information about people and situations in our daily lives. Elicit some examples, such as a person's job or social status based on the kind of clothing they wear or car they drive.

A

- Ask the students to think of the most they've ever spent on a glass or bottle of water. Then elicit their responses, asking if anyone has spent more on each, until you reach the highest amount spent and where.

B

- Tell the students they are going to read an article about some special types of bottled water.
- Have the students read the title of the article and elicit a few predictions about what the article is about. Ask the following questions to help them.
  Why do you think some companies might charge a lot of money for their bottled water?
  What kinds of people would pay up to £1,000 for a bottle of water?
  Why would they want to pay so much?
- Give the students time to read the article.
- Put the students in pairs and have them summarise the article in their own words.
- Elicit a few sentences from the class to summarise the article. Then ask the students to share their opinions about the products mentioned in the article. Get them to say whether they would buy them (giving reasons why or why not).

C

- Ask the students what they can tell about the writer's opinions based on the reading.
- Elicit that the writer does not directly say whether he approves or disapproves of 'exclusive' bottled water or its prices, but we can infer his opinion from some of the words or phrases he uses.
- Put the students in pairs to discuss the questions. Encourage them to discuss any other clues in the text about the writer's attitude. When they finish, have them compare answers with another pair.
- Check the answers with the class.

Something in the water UNIT 5 43

Answers

1 The writer has a negative opinion of exclusive bottles of water. Students might mention evidence in the text such as:
Believe it or not, there are brands of bottled water that range from around £10 to £1,000 per bottle!
In truth, no type of water can produce miracles; …
The advertisers all claim that their water is extremely pure and beneficial to our health in some way or another. But is it really? And does that make their water worth up to £1,000 a bottle?
In many cases, the spring water itself is not actually considered to be worth £1,000. The high price tags are often more about the bottle than the water that comes in it.
Even so, why are some people prepared to pay so much just for a drink of relatively ordinary spring water? Well, I can only guess …
Finally, some may even believe the health claims of the advertising companies.

2
a) The writer thinks the reader is likely to be surprised by the fact that there is a bottle of water that costs £1,000.
b) The writer thinks that the water should contain something special to justify the high expense.
c) The writer has no evidence that the water is pure and beneficial to health.
d) The writer feels that it would be naïve/ignorant to believe the claims.

Extra: homework

Have the students research various brands of bottled water and compare the claims different companies make about what makes them better or different from other brands. Alternatively, have them research other goods with high prices mainly because they are status symbols. Ask them to research the company's background, philosophy, marketing tactics, how the product became a status symbol and what customers say about it. The students should then prepare a poster presentation about the product and the company and present them in class.

D

- Direct the students' attention to the phrases in the box. Then have the students read the sentences and think about which phrase best completes each one.
- Go over any unfamiliar vocabulary. Then give the students time to complete the sentences. Make sure the students understand that they may need to change the forms of the verbs to fit the sentences.
- Check the answers with the class.

Answers

1 <u>market</u> water <u>as</u> **2** <u>ranged from</u> £1.50 <u>to</u> £3
3 <u>specially-designed</u> **4** <u>make</u> a product <u>worth</u> a higher price **5** <u>more about</u> the packaging <u>than</u> the product itself **6** <u>limited-edition</u>

E

- Put the students in groups to discuss the statements in Ex. D. Encourage them to say whether they agree or disagree, supporting their opinions with examples and evidence where possible.
- Review the phrases from Unit 3 for clarifying misunderstandings. Encourage the students to use them in their discussions.
- To conclude, extend the discussion with the whole class. Have the students share their opinions, then expand on the topic by discussing the following questions:
Do you buy any 'limited edition' or 'exclusive' products?
Do you think a higher price generally means a product is of better quality?

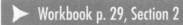 Workbook p. 29, Section 2

 Workbook p. 30, Section 3

Writing: contributing to an online debate (p. 60)

Lead-in

Ask the students how often they read news articles online and which websites they use. Ask whether anyone in the class reads the comments section frequently included at the end of online news articles, where readers can post their opinions and respond to others' opinions. Explain or elicit that frequently readers use these forums to debate a topic and to persuade others to agree with their view. Tell them they are going to read and practise participating in an online debate.

A

- Have the students read the topic of the debate. Elicit what the word *really* indicates in the debate question. Remind the students that often a single word can be enough to enable us to infer someone's opinion or attitude.

Answer

Really suggests a negative attitude toward bottled water.

B

- Have the students read the contributions to the online debate. Remind them that they should read each one to find out the writer's opinion about drinking bottled water, inferring the information when needed. Encourage the students to underline any words or phrases that offer clues about each writer's opinion.
- Have the students compare their ideas in pairs, referring to the text to support their answers.
- Call on individual students to summarise each writer's post in their own words, including the opinion expressed.

Answers

Writer 1: Against it, because his country has a good public water supply.
Writer 2: For it in countries where they don't have a good public water supply, but against it in countries that have safe drinking water.
Writer 3: For it in countries where drinking water is not available, but only if it becomes more affordable.

C

- Encourage the students to consider the opinions presented in the online posts and think about their own opinions on drinking bottled water. They should consider factors in their own country, such as availability of safe drinking water, as well as costs, environmental effects, etc.
- Elicit the students' ideas about some of the positive and negative points of drinking bottled water. List them on the board.
- Give the students time to make some notes on their own opinions and then explain that they will write a paragraph expressing their ideas.
- Review paragraph format and if needed write a guide for the paragraph's format on the board, for example:
  1) introductory topic sentence
  2) two reasons for your opinion
  3) one or two supporting details or examples for each opinion
  4) concluding sentence
- Put the students in groups to compare their ideas. Encourage them to debate the topic and include evidence to support their opinions.

Pronunciation: word stress in adjective + compound noun phrases (p. 60)

A 1.24

- See the Student's Book for the **audioscript**.
- Give the students time to read the phrases. Explain or elicit that when a word has stress, it is said with more emphasis.
- Play the audio once and have the students listen. Ask them to tell you which word is stressed in each pair (the second word). Then play the audio a second time and have the students repeat each phrase.
- Put the students in pairs and have them practise saying the phrases with the correct stress.

B 1.25

- See the Student's Book for the **audioscript**.
- Give the students time to read the sentences and think about which words should be stressed.
- Have the students practise the sentences in pairs, saying them to each other with the correct word stress.
- Play the audio to check and have the students repeat the sentences.

Extra: news reports

Have the students work in pairs to write a news article related to the topic of water, to include at least five of the phrases from Ex. A and Ex. B. Combine pairs to form groups of four and have the students deliver their news reports, focusing on the correct word stress.

Grammar: expressions of purpose (p. 61)

A

- Have the students close their books. Tell them you are going to ask them some questions related to humans and water. Ask the FAQs from the text and call on individual students to tell you the answers. Encourage them to make guesses. Write their guesses on the board.
- Have the students open their books and read the text.
- Ask the students which answers were close to their guesses and which facts they found most surprising.

NOTICE!

- Direct the students' attention to the **Notice!** box.
- Ask them to look at the underlined phrase and say what it expresses.

Possible answers

to control all of our body's functions, (purpose)
In order to be healthy, (reason)
So as not to suffer from this dangerous condition, (reason)
for washing and flushing the toilet! (reason)
so that these electrolytes are replaced. (purpose)

B

Form & Function

- Have the students read the text again, paying attention to the expressions of purpose.
- Direct the students' attention to the table and present it from left to right. Ask the students to complete the table individually with examples from the text.
- Put the students in pairs to compare answers. Then check the answers with the class.
- **Highlight** an important difference between *to* + infinitive and *so (that)* + (pro)noun + clause. To express purpose, *to* + infinitive can only be used when the subject of the main clause is the subject of the clause expressing purpose. If the subjects are different, it is necessary to use *so (that)* + (pro)noun. Compare:
I walked to work. I wanted to save money. = *I walked to work to save money.*
with:
I walked to work. My husband wanted to use the car. = *I walked to work so that my husband could use the car.*
NOT *I walked to work my husband to use the car.*

Something in the water UNIT 5

Answers

1 … most of the water is used for washing and flushing the toilet!
2 Because we need water to control all of our body's functions, …
3 In order to be healthy
4 So as not to suffer from this dangerous condition
5 … so that these electrolytes are replaced.

C

- Give the students time to read the instructions and the sentences, and to think about the correct expression of purpose for each.
- Have the students work individually to complete the sentences. Then compare answers in pairs.
- Check the answers with the class.
- Direct the students' attention to the **What's right?** box. Elicit/explain that the second sentence is incorrect because the preposition *for* needs to be followed by a gerund in expressions of purpose.

Answers

1 in order 2 keep 3 to get 4 helping 5 so that
6 so as to 7 to 8 so as

D

- Ask the students to think about the opinions they read in Ex. A.
- Give the students time to read the questions and think about their answers. Have them make some notes if they wish.
- Put the students in pairs and have them discuss the questions. Circulate and monitor, checking that expressions of purpose are used correctly.
- To conclude and assess the students' grasp of the target grammar, ask for a few volunteers to report on their discussions to the class.

Extra: grammar practice

Have the students generate more statements with the expressions of purpose. Give the students several questions to discuss in groups, or to write about for homework, for example:
Why is it important for people to conserve water?
What are some reasons people should stop drinking bottled water?
What are some creative uses for plastic water bottles?
Encourage them to try to use a variety of expressions of purpose in their discussions/writing.

▶ Workbook p. 31, Section 5

Listening: to an interview (p. 62)

Lead-in

Write the phrase *water poverty* on the board and ask the students to tell you what they think it means (poverty and lack of opportunities caused by lack of access to clean water). Ask the students to name some areas of the world where this is a problem and to discuss how they think/know it affects people in those regions.

A 🎧 1.26

- See p. 124 for the **audioscript**.
- Tell the students they are going to listen to a radio interview with a representative from an organisation called *Water Watch*. Elicit a few predictions about what the organisation is/does.
- Give the students time to read the questions. Remind them of, or elicit from them, the meaning of *charity* (an organisation to which you give money so that it can give money and help to people who are poor or sick, or who need advice and support).
- Play the audio. Tell the students they can take notes as they listen if they wish.
- Put the students in pairs to discuss their answers to the questions.
- Elicit the answers from the class.

Answers

1 To prevent water poverty
2 To improve hygiene, education and standard of living
3 They have to travel long distances to collect water for their families.
4 Volunteers

Culture note

A charity is a type of non-profit organisation (NPO). The purpose of a charity is to make improvements to peoples' lives, living conditions, health and well-being; or to improve or protect the environment or the welfare of animals. Charities depend on donations from individuals and companies. Some of the world's leading charities include Médecins Sans Frontières; The International Red Cross; the World Wildlife Fund and the Salvation Army.

B

- Give the students time to read the notes. **Highlight** the fact that this time they are listening specifically for numbers and, like scanning when they are reading, they do not need to listen to everything the speakers say. Instead, they should focus their listening on the phrases from the prompts and the numbers.
- Play the audio and have the students complete the notes. Check whether they need to listen one more time.
- Have the students compare answers in pairs.

- To check the answers, call on individual students to write the correct numbers on the board. Make sure the students have all written the numbers correctly and review any difficulties they had with number format.

Answers
1 884 million 2 £25 million 3 25.5 million 4 £1

C
- Put the students in pairs to discuss any of the bold words or phrases they already know, and to share their meanings.
- Have the students complete the matching exercise, referring to the text to check their answers and using the context to figure out any words they don't know. They could also use a dictionary to help them.
- Have the students compare answers with another pair. Then check the answers with the class.

Answers
1 c 2 a 3 b 4 d 5 h 6 g 7 f 8 e

D
- Give the students time to read the questions and think about their opinions.
- Put the students in pairs to discuss the questions.
- Direct the students' attention to the examples in the **How to say it** box and encourage them to use the expressions in their discussion. Encourage them also to use expressions of purpose and to support their ideas using the statistics and facts from the interview if appropriate.
- Have the students share their ideas. Ask them to use as many of the new words and phrases from Ex. C as they can.
- To conclude, lead a class discussion. Call on individual students to share their ideas and encourage the rest of the class to ask follow-up questions.

Extra: homework
Have the students write an essay responding to the questions in Ex. D.

▶ Workbook p. 31, Section 6

Speaking: suggesting alternatives (p. 63)

Lead-in
Ask the students if they have ever donated to a charity or taken part in or supported a charity in some way. Elicit some of the students' experiences, what kind of work the charity did and why they wanted to take part in it. Share any experiences you have had with charity or volunteer work, or any charities you support and your reasons for doing so.

Ask the students to read the information in the skills panel. Explain that in this lesson they will practise phrases for suggesting alternatives.

A
- Draw the students' attention to the photos.
- Have the students work in pairs to match the photos with the advertisements below.
- Then ask them to describe the problem or issue shown in each photo.
- Check the answers with the class.

Answers
1 B 2 A 3 C

Extra: class discussion
To expand on the topic, lead a brief class discussion about the ads. Ask the students which problem they think is the most serious. Ask whether they have similar issues in their country, what is being done about them and whether they think ads like these would help. Ask them to tell you which ad they think is most effective and why.

B 1.27
- See p. 125 for the **audioscript**.
- Tell the students they are going to listen to two people discussing ways they can help solve one of the problems presented in Ex. A.
- Play the audio and have the students listen. Ask which problem the discussion is about (water pollution: photo 2).
- Play the audio again. Have the students tick the phrases that are used.
- Have the students compare answers in pairs. Then check the answers with the class.

Answers
Students tick:
What if we do … instead?
There's always …
We could try …
I'd suggest …

Extra: creating ads
Have the students research local charities that help people who have been affected by natural disasters. Encourage the students to create their own ads as though they are employees of that charity. Have the students present their creations to the class. Take a vote. Whose ad does the class prefer: the charity's ad or the student's ad?

Something in the water   UNIT 5   47

Extra: in your own words

Have the students work in pairs to re-create the conversation in their own words from memory. Then have them practise it using the phrases for suggesting ideas. Ask for volunteer pairs to perform their conversations for the class.

C

- Give the students time to read the instructions and think about which charity they would like to support.
- Elicit from the class the suggestions the people in the conversation made for how to help the charity and list them on the board.
- Put the students in pairs to decide on a charity and suggest ways to support it. Have them come up with four or five alternatives for ways to support the charity. Encourage them to be realistic and creative and to think of suggestions that would work well and be successful.
- When the pairs have finished, have them present their suggestions to the class, giving reasons for the ideas they chose.

 Workbook p. 30, Section 4

LifeSkills: developing empathy (p. 64)

Step 1: Think of an experience that you have had that is similar to another person's situation. (Ex. A, Ex. B, Ex. C, Ex. D)
Step 2: Compare the difficulty of your experience with that of the other person. (Ex. E)
Step 3: Imagine how you would feel in the other person's situation. (Ex. E)

Lead-in

Read the target skill aloud and invite the students to tell you what they think developing empathy means. Elicit a definition from the class for the word *empathy* and then read the definition in the book. Give or elicit examples of situations relating to **Self and Society** in which empathy might be helpful (*forming relationships and personal bonds with others, supporting a family member or a friend in crisis*, etc).

Then **highlight** the three-step strategy to develop the skill of *developing empathy*. Point out that this skill is highly useful in relationships and social interactions with others and it is also useful in the domain of **Work and Career**. Ask the students to think about a time when someone showed empathy toward them. Ask who the person was and how it made the student feel to know that that person understood their feelings. Elicit that empathy helps people feel accepted and that they are not alone.

A

- Ask the class to tell you some of the ways they have used water today before class, for example, take a shower, wash dishes, use it to cook breakfast, flush the toilet, etc. Encourage the use of the expressions of purpose from the Grammar section (*I used water in order to boil an egg this morning; I use a lot of water for showering*, etc). List their responses on the board.
- Put the students in pairs to discuss all the ways they use water in an average day and to estimate how much they use. Tell them to use the list showing average water usage for different activities to help them.
- Have the pairs share their responses with the class and compare their levels of water usage. If any pairs use exceptionally more or less water, have them discuss the reasons why. Encourage the students not to be judgmental if they think their classmates use too much water.

Alternative

Ask the students to form small groups to discuss how much water they use compared to other members of the group. Remind them to use comparative and superlative adjectives in their comparisons.

Extra: grammar practice

Put the students in small groups. Ask them to select one or two expressions of purpose and use them to write sentences about their daily water use. Encourage the students to write sentences saying how much water they use for different functions each day.

B

- Have the pairs combine to form groups of four.
- Give the groups time to discuss any water-related problems the students may have experienced and how they felt if they had limited access to water.
- Direct the students' attention to the examples in the **How to say it** box and encourage them to use the expressions in their discussion.
- Call on volunteers to share the group members' experiences and feelings. Ask the rest of the class if they have experienced any similar situations.

Extra: homework

Ask the students to write a short paragraph explaining how much water they use in a day. Encourage them to think of ways in which they could cut down the amount of water they use and to include these ideas in their paragraph.

C
- Draw the students' attention to the photo. Ask the students to describe the situation and where they think it is (Africa – Ethiopia).
- Elicit some predictions about what the information will say about the woman.
- Have the students read the information.
- Put the students in pairs to estimate how much water Shartati and her family use. Remind them to refer to the notes in Ex. A.
- Elicit some estimates from the class and ask the students to predict some other information they might hear about Shartati and her family.

Possible answer
for having a shower = 0
for having a bath = approx. **5** litres (They probably wash with water they collect.)
for brushing teeth = 0 (They probably don't have running water.)
for flushing the toilet = 0 (They probably don't have running water.)
for washing clothes = **10** litres (Or 0 if they take their clothes to a river to wash.)
for cooking and drinking = **5** litres
Total: about **20** litres

D 🎧 **1.28**
- See p. 125 for the **audioscript**.
- Play the audio and encourage the students to take notes about how much water the family uses.
- Put the students in the same pairs as in Ex. C to come up with a brief summary of the listening in their own words and to discuss how much water the family probably uses.
- Elicit some of the pairs' original guesses and compare them with the actual amount of water used by the family.

Possible answer
It appears that they sometimes use about 10 litres and sometimes a bit more.

E
- Have the students read the discussion questions and think about their answers.
- Put the students in groups to discuss the questions.
- When the groups finish, elicit some responses to each question and lead a class discussion about questions 3 and 4.
- Ask the students to think about other situations in their country or around the world that might be improved if more people knew about them and empathised with the people who lived there.

F
- Put the students in groups to discuss the questions. Encourage the students to think of reasons as they answer them.
- Ask for feedback from the groups and focus on their reasons. Then lead a class discussion about why the skill of *developing empathy* is useful in the domain of **Self and Society**.

 REFLECT
- Discuss the question with the whole class. Ask the students to say what they feel are the most useful points they learned from this lesson and how the skill of *developing empathy* might be useful in the domains of **Study and Learning** and **Work and Career**, either now or in the future.
- Elicit the following ideas: *trying to understand the views and experiences of others, helping make useful suggestions and positive changes at home, school or in their community*, etc.

Extra: focus on the issues
Provide the students with regular opportunities to continue to develop their ability to express empathy in English. Present case studies or bring in articles about issues from the local community, region, country or around the world. Have the students discuss the issues and think about the way people in those places are being affected by the issues.

🔬 **RESEARCH**
- Go through the task and check that the students are clear about what they have to do.
- Suggest a water-related charity or specific issues or articles for the students to explore.
- Have them do research and make notes on the problem and its effects, and make suggestions for how to improve it in a report to the class.

Language wrap-up (p. 66)

For notes on how to approach the exercises in the Language wrap-up section, please see page 9.

1 Vocabulary

A
- Go over the phrases in the box.
- Encourage the students to read through the ad and focus on the overall meaning before they choose the correct word or phrase for each blank.
- To check the answers, call on individual students to read the sentences aloud, inserting the correct answers. Ask the rest of the class to say whether the sentence is correct or not.

B
- Give the students time to read through the text before they choose their answers.
- To check answers, call on individual students to read the sentences aloud, inserting the correct answers. Ask the rest of the class to say whether the sentence is correct or not.

Something in the water | **UNIT 5**

2 Grammar

A
- Before the students begin, tell them to think about the rules for forming the passive. Elicit one or two examples of verbs in the passive in different tenses and write them on the board.
- To check the answers with the class, call on individual students to write their rewritten sentences on the board. Ask the class to say whether each sentence is written correctly.

B
- Point out to the students that there may be more than one correct answer.
- Ask the students to read each sentence through first before completing the exercise. Encourage them to say each sentence silently to themselves before deciding on their answers.
- Check the answers with the class by asking individual students to read the sentences aloud. Where possible, elicit the alternative structure(s) for the sentence.

Writing workshop: interpreting data (p. 67)

A
- Write the target skill *interpreting data* on the board and elicit what it involves (analysing and understanding different types of information, such as facts, figures and statistics).
- Explain that the students are going to review a writing assignment for which a student has interpreted and summarised data about bottled water consumption in the USA.
- Ask the students to read the assignment and look at the table. To ensure that the students understand the assignment, ask for volunteers to summarise it in their own words. Elicit some predictions about some of the key information the student might include in the report.
- Ask a few questions to orient the students to the information in the table, for example, ask how many years the data covers (11), ask about the overall trend in bottled drinking water in the USA. (It has increased.) Ask which years saw a decrease (years 6 and 7).
- Give the students time to read the student's report. Have them discuss in pairs whether the student answered the question in the assignment fully.
- Then check the answer with the class.

> **Answer**
> The student has presented the main points of the data and represented the data correctly in written form.

B
- For item 1, have the students look at the vocabulary in bold in Ex. A and make sure they understand the terms. Encourage them to refer to the data in the table in order to deduce the meaning of any unknown terms.
- For item 2, look at the structure of the model report. Elicit the information included in each of the paragraphs.

> **Possible answers**
> 2 Paragraph 1 gives a general summary or overview of the information in the table.
> Paragraph 2 gives more specific information about fluctuations between particular years.
> Paragraph 3 gives the overall conclusion of all of the data.

C
- Have the students read the instructions and the information in the table.
- Ask the students to give you an overview in their own words of what the data in the table shows.
- Give the students time to make some notes for their reports. Remind them of the structure of the model report in Ex. A and encourage them to organise their notes according to that same structure.
- You could put the students in pairs to compare their notes.

D
- Make sure the students understand the assignment – that they should write three paragraphs following the structure in Ex. A.
- Have the students write their report in class or for homework. Remind them to write about 200 words.
- Award an extra mark or marks for including the bold terms from the model report as well as reported speech or other new vocabulary from the unit.

How are you doing?
- Ask the students to read the statements and tick the ones they believe are true.
- Ask them to discuss their essay with another student in the class and identify things they could improve on next time.

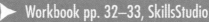 Workbook pp. 32–33, SkillsStudio

UNIT 6 LIVING TRADITIONS

The expression *living traditions* refers to beliefs or customs about the way we live which have been passed down within a family, group, society or culture. Traditions have a special meaning for us and can include a range of things, such as clothing, music, dances, ceremonies, festivities or holidays. The idea of a tradition is to remember and respect a previous time.

Unit plan

Unit opener	(p. 68)	20 min.
1 **Grammar:** *be used to / get used to*	(p. 70)	40 min.
2 **Listening:** for main ideas	(p. 71)	30 min.
3 **Reading:** a book excerpt	(p. 72)	30 min.
• Vocabulary: institutional traditions		15 min.
4 **Grammar:** verb + object + infinitive	(p. 73)	40 min.
5 **Pronunciation:** stress in words with *-tion/-sion*	(p. 74)	15 min.
6 **Speaking:** talking about personal rituals	(p. 74)	30 min.
• Vocabulary: phrasal verbs for personal rituals		15 min.
7 **Writing:** avoiding run-on sentences	(p. 75)	30 min.
LifeSkills: managing distractions (Study and Learning)	(p. 76)	50 min.
• Optional downloadable *LifeSkills* lesson (Self and Society)		50 min.
• Optional downloadable *LifeSkills* lesson (Work and Career)		50 min.
Language wrap-up	(p. 78)	15 min.
Speaking workshop	(p. 79)	20 min.
Video and downloadable video worksheet		45 min.

Unit opener (p. 68)

Lead-in
Ask the students to look at the unit title and the photos and to predict what the unit will be about. Draw attention to the background photo of an American-style parade. Ask the students if anyone has been to a parade like this. Ask the students to describe other types of parades they know about. If the students are from a variety of cultures, make a list on the board. If the students are from the same culture, ask them to list a type of dress that is common for their culture. Direct the students' attention to the points in the unit objectives box and go through the information with them. To get your students to think about the skills being developed in this unit, ask them to look at the questions in the cogs.

Listening: for main ideas
- Survey the students to find out how many of them are concerned when they don't understand every word in English. Tell them that understanding details might not always be important. Present the question and give the students time to make a list of situations. Compare their answers as a class.

Writing: avoiding run-on sentences
- Put the students in small groups to answer the question. Ask each group to present its list of comma uses.

LifeSkills: managing distractions
- Give the students a few minutes to read the survey and to check the option that best describes them. Take a survey of the class and list the results on the board.

Common European Framework: unit map

Unit 6	Competence developed	CEF Reference (B2 competences)
Grammar	can use and understand *be + used to* and *get + used to* structures	Table 1; Table 2; Sections 5.2.1.2; 6.4.7.7; 6.4.7.8
Listening	can listen for main ideas	Table 1; Table 2; Section 4.4.2.1; Section 4.5.2.2
Reading	can read and understand an excerpt from a book	Table 1; Table 2; Sections 4.4.2.2; 4.4.2.4; 4.5.2.2
Grammar	can use and understand verb + object + infinitive structures	Table 1; Table 2; Sections 5.2.1.2; 6.4.7.7; 6.4.7.8
Pronunciation	can correctly apply stress in words ending in *-tion* and *-sion*	Section 5.2.1.4
Speaking	can talk about personal rituals	Table 1; Table 2; Sections 4.4.1.1; 4.4.3.1; 4.4.3.5; 4.5.2.1; 5.2.1.1; 5.2.1.2; 5.2.3.2
Writing	can avoid run-on sentences	Table 1; Table 2; Sections 4.4.1.2; 4.5.2.1; 5.2.1.6

Living traditions UNIT 6 51

A

- Put the students in pairs. Draw attention to the photos and explain that these people are all wearing traditional dress from their countries. Ask the students to match the photos with the countries and to use their own words to describe each kind of traditional dress.
- Listen to their ideas as a class and then check the answers.
- If there are students familiar with any of the cultures pictured, ask them to give more details of the traditional dress. Ask if the students know of any other traditional dress from around the world. Elicit examples and the countries they come from.

Answers

1 Norway 2 Wales 3 Albania 4 Morocco 5 Ecuador
6 Kenya

Extra: discussion

Bring in a map and ask the students to locate the countries in Ex. A. Albania is in southeastern Europe, Ecuador is in South America, Kenya is in Africa, Morocco is in Africa, Norway is in Scandinavia and Wales is in the United Kingdom.

Extra: homework

Choose one country for each student and ask them to do some research about the country. Ask them to write a short report on the country's facts, such as population, size, government, capital and official languages, to share with the class.

B

- Have the students continue working with their partners or hold a whole-class discussion to answer the questions.
- Listen to their ideas as a class. Note that there could be a wide variety of answers and that even students from the same country might answer differently based on regions, religions or other factors.

Alternative

Ask the students to bring in photos of traditional dress from their country or region, or from another country or region they are familiar with. Ask them to point out the features of the clothing and to discuss for which events or in what settings the clothing is worn.

Grammar: *be used to / get used to* (p. 70)

Lead-in

Before opening the book, set a time limit of three minutes and ask the students to list as many traditional European festivals as they can. Make this a team event and see which group can think of the most. Afterwards, ask the class to help you write a list of their ideas on the board. Then ask them to open their books. Refer them to the photo and see if they can guess what event this is.

A 1.29

- See the Student's Book for the **audioscript**.
- Have the students read the question first. Then play the audio.
- Ask them what traditions were mentioned. Ask them if they are familiar with them and if they learned anything new. Extend the discussion by asking if they have participated or would like to participate in these traditions.

Alternative

Ask the students to keep their books closed. Write the following question on the board: *What two traditions do Tao and Daniel talk about?* Play the audio once and ask the students to note their answers. Then ask them to open their books and read the conversation to check their answers.

Answers

The traditions mentioned are:
Halloween: people, especially children, dress up and go trick or treating.
Bonfire Night: people make fires and let off fireworks. They burn a figure on top of the bonfire.

Culture note

Halloween is celebrated annually on 31st October. It is thought to have come from the Celtic Festival of Samhain from over 2000 years ago when it was celebrated as a day when people believed that the living and dead could meet. On Halloween it is traditional for children to go out 'guising' – going round the houses in the local area offering to entertain their neighbours either by singing, reciting a poem or telling a joke in exchange for some sweets, chocolate or fruit (satsumas and peanuts in the shell are common). Some people have Halloween parties where the hosts and guests dress in scary costumes. Symbols associated with Halloween include pumpkins, ghosts, witches, goblins, black cats, spiders and vampire bats. Many people like to watch horror films at Halloween. Other countries that celebrate Halloween include Australia, Canada and the United States.

Guy Fawkes, also known as Guido Fawkes, is a well-known historical figure. He is most famous for the 1605 Gunpowder Plot in which he tried to assassinate King James I by blowing up the Houses of Parliament – the base of English politicians by the River Thames in London. The plot failed and Guy Fawkes was captured in the cellar of the parliament building on 5th November 1605. He was found guilty of treason and sentenced to death. He was hanged on 31st January 1606.

NOTICE!

- Direct the students' attention to the **Notice!** box.
- Explain that there are examples of the common phrases *be used to* and *get used to* in the conversation. Give the students time to underline them.
- Ask the students to notice what part of speech follows each instance of *used to*.

Answer

Underline: I'm used to parties; I'm not used to dressing in fancy-dress costumes; I don't think I'll ever get used to some aspects of life in the UK; I'm sure I'll never get used to the British sense of humour; You'll have to get used to a lot more than that
A noun gerund, or noun phrase follows *used to*.

B

Form

- Ask the students to read the conversation again, paying attention to the phrases with *used to*.
- Ask the students to complete the table using examples from the text in Ex. A.
- **Highlight** the fact that in the present tense, we use *get (used to)* in the continuous rather than the simple form: *She's getting used to driving on the left after three weeks in the UK.* (NOT *She gets used to …*).
- Direct the students' attention to the **What's right?** box. Remind them that *be/get used to* is followed by the gerund and not the infinitive.

Answers

1 I'm used to parties
2 I'm not used to dressing in fancy-dress costumes
3 I don't think I'll ever get used to some aspects of life in the UK
4 I'm sure I'll never get used to the British sense of humour
5 You'll have to get used to a lot more than that in my country.

Function

- Ask the students to name something that they are already familiar with. Elicit answers such as *how to play a game* or *how to do maths*. Then ask them if they are learning how to do something new right now. Accept any reasonable answers, e.g. *living in another country*. Explain that these functions have different grammatical forms. Ask the students to choose the correct option to complete the rules.

Answers

1 be; are OR get; are not   2 get

C

- Ask the students to complete the exercise individually.
- When you check the answers, make sure the students understand why they needed to use the negative form.

Answers

1 get used to   2 are used to   3 got used to   4 aren't used to   5 get used to   6 will/'ll get used to

Extra: grammar practice

If the students need extra practice with *be used to / get used to*, schedule time for a quiz. Write these fill-in-the-blank questions on the board or type them for distribution as a written test.

1 We always go to the same restaurant. I _____ to the spicy food.
2 I didn't drive my car much at all last year. I _____ walking everywhere.
3 My parents _____ visiting me every summer.
4 I have a new job, but I am _____ getting up at 7am yet!
5 I have to _____ getting up early since my boss expects me at the office at 8.
6 My sister is _____ dancing, so she is tired after dance class every night.

Answers

1 am used to   2 got used to   3 are used to
4 not used to   5 get used to   6 not used to

D

- Explain to the students that they are going to describe a time when they were in a new situation. Then put them in pairs and ask them to discuss the questions.
- Remind them to use *be used to* and *get used to* and to use the correct tense and negative forms as appropriate.
- Ask each pair to share some of their experiences with the class. Correct any errors in the use of *be used to* and *get used to*.

Extra: homework

Ask the students to write a short paragraph about another tradition in their country, explaining what they look forward to, enjoy and/or dislike about it.

 Workbook p. 34, Section 1

Listening: for main ideas (p. 71)

Lead-in

Write the words *fantastic* and *terrible* on the board. Ask the students to brainstorm as many other positive and negative adjectives as possible. Make a list on the board for each category. Elicit answers such as *great, splendid, fabulous* (positive) and *disgusting, boring, miserable* (negative). Ask the students to think of verbs of attitude and signal words and phrases as well. Expect answers such as *love, hate, want, can't stand, dislike* for verbs, and *such as, but, so, that said, and, also, because* for signal words.

Ask the students to read the information in the skills panel. Remind them that it is not always important to notice all the details. Emphasise the importance of prediction in making listening easier. Explain that key words and phrases help us understand main ideas, while signal words like *but* and *so* help us follow the speaker's ideas.

Living traditions   UNIT 6   53

Culture note

In the UK, some weddings are traditional and others are more informal. In a traditional wedding, the bride usually wears a white wedding dress, sometimes with a veil. Guests throw uncooked rice at the newlyweds as they leave the place where the ceremony was held. Often a reception follows the wedding and includes the symbolic cutting of the wedding cake. The newlyweds hold the knife in both their hands and cut the cake together. Before they leave for their honeymoon, the bride tosses her bouquet of flowers over her shoulder to the unmarried female guests. It is tradition to say that the woman who catches the bouquet will be the next to be married. Sometimes, people attach cans and ribbons to the back of the couple's car. They may also hang a sign that says 'Just Married' on the back of the car.

A

- Ask the students to look at the photo and read the excerpt from the online guide. Then ask them to read the questions and note possible answers. Listen to their suggestions as a class.

Possible answers

1 Common traditions such as weddings, funerals and holidays. Verbs of attitude (*love*, *hate*, etc) and adjectives (*great*, *splendid*, etc).
2 They help to maintain family and community unity, make us feel secure and are important for cultural identity.
3 Younger generations may not be interested in old traditions. Families tend to live in different places now.

Extra: discussion

Have the students brainstorm a list of traditions that are important to them. In pairs, have the students compare lists and discuss any similarities or differences. Invite the students to share an important tradition with the class.

B 🎧 **1.30**

- See p. 125 for the **audioscript**.
- Explain to the students that they have two things to do for each interview: first, decide if the person thinks traditions should be maintained; and then, decide which of the statements best summarises the main idea of what they say.
- Play the audio. Then ask the students if they want to hear the audio again before checking the answers.

Answers

Interviewee 1: ✗, c
Interviewee 2: ✗, b
Interviewee 3: ✓, a
Interviewee 4: ✓, b

C

- Explain that you will play the audio again and this time the students should listen for and write the reasons the people give for their opinions.

- Ask them to compare their answers in pairs before checking the answers as a class.

Answers

Interviewee 1: Young people are not interested in old traditions because they want to do things in new, creative ways.
Interviewee 2: Each generation makes changes in order to make the tradition relevant to their own lives.
Interviewee 3: Traditions give us a sense of history and continuity.
Interviewee 4: Traditions give a society its identity and connect one generation to another.

D

- Put the students in groups. Ask them to discuss the opinions of the people in the interviews and whether they agree or disagree with them.

▶ 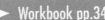 Workbook pp.34–35, Section 2

Reading: a book excerpt (p. 72)

Lead-in

Write the phrase *institution* on the board. Hold a brainstorming session for the students to call out types of institutions they are familiar with. Elicit answers such as *schools, hospitals, banks, the military* or *businesses*. Write the phrase *institutional tradition* on the board. Ask the class to say what they think this term means and to give some examples. (An institutional tradition is a tradition within a formal organisation rather than within a family, community or country; some organisations that typically have strong traditions are schools, colleges/universities and the military.)

A

- Refer the students to the photo and ask them to discuss why the women are wearing red gowns.
- Ask them to read the paragraph and check whether their ideas were correct. When you check the answer, point out that undergraduate students studying Arts and Science subjects at St Andrews wear red gowns at special events at the university. Be prepared to explain that PH are the initials of Patrick Hamilton who was martyred in 1528.

Answer

It shows university students (at the University of St Andrews in Scotland, where Prince William studied).

Culture note

St Andrews University is a public university in Scotland. It is the third oldest university in the world and was founded between 1410 and 1413. It has a very diverse student population, with students from over 100 countries. Some of its most notable alumni include Prince William and Catherine, Duke and Duchess of Cambridge.

B

- Explain that the students are going to read an excerpt from a book. Draw attention to the questions and ask the students to work in pairs to find the answers in the excerpt.
- When you check the answers, check that the students know what a *raisin* is (a dried grape).

Possible answers

Academic Family: Freshers become part of an academic family. Their academic father and mother act as their mentors during their time at university. This tradition helps students form strong bonds with others of varying levels of academic experience. This makes their university experience richer, as they are in a supportive environment.

Raisin Weekend: Academic mothers are given presents (usually a pound of raisins). They host a party on the morning of 'Raisin Sunday'. Academic fathers hold parties in the evening. The following day is 'Raisin Monday' when the fathers give receipts for the mothers' presents. The receipt must be carried by the academic son or daughter all day – this receipt could be written on anything at all (that is the challenge). The weekend ends in a massive foam fight. All the events on Raisin Weekend act as ice-breaking and bond-forming activities amongst old and new students at the university.

C

- Ask the students to work individually to match the words with the definitions.
- When you check the answers, go over the pronunciation of each word. Point out the word stress on these words: <u>ri</u>tual, sym<u>bo</u>lic, <u>mas</u>cot and ini<u>tia</u>tion.

Answers

1 d   2 f   3 e   4 a   5 b   6 c

D

- Ask the students to read the questions and check that they understand them. Give them a few minutes to think about what they are going to say and to make a few notes. Then put them in groups and ask them to discuss the questions.
- Listen to some of their ideas as a class.

Extra: homework

Ask the students to write a paragraph about an initiation ritual or mascot in their country. Encourage them to use some of the vocabulary from Ex. C when writing their paragraph.

 Workbook p. 35, Section 3

Grammar: verb + object + infinitive (p. 73)

Lead-in

Write *traditional* and *non-traditional* on the board. Ask the students if they know what these words mean. Add the phrase *work environment* to the board. Ask the students what characteristics each of a traditional and a non-traditional work environment might have. See if they think they prefer one over the other.

A 🎧 1.31

- See the Student's Book for the **audioscript**.
- Ask the students to read the question. Then play the audio and have them listen and follow the conversation in the book.
- After you check the answer, ask the students to describe how the woman's new job is less traditional than her previous job.

Answer

Her previous job was more traditional. She talks about how her new job is unstructured and gives examples of the newer, less traditional working models: people can arrive and leave at any time and they don't have to work if they're not feeling creative. They are not supposed to work at their desks all day and they are supposed to move around and talk to people. They also text you if they need you to do something.

NOTICE!

- Direct the students' attention to the **Notice!** box.
- Ask the students to find and underline the verbs in the text that are followed by an object and then an infinitive.
- Point out the underlined verb and elicit the object (*people*) and infinitive (*to arrive*) that follow it.
- Ask the students to notice where *not* and *don't* go in these types of structures.

Answers

allow people to arrive, don't ask us to work, don't force people to work, ask us not to work, encourage us to move, needs you to do. The word *not* goes before the infinitive. The word *don't* goes before the verb.

Culture note

There are two kinds of office space: open and closed. In an open-plan office, the majority of the employees share large, open spaces. There are few small, enclosed rooms or cubicles. To explore the concept of open-plan working, ask students what they think the advantages and disadvantages of working in an open-plan office might be. Answers may include: The advantages include better teamwork, less division between management and employees and better relationships among employees. The disadvantages include more noise, less privacy and weaker performance due to distractions.

Living traditions   UNIT 6   55

B

Form

- Ask the students to read the conversation again, paying attention to the verb + object + infinitive structure.
- Draw attention to the three forms presented in the table. Ask the students to complete the table with examples from the conversation.
- When you check answers, have the students look at the verbs in column 4 of the table. Point out that the same structure is used with these verbs. Write the example *I want you to go*. Point out that we don't use *that* after these verbs when they are followed by an object, except with *advise, persuade, tell* and *warn*. In these cases, we often use *that* + *should* + infinitive, e.g. *He advised me that I should leave immediately*.
- Explain the differences between the examples in column 2 and column 3. Write these two contrasting examples on the board: *She didn't ask us to talk* and *She asked us not to talk*. Ask the students to explain the difference in meaning (in the first example, she didn't say that we should talk; in the second example, she specifically requested that we not talk).
- Direct the student's attention to the **What's right?** box. Elicit why the first sentence is incorrect (we can't use *don't* to form the negative infinitive).

Answers

1 people to arrive 2 us to work 3 us not to work

Function

- Point out the beginning of the sentence above the six options. Explain that this structure is used for several reasons, then ask the students to tick the statements that are true.

Answer

Students should tick all except *emotions*.

C

- Ask the students to complete the exercise individually. You may want to let them compare their answers in pairs before checking the answers with the class.
- Elicit some further examples with these and other verbs from column 4 of the table to ensure that the students understand how to use each verb.
- Check the answers with the class.

Answer

1 The army forces people to show respect for higher-ranking members.
2 Many universities encourage freshers to join an organisation.
3 Doctors warn people not to look at a computer screen for too long.
4 I need someone to help me with this project.
5 Some universities don't allow freshers to live off campus.
6 Our boss advises us not to eat lunch at our desks.

D

- Give the students a few minutes to work individually to think of more advantages of working both in a traditional and a non-traditional setting, and to decide which way of working would suit them best.
- Put them in pairs to share their ideas.
- Listen to some of their ideas with the whole class. Correct any errors in the use of verb + object + infinitive.

Extra: homework

Ask the students to write a short paragraph about changes in traditional working models. Encourage them to use as many verbs from column 4 of Ex. B as possible.

▶ Workbook p. 36, Section 4

Pronunciation: stress in words with *-tion/-sion* (p. 74)

A 1.32

- See the Student's Book for the **audioscript**.
- Ask the students to look at the group of words and notice that the last syllable is *-tion* or *-sion*, which have the same sound.
- Play the audio and ask the students to tell you where the stress falls in each word (the syllable before *-tion* and *-sion*).
- Play the audio again and ask the students to repeat the words.

B 1.33

- See the Student's Book for the **audioscript**.
- Play the audio as the students read along. Then put the students in pairs and ask them to take turns reading the text aloud to their partner. Remind them to pay attention to the stress in the words ending in *-tion* and *-sion*.

Speaking: talking about personal rituals (p. 74)

Lead-in

Write examples of your daily rituals on the board, but in the wrong order, e.g. *lock the door, walk to work, feed the dog, have coffee, get up, read email*. Ask the students to work in pairs to put the activities in a logical order. Listen to their ideas and then tell them what the actual order is.

A

- Ask the students to work in pairs and talk about whether or not they think that most people follow rituals in their everyday lives.

- Ask the students to read the text. Then ask how many pairs had predicted the answer correctly.

Answer
According to the paragraph, everyone has personal rituals.

B

- Remind the students that a phrasal verb is a two- (or three-) word verb that contains a verb and a particle (preposition). Point out that phrasal verbs are common in spoken English. Explain that they should do the task and check the meanings of the phrasal verbs in their dictionaries if necessary.
- Check the answers. Make sure that the students understand the meaning of all the phrasal verbs. Elicit another example sentence or two for each verb if necessary.

Answers
1 put   2 write, cross   3 go   4 go, work   5 clean
6 line

C 1.34

- See p. 126 for the **audioscript**.
- Tell the students that they will hear three people talking about their personal rituals. Ask them to listen and take notes on the rituals that each person mentions.
- Play the audio and check progress. If necessary, play the audio again.
- Check the answers. Ask the students if they ever do any of the things mentioned in the conversation. Point out that another phrasal verb, *try on*, is used toward the end of the conversation. Play the recording again if necessary to demonstrate.

Answers
Speaker 1: eats three biscuits while watching the news. Before going to bed, the speaker plans the next day by writing down the things that must be done the next day. In the morning, the speaker goes over the list.
Speaker 2: goes through the post while eating breakfast and puts it into three piles. The speaker always gets the same kind of coffee at the same café every day and drinks it in the car on the way to work.
Speaker 3: tries on her work clothes the day before she plans to wear them.

D

- Ask the students to work individually and make notes about their personal rituals. Tell them that these could be in a personal context (their daily routine), at work or about their leisure or free-time activities (when they play sports, for example). Remind them that they do not have to mention any rituals that they don't feel comfortable sharing with the class.

E

- Put the students in pairs. Explain that they should take turns talking about their rituals using the notes they made. They should each speak for about one and a half minutes. While one student talks, the other should listen and take notes but should not interrupt or ask questions.

- Ask the students to use their notes to tell the whole class about their partner's rituals.

▶ Workbook pp. 36–37, Section 5

Writing: avoiding run-on sentences (p. 75)

Lead-in

Write the word *punctuation* on the board. Put the students in pairs and ask them to write and name as many different examples of punctuation as they can. Set a time limit of two minutes. Listen to their suggestions as a class and write the punctuation and the corresponding words on the board:
. = *full stop* , = *comma* ? = *question mark*
! = *exclamation mark* : = *colon* ; = *semicolon*

Ask the students to read the information in the skills panel. Check that they understand the concept of run-on sentences.

Teach the students the different ways of avoiding run-on sentences. Point out that the simplest way is to use a full stop and make two complete sentences. Explain that two independent clauses that are closely related can also be separated by a semicolon. The students can also use connectors such as *and*, *but* and *or* to connect independent clauses. Other connectors include *while*, *if*, *when* and *although*. Remind them that using connectors in writing makes the writing more fluent. Write these sentences on the board as examples:

Independent clause: *We are having a family meeting.*

Independent clause with a complement: *We are having a family meeting about our plans for the weekend.*

Run-on (two independent clauses connected by only a comma): *Our family has a lot of little traditions, they bring us closer.*

Avoid run-ons by using:

a full stop: *Our family has a lot of little traditions. They bring us closer.*

a semicolon: *Our family has a lot of little traditions; they bring us closer.*

connectors *and*, *but*, *or*: *Our family has a lot of little traditions, and they bring us closer.*

connectors *before*, *because*, *while*, *if*, *when*, *although*, etc: *Our family maintains a lot of little traditions because they bring us closer.*

A

- Ask the students to read the six sentences and decide if they are correct or if they are run-ons.
- Have them compare their answers in pairs and decide how to correct the run-ons.
- Check the answers. Ask why the correct sentences are correct (1 is connected by *and*; 4 is connected by *when*; 6 is connected by *in which*).

Living traditions   UNIT 6   57

> **Possible answers**
> 1 C
> 2 RO Some of our family traditions are normal, <u>but/although</u> some of our traditions might seem strange to other people.
> 3 RO Some families are used to doing things in a certain way <u>and/so</u> they don't like to change.
> 4 C
> 5 RO One tradition in my family is Sunday dinner, <u>when</u> we all relax and talk about our week.
> 6 C

B
- Ask if the students are familiar with blogs. Define a blog as a combination of the words *web* and *log* and explain that it is a discussion or collection of information written online.
- Explain the task and ask the students to work individually to find examples of run-on sentences in the blog entry. Ask them to think of one or two different ways of correcting these.
- Have the students compare their answers in pairs and discuss different ways of correcting the run-on sentences. Check the answers as a class. Include different ideas for making the corrections.

C
- Put the students in pairs to discuss their family traditions. Encourage them to explain where the traditions came from.
- Give them time to make some notes before their discussion if they wish.

D
- Tell the students that it is their turn to be bloggers. Ask them to write a comment responding to the blog entry using their notes and ideas from the discussion in Ex. C. Remind them to check for run-on sentences.
- Schedule time for a peer review in which partners can check for run-on sentences before the students submit their work.

 Workbook p. 37, Section 6

LifeSkills: managing distractions (p. 76)

Step 1: Recognise your main distractions. (Ex. A, Ex. B, Ex. D)
Step 2: Find out ways to change habits and choose ones that work for you. (Ex. C, Ex. D)
Step 3: Make a plan for managing distractions. (Ex. D)

Lead-in
Read the target skill aloud and invite the students to tell you what they think *managing distractions* means.

Ask the students what a *distraction* is (something that interrupts your concentration when you are trying to do something like work or study). Ask them to give some examples of distractions (people talking to you, phone calls/texts, TV, social networking sites, etc).

Then **highlight** the three-step strategy to develop the skill of *managing distractions*.

A
- Explain that *distracted* is the adjective form of *distraction* and that it means *not being able to concentrate on something, often because you are thinking about something else*. Give or elicit the opposite of *distracted* (focused).
- Draw attention to the photo. Ask the students what is happening in the photo. Invite volunteers to say if they've ever done the same thing as the young man in the photo.
- Ask the students to read the excerpt from a website aimed at university students. Check that they understand *bombarded with* (hit with a large amount of something, in this case, information).
- Then ask them to read the statements in the quiz and tick the ones that are true for them. Ask them to estimate the amounts of time they spend on each activity and to write the minutes or hours in the spaces.
- Have the students report back to the whole class. Find out which of the statements in the quiz are true for most students. Calculate the total amount of time spent by the class on these electronic activities.

Extra: discussion
Point out that *focused* is the opposite of *distracted*. Ask the students to share the steps they take to stay focused when they are studying or doing something that requires concentration. Write the students' ideas on the board. When you have finished, read each idea aloud and ask the students to raise their hand if they use this method to help them focus. As a class, identify the three most popular methods to help the students stay focused.

Extra: class survey
Have the students share the results of the quiz. Ask them to stand up and circulate to find out the following information from the other students: a) total time spent on the activities, b) the three activities that take up most of their time, c) any activities that they don't do. Have them work in groups to calculate the average time per day spent on the activities, the activities that the students spend the most time doing and any common activities that no or few students do. Ask them to write a brief report of their findings for homework to hand in during the next lesson.

B
- Put the students in pairs and ask them to compare their lists of distractions from Ex. A on p. 76. Ask them to tell their partner how much time they spend each day on the various activities.
- Ask the students to work individually and think about their answers to the questions. Give them two or three minutes to make some notes.
- Ask them to compare and discuss their answers to the questions with their partner. Then ask some of them to share their answers with the whole class.

C

- Have the students continue working in the same pairs. Draw attention to the photo. Ask the students if they can relate to this student and/or if they have ever been distracted in this same way.
- Tell the students that the rest of the article contains some ways to avoid being distracted. Ask them to read the next section of the article and to make a list of ideas that the website might make.
- When the pairs have made their lists, have them combine to form groups of four and share their ideas.

> **Possible answers**
>
> - Be aware of how often you are distracted and by what.
> - Don't take every opportunity for a distraction. Ask yourself if you really need to answer that text message instantly or have a cup of coffee right now.
> - Avoid being exposed to distractions. Work away from other people. Turn off your mobile phone. Turn off your messaging app, etc.
> - Don't try to force yourself to give up all distractions. Allow yourself to take breaks, but schedule them and set time limits for them. For example, respond to messages for ten minutes, three times a day.

D

- Have the students work in the same pairs as before. Explain that they each need to identify their three main distractions and help each other create an action plan for managing them.
- Refer the students to the **How to say it** box. Explain that these expressions are all useful ways of giving advice to someone. Briefly check that they know which ones are followed by the gerund (the first and the third). Encourage them to use some of these expressions when discussing their action plans.
- Give the students time to read the model conversation. Then ask them to work together on each other's action plans. Point out that they can use ideas from the text in Ex. C and/or their own ideas.
- Invite several students to share their action plans with the class.

> **Extra: homework**
>
> Ask the students to carry out their action plan for managing distractions and report back on its effectiveness. Schedule a due date.

E

- Put the students in pairs to discuss the questions. Encourage them to focus on the domain of **Study and Learning**.
- Combine the pairs to form groups of four and share their ideas.
- Focus the students on what they still need to work on in order to improve the skill of *managing distractions*.
- Elicit some suggestions from the class for how the students might continue to practise and develop this skill, for example, by *setting time limits, keeping their calendar up-to-date*, etc.

REFLECT

- Discuss the question with the whole class. Ask the students to say what they feel are the most useful points they learned from this lesson, and how the skill of *managing distractions* might be useful in the domains of **Work and Career** and **Self and Society**, either now or in the future.
- Elicit the following ideas: *accomplishing more in a shorter time, making more money, completing work earlier*, etc.

RESEARCH

- Go through the task and check that the students are clear about what they have to do.
- Have the students conduct research on avoiding distractions and ask them to choose one technique they think will be effective. Ask them to be prepared to explain this technique to the rest of the class.
- Have them share their findings in class. Lead a class discussion about the advantages of each technique.

Language wrap-up (p. 78)

For notes on how to approach the exercises in the Language wrap-up section, please see page 9.

1 Vocabulary

- Ask the students to read the whole email for general understanding and to gain an idea of the context before filling in the blanks with the words or phrases from the box. Point out that they need to think about the correct form of the verb.
- Have the students complete the task individually and then compare answers in pairs.
- Call on individual students to say the sentences, inserting the correct answers. Ask the rest of the class to say whether the sentence is correct or not.

2 Grammar

- When checking the answers with the students, remind them that *be used to* is used to talk about things we are already familiar with, and *get used to* is used to talk about the process of becoming familiar with something.
- Remind them of the form of the verb + object + infinitive structure and its function (to report advice, requests, warnings, encouragement and commands).

Speaking workshop: comparing photos (p. 79)

Lead-in

Ask the students if they like to take photos of food. Ask if they have ever taken a photo of a meal that they have been served at a restaurant. Continue the discussion by asking the students if they have any family photos from a holiday dinner or special event.

Living traditions | UNIT 6 | 59

Alternative

Ask the students to bring in a personal photo of a family dinner or special event. Invite them to share the tradition behind the photo.

A 🎧 1.35

- See p. 126 for the **audioscript**.
- Explain that comparing and contrasting is an important concept in academic studies. Give examples of assignments such as writing a compare/contrast essay or giving a presentation comparing and contrasting two objects.
- Tell the students they will listen to someone comparing the two photos and answering the question *Why might these traditions be important to these people?* Ask them to take notes about the main points the speaker makes.
- Play the audio once. Play it again if necessary.
- Put the students in pairs to compare notes. Then discuss their answers as a class.

Answers

The speaker makes the following points:
Both photos show people doing something together.
The first is a family, while the second is a community.
Both of them show people enjoying themselves in a traditional way.
The first may involve particular food, while the second may involve a particular dance.
The first shows people in casual clothes, while the second shows people in traditional dress.
The traditions remind the people of their family and national histories.

Extra: vocabulary expansion

Point out that we use specific words and phrases when we compare and contrast two items. List these words and phrases on the board: *both, similar, unlike, have in common, alike, different, in contrast*. Ask the students to work in pairs to make two lists: one with words and phrases that compare, and another with words and phrases that contrast. Challenge them to use as many of these words and phrases as they can to compare or contrast two items.

B

- Ask the students to look at the phrases and point out that the speaker used them to compare the photos. Play the audio again. Ask the students to listen for the missing words and write them in the blanks.
- Repeat the audio only if necessary.
- Check the answers with the class.

Answers

1 Both 2 While 3 in common 4 while 5 similar
6 In contrast to

Alternative

Ask the students to try to fill in the blanks before the audio is played. Have the students check their answers as the audio is played.

C

- Explain that the students will now prepare their own comparison of the two photos in Ex. A. Encourage them to follow the same process by making notes about their own ideas in the table.
- Point out that they can refer to the first photo as A and the second as B.
- Give the students time to think and make notes. Then put the students in pairs to compare their ideas. Remind them that they will present their comparison orally.

D

Activity

- Put the students in groups. Schedule enough time for each student to present their comparison of the photos to their group. Each student should talk for about one minute.
- Remind the students to discuss the answer to the question in Ex. A.

Extra: roleplay

Put the students in two groups: one is a family eating a traditional meal in a restaurant, as in photo A. The other is people in the community wearing traditional dress and marching in a parade, as in photo B. Give the groups a few minutes to talk about why these traditions are important to them. Then have the groups share their ideas. Encourage them to talk about how their reasons are the same and how they are different.

How are you doing?

- Ask the students to read the statements and tick the ones they believe are true.
- Ask them to discuss their talk with a member of their group and identify things they could improve on next time.

 Workbook pp. 38–39, SkillsStudio

UNIT 7 DESIGNED TO PLEASE

The expression *designed to please* refers to the fact that many items nowadays can be custom-made, meaning they can be designed for a specific client. Customers can choose the style, the size, the colour, etc of many things that they purchase.

Unit plan

Unit opener	(p. 80)	20 min.
1 **Reading:** inferring factual information	(p. 82)	30 min.
• Vocabulary: design		15 min.
2 **Grammar:** possessive apostrophe	(p. 83)	40 min.
3 **Listening:** to a radio phone-in show	(p. 84)	30 min.
• Vocabulary: phrasal verbs		15 min.
4 **Grammar:** past perfect vs. past perfect continuous	(p. 85)	40 min.
5 **Speaking:** distancing language	(p. 86)	30 min.
6 **Pronunciation:** 's after names that end in /s/, /ʃ/ or /z/	(p. 87)	15 min.
7 **Writing:** a biography	(p. 87)	30 min.
LifeSkills: showing initiative (Work and Career)	(p. 88)	50 min.
• Optional downloadable *LifeSkills* lesson (Self and Society)		50 min.
• Optional downloadable *LifeSkills* lesson (Study and Learning)		50 min.
Language wrap-up	(p. 90)	15 min.
Writing workshop	(p. 91)	20 min.
Video and downloadable video worksheet		45 min.

Unit opener (p. 80)

Lead-in
Ask the students to look at the unit title and the photos and to predict what the unit will be about. Ask the students to give examples of design features that make a product more desirable, for example, in relation to houses, cars, technology, fashion, etc. Direct the students' attention to the points in the unit objectives box and go through the information with them. To get your students to think about the skills being developed in this unit, ask them to look at the questions in the cogs.

Reading: inferring factual information
- Remind the students that *inferring* means *getting information from the text that is not directly stated*. Ask why this skill is important when they are reading: information may not be stated directly in a text; the reader can understand a text more fully. In Unit 5, the students inferred the writer's opinion; in this unit, they will infer facts.

Speaking: distancing language
- Ask the students to think about situations in which they would need to make a polite request: when asking a big favour of someone, asking a boss to leave work early, etc.

LifeSkills: showing initiative
- Ask the students what it means to show initiative and elicit some examples. Elicit reasons why it is useful or important to show initiative in our work lives. Ask the students whether they generally feel confident showing initiative, and to say why or why not.

Common European Framework: unit map

Unit 7	Competence developed	CEF Reference (B2 competences)
Reading	can infer factual information	Table 1; Table 2; Sections 4.4.2.2; 4.4.2.4; 4.5.2.2
Grammar	can correctly use the possessive apostrophe	Table 1; Table 2; Sections 5.2.1.2; 5.2.1.5; 6.4.7.7; 6.4.7.8
Listening	can understand a radio call-in	Table 1; Table 2; Sections 4.4.2.1; 4.4.3.1; 4.4.3.5; 4.5.2.2
Grammar	can use and understand the past perfect and the past perfect continuous	Table 1; Table 2; Sections 5.2.1.2; 6.4.7.7; 6.4.7.8
Speaking	can make a request or suggestion using distancing language	Table 1; Table 2; Sections 4.4.1.1; 4.4.3.1; 4.4.3.5; 4.5.2.1; 5.2.3.2
Pronunciation	can correctly pronounce the possessive apostrophe after names ending in /s/, /ʃ/ and /z/	Section 5.2.1.4
Writing	can write a biography	Table 1; Table 2; Sections 4.4.1.2; 4.5.2.1; 5.2.1.1; 5.2.1.2; 5.2.1.6; 5.2.3.2

A

- Ask the students to raise their hands if they are wearing designer clothing or accessories, or have designer goods with them. Ask for volunteers to say why they chose the product and what it is about its design that makes it special or different from a non-designer brand.
- Have the students look at the photos and describe the design of each item shown. Elicit their overall reactions to each design, whether they like it, whether they would buy it, and why or why not.
- Give the students time to read the questions and think about their responses.
- Put the students in pairs and ask them to discuss how design is important in people's lives. Have the pairs list as many ways as they can think of for each photo. To help the students get started, you may wish to share some of your own ideas about which design types are important in your life.
- Have the pairs rank the types of design in order of their importance. As the ranking task is somewhat subjective, and the students may not agree on all of the rankings, encourage them to support their opinions with reasons and examples.
- Combine the pairs to form groups of four. Ask the students to share their rankings and talk about which types of design are important in their lives.

Extra: class discussion

Extend the conversation about the importance of design by having the class focus on how different design features are important depending on the person. Lead a class discussion about what design-related factors may be more important to:
men vs. women
single people vs. married people
younger people vs. older people
taller people vs. shorter people
parents vs. non-parents
people who live in cities vs. people who live in the country
people who live in warmer regions vs. people who live in colder regions
university students vs. working people.

B

- Ask the students to think about people or factors that influence design. Elicit several examples from the class. Some examples could be:
  Technology
   the iPhone/iPad – Apple Inc./Steve Jobs
   the internet – Sir Tim Berners-Lee
  Architecture
   the Guggenheim Museum – Frank Lloyd Wright
   the Eiffel Tower – Gustave Eiffel
   the Pyramide du Louvre – I.M. Pei
  Art
   the statue of David – Michelangelo
   Seated Woman – Picasso
   Campbell's Soup Can (Tomato) – Andy Warhol
   The Starry Night – Vincent Van Gogh
  Automobiles
   the Beetle – Volkswagen
   Lamborghini – Ferruccio Lamborghini
   the Smart Car – Daimler AG
  Fashion
   Coco Chanel
   Run-DMC/Ice-T/LL Cool J
   Jacqueline Kennedy Onassis
   Kurt Cobain
   Issey Miyake

Alternative

If possible, bring in photos to represent some of the top design influencers throughout history. Ask the students to identify them and discuss what makes them unique and fashionable.

- Put the students in groups to discuss the first question. Have the students try to come up with at least two influences for each type of design represented in the photos. Then ask for a volunteer from each group to share the group's ideas.
- Ask the students to discuss what they think makes a design popular or fashionable. Again, have them try to come up with at least two ideas for each design type pictured.

Extra: design differences

Ask the class to brainstorm some everyday items, for example, cars, telephones, TVs, computers, shoes, books, etc and list them on the board. Have the students discuss the ways the design of each has changed over the years. If possible, allow them to go online and find pictures to exemplify some of the older designs. Compare them with the features of the newer designs. Have the class discuss the possible reasons behind the design changes.

Extra: homework

Have the students choose a product that they own. For homework, have them think about ways the design could be improved. In the next lesson, have them present their product and suggested improvements to a partner or small group.

Reading: inferring factual information (p. 82, p. 59 ⓞ)

Lead-in

Remind the students that they practised inferring – opinion – on p. 59. Give the students time to read the information in the skills panel. Explain that in this section they will practise 'reading between the lines' to infer facts. Elicit/explain that *making deductions* means using the information that is stated in a text to infer other information that is not stated.

To lead into the article, elicit what the students know or have heard about the process of 3D printing from articles in the news, online, etc.

A

- Focus the students' attention on the title of the article. Elicit the meaning of the phrase *revolutionising the design process* (completely changing the design process).
- Ask the students to read the article and think about how 3D printing is changing the way objects and products will be designed in the future.
- Put the students in pairs to summarise the article.
- To conclude, ask for a volunteer to describe the 3D printing process. Lead a brief class discussion about the ways 3D printing is changing the design process.

Answer

It's changing the design process by allowing customers to be involved in the design process and allowing designers to manufacture products from digital templates using plastic, paper and many other types of materials.

B

- Give the students time to read the statements. Remind them that the statements are inferences that are not directly stated in the article. They will need to use the information given in the text to deduce this information. If further clarification is needed, do the first item with the class as an example.
- Have the students read the article again and note down which paragraphs contain the information needed to make the inferences.
- Have the students compare answers in pairs using information from the text to support their answers.
- Check the answers with the class.
- To expand the task, ask the students to share any other facts they can infer from the text.

Answers

1 3 and 5 **2** 1 **3** 2 **4** 5 **5** 3

C

- Go over the pronunciation of the bold vocabulary words in the article. Call on individual students to read the words aloud. Correct their pronunciation as needed.
- Give the students time to read the partial sentences. Remind them to use the context of the sentences and the full reading text to figure out the general meanings of the words.
- Have the students complete the sentences and then check their answers in pairs.
- Check the answers with the class.

Answers

1 template **2** affordable **3** unique **4** manufacture
5 miniature **6** personalised **7** top quality
8 innovative

D

- Give the students time to read the questions and think about their responses.
- Put the students in pairs to discuss the questions. Encourage them to support their responses with details, reasons and examples.
- When the pairs finish their discussions, go over the questions with the class and elicit a few responses to each one.

Alternative

For question 3, ask the pairs to come up with an idea for a 3D-printed product they would like to see for each of the design categories in the Unit opener. Encourage them to be creative. Have the pairs write a brief description of each idea. Then combine the pairs and have them present their ideas in groups.

Extra: homework – the future of design

Have the students write a short essay on the future of design, predicting and describing new types of design possibilities brought about by the 3D-printing process. In their essays, have the students discuss the possible applications of 3D printing for the types of design shown in the photos on the Unit opener page.

 Workbook p. 41, Section 3

 Workbook p. 40, Section 1

Grammar: possessive apostrophe (p. 83)

Lead-in

Direct the students' attention to the photo. Elicit some predictions for what the text will be about. Elicit any information the students know about the celebrity couple, David and Victoria Beckham (see page 35 for a photo of Victoria).

A

- Give the students time to read the article with the question in mind.
- Put the students in pairs to summarise the article and discuss why the designer sale was so popular.
- Elicit the reason why the sale was so popular.

Answer

This designer clothing sale was so popular because it had clothes from celebrities Victoria and David Beckham for sale.

NOTICE!

- Direct the students' attention to the **Notice!** box.
- Have them look at the underlined phrases in the text, and determine which things the couple owned separately and which things they owned together.
- Discuss the answer as a class, noting how the apostrophe provides this information.

Answer
Victoria and David own the suits separately. They own the designer collection together.

B
Form

- Briefly review the two possessive forms used in the text. Have the students read the article again, focusing on the use of the possessive apostrophe.
- Give the students time to complete the table individually with examples from the text. Then check the answers with the class.
- **Highlight** the fact that the 's in the word *It's* in the quote in the second paragraph is not a possessive form. Elicit that it is the contracted form of *It + is*.
- Explain the following rules:
  1. Use ' after plural nouns, e.g. *her parents' car*, and proper nouns ending in -s, e.g. *James' sister*. But note that *James' sister* and *James's sister* are both acceptable and are pronounced differently.
  2. With compound nouns, use 's after each noun to express each person's possession separately, e.g. *Maria's and Javier's dogs* (they own different dogs). Use 's after the second noun to express joint possession, e.g. *Maria and Javier's dogs* (they own the dogs together).
  3. Possessive + gerund, e.g. *the shop's opening*, is more formal and the noun without 's is often preferred.
- Direct the students' attention to the **What's right?** box. Elicit that although *women* is plural, the possessive apostrophe comes before -s.

Answers
Form
1 store's 2 bargain hunter's 3 Victoria's
4 celebrities' 5 Beckhams' 6 Victoria's and David's
7 Victoria and David's 8 the couple's sons'
9 the store's opening

C

- Have the students work individually to rewrite the sentences using the correct possessive forms. Then check the answers with the class. Ask the students to support and explain their reasons for choosing each form, referring to the table in Ex. B.

Answers
1 My friends' new art gallery is beautiful.
2 The couple's daughter('s design) won first prize in the competition.
3 Patricia and Jenny's friend's father works in the fashion industry.
4 Lorraine's and Julia's shoes cost a fortune.
5 Women's fashions are in shades of green and grey this autumn.
6 Teenagers' fashion-buying habits are changing.

Extra: grammar practice
Have the students write additional sentences using the target possessive forms. Encourage them to personalise the sentences using the names of family members or other students in the class.

D

- Give the students time to read the questions and think about their responses. Encourage them to make notes about the topics.
- Put the students in pairs to discuss the questions. Encourage them to support their ideas with details, reasons and examples, and to ask follow-up questions to find out more about their partner's ideas.
- Elicit responses from the class. Ask the students to name celebrities whose items they would like to own, and to say why.
- Discuss some examples of celebrities who are known for supporting charities, for example, Oprah Winfrey, Angelina Jolie, Lance Armstrong, etc. Discuss the pros and cons of celebrities supporting charities, and elicit examples of situations when celebrity support of a charity organisation might cause problems (for example, in 2013 when Lance Armstrong was found guilty of taking performance-enhancing drugs, his cancer charity 'Livestrong' saw a drop in donations from supporters).

 Workbook pp. 40–41, Section 2

Listening: to a radio phone-in show (p. 84)

Lead-in
Ask the class to name any celebrities they know of who, like Victoria Beckham, have used their fame to start other businesses, such as a line of clothing, cosmetics, etc. Give a few other examples to help them get started. Elicit several examples and lead a brief class discussion about the reasons why many people choose to buy products associated with a celebrity's name.

A

- Tell the students they are going to listen to a radio phone-in show. Explain that callers are giving their opinions about three celebrities who have started their own designer fashion companies.

- Put the students in pairs and ask them to talk about what they know about the three celebrities in the photos. Have them discuss what each celebrity is famous for and list any films, TV shows or songs they know featuring each person.
- Elicit some of the students' opinions about the celebrities' fashion style.

Answers
Lady Gaga, Johnny Depp, Gwen Stefani

B 2.01

- See p. 126 for the **audioscript**.
- Explain to the students that they will hear two callers during the radio show: Tony and Marianne.
- Give the students time to read the statements. Elicit some predictions from the class about whether the statements are true or false.
- Play the audio and have the students mark the statements true or false.
- Have the students compare answers in pairs. Then check the answers with the class.
- Call on individual students to correct any false statements.

Answers
1 F 2 F 3 T 4 F

Extra: agree or disagree
After checking the true/false answers, have the students say whether or not they agree with the callers' opinions and to explain their reasoning.

C

- Remind the students that they studied phrasal verbs in Unit 6, and elicit that a phrasal verb is a two- or three-word verb + a particle. Draw the students' attention to item 1 and ask them to change *their own ranges of products* to a pronoun (*them*). Elicit that when some phrasal verbs are used with a pronoun, the pronoun comes between the verb and particle (*What do you think of celebrities who bring them out?*). Ask the students to do the same with item 4: *I think a lot of the time they don't even draw them up themselves.*
- Explain that phrasal verbs are idiomatic because their meaning usually cannot be deduced from the meaning of the words in the phrase.
- Give some examples like the one below to clarify the difference between a verb + preposition and a phrasal verb.

  Verb + preposition   Phrasal verb
  John is <u>getting into</u> the car.   John is <u>getting into</u> jazz music.

- Draw the students' attention to the sentences from the audio that contain a phrasal verb.
- Have the students match the phrasal verbs with their definitions. Remind them to use the context of the audio to help them.
- Check the answers by saying a phrasal verb and inviting individual students to give the definition.

Answers
1 d 2 a 3 f 4 b 5 e 6 c

Extra: separable and inseparable phrasal verbs
Write *separable*, *inseparable* and *no object* on the board. Tell the students that the verbs in Ex. C can be divided into these categories. Explain that some phrasal verbs can have the object between the verb and particle (separable) and others cannot (inseparable). Point out that when the object is a pronoun, it has to come between the verb and particle of a separable phrasal verb. Explain that some other phrasal verbs do not take objects. Have the students work in pairs to divide the verbs into the three categories. Check the answers with the class.

Answers
1 separable 2 no object 3 inseparable
4 separable 5 no object 6 inseparable

D

- Put the students in pairs to complete the questions. Then check the answers with the class.
- Have the pairs answer the questions and discuss them, giving reasons for their opinions.
- When the pairs finish their discussions, elicit responses to each question from the class.

Answers
1 look up to 2 come up with 3 takes off
4 draw up / come up with

▶ Workbook p. 42, Section 4

Grammar: past perfect vs past perfect continuous (p. 85)

A

- Have the students look at the photo, tell you who the celebrity is (Jennifer Lopez) and say what they know about her. Have the students say what they think she is famous for.
- Have the students read the biography and check their answer. Then ask them to tell you any new information they learned about her.

NOTICE!
- Direct the students' attention to the **Notice!** box.
- Have them find and circle the date 1997 in the text.
- Have the students work individually to underline the events that happened before 1997. Then have them compare answers in pairs and say how they know these events happened before 1997.

Answer
The verbs *had been working* and *had already appeared* show that these things happened before 1997.

Designed to please UNIT 7   65

- To clarify the answer, **highlight** that both events happened before 1997 and that, in order to talk about events before a certain point in the past, it is often necessary to use the past perfect or past perfect continuous. Also point out that the past perfect continuous is often followed by the preposition *for* + a time expression.
- **Highlight** that we often use the preposition *by* with the past perfect, e.g. *by 1997*. We can also use *by* with *the time* and a clause, e.g. *By the time she arrived, her friend had left.*

B
Form & Function

- Ask the students to read the biography again, paying attention to the past perfect and past perfect continuous.
- Ask the students to complete the table using the biography text as a reference.
- **Highlight** that *had been working as an actor* refers to activity that continued steadily over a period of time. *She had already appeared* in seven films refers to seven completed actions.
- Check the answers with the class.
- Direct the students' attention to the **What's right?** box. Elicit that the first sentence is incorrect because it uses the continuous for a single, completed action that can't continue over a period of time.

Answers
1 *had* 2 *had + been*

C

- Have the students complete the sentences with the past perfect or past perfect continuous. Review the function of each tense and encourage the students to think about whether the action in the sentence is complete or whether it continued over a period of time.
- Check the answers with the class.

Answers
1 had been working 2 had finished 3 had appeared
4 had been running 5 had started 6 had been designing
7 had been considering 8 had taken off

Alternative
Go over each sentence with the whole class first and ask the students to decide whether the verb should be in the past perfect or past perfect continuous. Refer them to the table in Ex. B. Then have them work in pairs to write each verb in the correct form.

D

- Ask the students to identify the celebrity in the photo (Justin Timberlake). Ask them to say whether they are fans and to share anything they know about him.
- Put the students in pairs to read the notes. Explain that they should use the prompts at the bottom of the page to talk about the events in Justin Timberlake's life using the past perfect and past perfect continuous.

- Give the students time to discuss the notes using the prompts and the correct form of the verb. Remind them that the past perfect continuous is often followed by the preposition *for* + a time expression.
- Elicit responses from the class, correcting the students' use of the verb forms as needed.

Possible answers
By 2002, he had been singing with 'N Sync for seven years.
By 2006, he had been singing with 'N Sync for eleven years and had released two solo albums.
By 2010, he had brought out the William Rast clothing line and had appeared in several films.
By 2012, he had married Jessica Biel.

Extra: grammar practice
Write various dates on the board, e.g. 1998, 2002, 2010, 2013, etc. Ask the students to write sentences or make statements about themselves or their family members using the past perfect and past perfect continuous, e.g. *By 1998, my parents had had two children. By 2010, I had been studying English for five years. By 2013, I had been working for several years. In 1990, I had not been born yet.*

 Workbook pp. 42–43, Section 5

Speaking: distancing language (p. 86)

Lead-in

Ask the students to read the information in the skills panel. Ask them which tenses are often used to make requests or suggestions (past tenses). Explain or elicit that using the past tense distances our request or suggestion from the present so that it seems less direct and therefore more polite.

Write the following categories of people on the board: *parent, teacher, boss, neighbour, brother/sister, classmate, friend*. Ask the students for some examples of *requests* they might make of each person, then list their ideas on the board. Ask the students for some *suggestions* they might make to those same people and list those on the board. Clarify the difference between a *request* (asking someone to do something for us) and a *suggestion* (asking someone to do something differently from the way they have done it). Ask the students how comfortable they feel making requests of / suggestions to the people on the board. Point out that making requests and suggestions can be difficult, especially if the relationship is very formal or if we don't know the person well. If we are not careful, the way we make a request or a suggestion can sound rude or offensive to a listener, so it is important to know how to make requests and suggestions politely.

A 🎧 2.02

- See the Student's Book for the **audioscript**.
- Direct the students' attention to the conversation. Play the audio and have them follow along.
- Put the students in pairs to discuss what Austin's job involves, based on the conversation between him and Celine.

Answer

Paul gives people advice about colour schemes and furniture designs they might use in their homes.

B

- Have the students stay in their pairs to look back at the conversation and find the four phrases.
- Call on individual students to tell you the answers.
- Refer the students to the conversation and ask them what verb (or modal) form comes after each of the phrases (*I was wondering if – could; I was hoping – might; I was thinking – might; I wanted to suggest – gerund [-ing form]*).

Answers

1
I was wondering if …
I was hoping you might …
2
I was thinking you might …
I wanted to suggest …

C

- Direct the students' attention to the sentences. If needed, do the first sentence with the class as an example.
- Give the students time to rewrite the sentences and then have them compare answers in pairs before checking the answers with the class.

Answers

1 I was hoping you would help me.
2 I was thinking you should paint the walls green.
3 I was wondering if you could help me paint my bedroom.
4 I wanted to suggest looking on the internet for ideas.

D

- Tell the students that they are going to roleplay a situation using distancing language to make a request.
- Put the students in pairs and have them choose Student A and Student B roles. Before they begin, give the students time to read the situation and their roles and to think about what they are going to say. Encourage them to note down any specific requests or suggestions using distancing language.
- When the pairs have had enough time to practise, call on a few to perform their roleplays for the class.

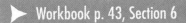 Workbook p. 43, Section 6

Pronunciation: 's after names that end in /s/, /ʃ/ or /z/ (p. 87)

A 🎧 2.03

- See the Student's Book for the **audioscript**.
- Have the students read the introduction and the phrases with the possessives.
- Play the audio once and have the students listen. Then play it a second time and have the students repeat the phrases.
- Call on individual students to say the phrases. Correct pronunciation as needed.

B 🎧 2.04

- See the Student's Book for the **audioscript**.
- Have the students practise reading the possessive phrases individually.
- Ask for volunteers to tell you which phrases add an extra syllable on the possessive.
- Play the audio and have the students check their pronunciation.

Answers

Extra syllable: Chaz's friend, Ros's teacher

Writing: a biography (p. 87)

Lead-in

Tell the students they are going to learn about a famous interior designer from New Zealand and write a *biography* about her. Ask the class for a definition of *biography* (a factual account of another person's life). Review some of the biographical information they read about celebrities earlier in the unit (Jennifer Lopez and Justin Timberlake).

A

- Direct the students' attention to the photos of the two hotels. Ask them to say which design they prefer and which hotel they would prefer to stay at. Encourage them to give reasons for their preferences and to use adjectives to describe the design and what they think it might be like to stay at each one.

B

- Have the students share anything they know about Anouska Hempel and her life and career.

Culture note

Anouska Hempel, born in 1941, is a New Zealand-born TV and film actress who has become a well-known hotelier and interior designer.

- Have the students read the biographical notes about Hempel and give them time to read the questions. Ask them to write their answers and remind them to use the past perfect and past perfect continuous tenses.
- Put the students in pairs to compare answers. Then elicit the answers from the class.

Designed to please UNIT 7 **67**

> **Answers**
>
> 1 She had been living in New Zealand and Australia.
> 2 By 1978, she had appeared in films and TV series and had moved to the UK.
> 3 By 1999, she had been acting for 36 years.
> 4 By 2010, she had designed two hotels.

C

- Tell the students that they are going to use their notes about Anouska Hempel to write a short biography, similar to the ones they read earlier in the unit.
- Have the students turn back to p. 85 and reread the biography of Jennifer Lopez. Elicit the examples of the past perfect and past perfect continuous in the text and remind the students that they should use those forms in their biographies as well.
- Point out the prompt. Tell the students that they should start their biographies with this partial sentence and then use the answers they wrote to the questions in Ex. B to complete the biography. Elicit a possible second sentence for the biography from the class.
- Circulate while the students are writing, making sure they are using the target verb tenses correctly and helping as necessary.
- Have the students exchange biographies and check their partner's usage of the past perfect and past perfect continuous.

> **Extra: homework**
>
> Ask the students to choose a building in their city or country, or a famous building somewhere in the world that has a unique design. Have them research the building's designer and then write a short biography of them using the past perfect and past perfect continuous.

LifeSkills: showing initiative (p. 88)

Step 1: Understand ways of showing initiative. (Ex. A, Ex. B)
Step 2: Identify opportunities to show initiative. (Ex. B, Ex. D)
Step 3: Be proactive and find practical solutions. (Ex. D, Ex. E)

Lead-in

Read the target skill aloud and invite the students to tell you what they think *showing initiative* means. Elicit a definition for *showing initiative* (being self-motivated and having the ability to think creatively and solve problems independently).

Give or elicit examples of what the students can do to show initiative: ask the teacher questions when they don't understand, review material regularly on their own, ask their peers for help solving problems, etc.

Ask the students to think about why it is important to show initiative and elicit some of the possible benefits. Explain that people who show initiative are often in leadership roles and are people who have the power to improve situations and make things work better. As a result, the ability to show initiative is often one of the traits employers look for when hiring or promoting employees.

Then **highlight** the three-step strategy to develop the skill of *showing initiative*.

A

- Give the students time to silently read the definition of *initiative* and say how it compares to their original definition.
- Ask the students to think of a time when they showed initiative in some aspect of their lives, for example, at school, at their job, in a relationship. Give them time to make some notes if needed.
- To help the students get started, you may wish to provide a model by sharing a few of your own personal anecdotes about showing initiative.
- Put the students in groups to explain how they showed initiative and what the results were. Circulate during the students' discussions and encourage the students to ask follow-up questions to find out more about their classmates' experiences.
- When the students finish their discussions, call on a few individuals to explain the ways they have shown initiative.

> **Alternative**
>
> The students may also discuss a time when they wished they had shown more initiative and the consequences of not showing initiative.

B

- Give the students time to read the paragraphs (pointing out that 3 and 4 are on p. 89). Remind them that they should think as they read about whether the person shows initiative, as well as what those who don't show initiative could have done differently or better.
- Put the students in pairs to discuss their ideas.
- When the pairs have finished their discussions, ask the class whether the person in each situation shows initiative, and why or why not.
- Elicit suggestions from the class for what Justin and Lauren could have done differently and list them on the board. Encourage the students to support their ideas with examples from personal experience. Ask for volunteers to say which ideas they think would work best and why.

> **Answers**
>
> 1 Lauren didn't show initiative. She could have asked for a message to give to her manager and then tried to contact him/her. Alternatively, she could have offered to help with whatever the client wanted. She could also have taken the client's number and offered to ring him/her back as soon as she contacted her manager.
> 2 Megan showed initiative.
> 3 Nathan showed initiative.
> 4 Justin didn't show initiative. He could have thought of useful tasks (cleaning, organising supplies, etc) to do when the café is quiet. He could also have suggested ways of attracting more customers at quiet times, perhaps with special offers.

C 2.05

- See p. 127 for the **audioscript**.
- Explain to the students that they are going to hear a man talking about a situation at work. Tell them they should listen for what the situation is and what the man is feeling worried about.

- Play the audio once and have the students summarise the situation with a partner. Then check whether the students need to hear it again.
- Elicit the reason why the man is feeling anxious.

Answer
He has an upcoming annual performance review (his first) and is unsure how to respond to questions about his leadership qualities and ways in which he shows initiative.

D
- Explain that the students are going to come up with a plan of action that will help the speaker in Ex. C prepare for his annual performance review.
- Put the students in pairs to complete the task. Go over the language in the *How to say it* box and encourage the students to use it in their discussions.
- Tell the students that they will need to report their plan to the class, so they should write down their ideas.
- Circulate during the students' discussions and offer help and suggestions as needed.

Possible answers
The man might:
- volunteer to give a presentation about the work of his department at the conference
- suggest setting up meetings with possible clients at the conference
- offer to help create posters or other publicity for an event
- go through local business directories to find possible new clients
- call possible clients and try to set up meetings with them
- arrange a dinner with a number of possible new clients

E
- Call on pairs to report their plans to the class. Following each pair's presentation, encourage the other students in the class to suggest which ideas they think were the best.

F
- Put the students in pairs to discuss the questions. Encourage them to think about the people in Ex. B and the man in Ex. C to help them decide how they would feel in certain situations.
- Have the pairs discuss their ideas as a class. Encourage them to say in what ways it is important to show initiative in the domain of **Work and Career**. Ask for examples from any jobs the students have done.

Alternative
You can also discuss with the students the possible negative consequences of not showing initiative.

Highlight the fact that what may come easily for some people in relation to showing initiative can be a challenge for others. Elicit that the students can reach out to others for help and support in situations when they feel it is difficult to show initiative at first.

REFLECT
- Discuss the question with the whole class. Ask the students to say what they feel are the most useful points they learned from this lesson, and how the skill of *showing initiative* might be useful in the domains of **Study and Learning** and **Self and Society**, either now or in the future.
- Elicit the following ideas: *solving problems more quickly and effectively, maximising their potential as a leader, improving challenging situations, making things go more smoothly in relationships with friends, family members and co-workers*, etc.

RESEARCH
- Go through the task and check that the students are clear about what they have to do.
- Suggest some newspapers, magazines or websites where the students may find examples of performance reviews.
- Have them share their findings in class. Lead a class discussion about what they found and how they think employees should prepare for a performance review.
- As an alternative, suggest that the students research films or TV programmes that are set in a workplace and have them watch for examples of people who show initiative (or a lack of initiative) and to note the results/consequences. Some possible ideas include *The Office, Parks and Recreation, 9 to 5, Office Space, Clerks, The Man in the Gray Flannel Suit*.

Language wrap-up (p. 90)

For notes on how to approach the exercises in the Language wrap-up section, please see page 9.

1 Vocabulary
- Go over the words and phrases in the box. Call on the students to say them aloud and correct pronunciation and stress as needed.
- Encourage the students to read through the whole text before they choose the correct word for each blank.
- Remind the students to use the context of the sentence to help them choose the correct words.
- Have the students complete the task individually and then compare answers in pairs.
- Call on individual students to say the sentences, inserting the correct answers. Ask the rest of the class to say whether the sentence is correct or not.

2 Grammar
- Encourage the students to read through the whole text first before filling in the blanks and correcting the mistakes. Encourage them to focus on the overall meaning and context of the story, and to choose the correct form to convey the meaning.
- Check the answers by calling on individual students to read the sentences of the paragraph aloud, inserting the correct forms.

Writing workshop: writing a review (p. 91)

Lead-in

Ask the students what a *review* is and what the purpose is (a written or spoken opinion about something – a film, book, restaurant, product, etc – which either recommends it to others or advises them against it). Ask the students whether they ever consult reviews before buying a product or using a service, and if so, what kinds of products/services.

Ask for a volunteer to talk about an experience when they stayed at a hotel and to say what they liked and disliked about the place. Tell the students that they are going to read a review of a hotel and then write their own.

A

- Have the students look at the photographs. Elicit some of the similarities and differences between them.
- Give the students time to read the review. Address any questions about unfamiliar vocabulary by encouraging the students to guess the meaning from context.
- Ask which place is being reviewed and elicit some of the words and phrases that indicate the answer, e.g. *decorated to look like one of Van Gogh's most famous paintings; done so effectively that I felt as if I had travelled back in time to when he painted it in 1888; simply furnished and the dominant colours were yellow and bright blue; furnishings of such unique character and atmosphere.*
- Ask the students about the reviewer's overall opinion of the place and whether they would recommend it to others. Ask which aspects of the place received positive reviews, and which received negative comments.

Answer
2

B

- Give the students time to review the prompts.
- Have them complete the phrases individually and then compare answers in pairs.
- Check the answers with the class.

Answers
Expressing approval
unique
delightful
enjoyed
Expressing disapproval
disappointing
disadvantage

Extra: alternative answers

Have the students work in pairs to come up with as many alternative words as they can to complete the blanks in Ex. B, for example:
Expressing approval: wonderful, delightful, thrilling, fantastic; great, amazing, enjoyable; liked, had a great time
Expressing disapproval: unfortunate, depressing; downside, disadvantage

Extra: online reviews

Have the students research travel review websites and list examples of additional useful phrases they can use to express approval and disapproval.

Extra: review practice

Put the students in pairs and give each pair a set of cards of written prompts about various aspects of a hotel. Include a '+' or a '–' to indicate whether they should make a positive or a negative review, for example:
the pool +
the room size –
the food at the restaurant +
the service at the restaurant –
Have the students take turns choosing a card and giving a review using one of the phrases in Ex. B.

C

- Have the students read the instructions.
- Elicit some additional categories to include in their reviews. Encourage the students to think of their own experiences if applicable.
- Give the students time to make some notes describing the aspects of the hotel.

Alternative

If the students have not stayed in a hotel recently, encourage them to write a review of a restaurant or other service they have used recently.

D

- Have the students write their reviews in class or for homework. Remind them to write about 200 words.
- Encourage the students to use new language and structures from the unit in their writing. Award an extra mark or marks for including the verb tenses or vocabulary from the unit.

How are you doing?

- Ask the students to read the statements and tick the ones they believe are true.
- Ask them to discuss their reviews with another student in the class and identify things they could improve on next time.

 Workbook pp. 44–45, SkillsStudio

UNIT 8 A FAIR DEAL?

The expression *a fair deal* refers to the notion that everyone in a society should have the same opportunities and rights. If something is fair, it is within and without bias. Some other expressions with *fair* include: *fair and square*, *fair play* and *fair's fair*.

Unit plan

Unit opener	(p. 92)	20 min.
1 **Grammar:** *would rather* and *would prefer*	(p. 94)	40 min.
2 **Reading:** biographical profiles	(p. 94)	30 min.
• Vocabulary: social issues		15 min.
3 **Listening:** for main ideas	(p. 96)	30 min.
4 **Pronunciation:** the contracted form of *would*	(p. 96)	15 min.
5 **Speaking:** talking about social justice	(p. 97)	30 min.
• Vocabulary: social justice		15 min.
6 **Grammar:** noun clauses as subjects	(p. 98)	40 min.
7 **Writing:** sentence variety	(p. 99)	30 min.
LifeSkills: understanding rights and responsibilities (Self and Society)	(p. 100)	50 min.
• Optional downloadable *LifeSkills* lesson (Study and Learning)		50 min.
• Optional downloadable *LifeSkills* lesson (Work and Career)		50 min.
Language wrap-up	(p. 102)	15 min.
Speaking workshop	(p. 103)	20 min.
Video and downloadable video worksheet		45 min.

Unit opener (p. 92)

Lead-in
Ask the students to look at the unit title and the photos and predict what the unit will be about. Ask them if they have ever seen similar housing or homeless people like the man pictured. Refer to the title and ask if they think homeless people are getting a fair deal. Direct the students' attention to the points in the unit objectives box and go through the information with them. To get your students to think about the skills being developed in this unit, ask them to look at the questions in the cogs.

Listening: for main ideas
- Remind the students that learning to listen for the main ideas will help them understand lectures better. Explain that speakers often use words or phrases before main ideas to help listeners recognise when a main idea is being delivered. Give them time to suggest phrases to answer the question.

Writing: sentence variety
- Tell the students they will learn ways to write a variety of sentences in this unit. Ask the question and elicit answers. Explain that using a variety of grammatical structures makes their writing more academic and more interesting.

LifeSkills: understanding rights and responsibilities
- Ask the students if they agree that we all have rights and responsibilities in the different roles we play. Ask them to think of the roles they have in their lives. Elicit other family relationship roles (*siblings*, *aunts/uncles*, *grandchildren*), specific work roles (*babysitter*, *office worker*, *employer*) and other answers.

Common European Framework: unit map

Unit 8	Competence developed	CEF Reference (B2 competences)
Grammar	can correctly use *would rather* and *would prefer*	Table 1; Table 2; Sections 5.2.1.2; 6.4.7.7; 6.4.7.8
Reading	can read and understand biographical profiles	Table 1; Table 2; Sections 4.4.2.2; 4.4.2.4; 4.5.2.2
Listening	can listen for main ideas	Table 1; Table 2; Sections 4.4.2.1; 4.5.2.2
Pronunciation	can correctly pronounce the contracted form of *would*	Section 5.2.1.4
Speaking	can talk about social justice	Table 1; Table 2; Sections 4.4.1.1; 4.4.3.1; 4.4.3.5; 4.5.2.1; 5.2.1.1; 5.2.1.2; 5.2.3.2
Grammar	can use and understand noun clauses as subjects	Table 1; Table 2; Sections 5.2.1.2; 6.4.7.7; 6.4.7.8
Writing	can use connectors to make writing more interesting	Table 1; Table 2; Sections 4.4.1.2; 4.5.2.1; 5.2.1.5; 5.2.1.6

A fair deal? UNIT 8

A

- Ask the students if they know what an infographic is. Define it if necessary (*a visual representation of a lot of complex information in a quick and easy way*). Give examples (weather maps, illustrations accompanying directions on how to make things, public transportation maps, etc).
- Put the students in pairs. Ask them to look at the photos and the infographic. Elicit or explain *vaccine/vaccination* (something put into the body, usually by injection, in order to provide protection against a disease) and *soup kitchen* (a place where food is given to people who are hungry). Give them time to discuss the questions.
- Listen to their ideas as a class. Point out that answers will vary depending on what they know about other countries. Remind them that everyone may have different opinions.

Culture note

Although modern technology has made it much easier to create infographics, they have existed for a long time. For example, in 1626, Christoph Scheiner wrote a book about the sun. In that book, he included illustrations showing how the sun rotates. The famous nurse, Florence Nightingale, used infographics to show the number and causes of death during the Crimean War. She used her infographics to persuade Queen Victoria to improve the conditions in the military hospitals.

Alternative

Ask the students which numbers they found most surprising and why. Encourage them to discuss any differences in opinion.

Culture note

A soup kitchen is a place where food is given to people who are hungry. The food is free or served at a very low price. Most soup kitchens are located in poor areas and are staffed by volunteers from local charitable organisations. Soup kitchens got their name because many locations only served (and still only serve) soup because soup is a low-cost and easy way to give nutritious food to a large number of people. The earliest soup kitchens date back to the 1790s. Soup kitchens are now available throughout the world.

B

- Have the students work in groups. Ask them to brainstorm ways to reduce social inequality both locally and in the world.
- Listen to their ideas as a class. Note that answers will vary and the aim is to encourage critical thinking and for the students to have the opportunity to express and explain their ideas.

Alternative

If students find answering the questions difficult, answer the first one together as a class. Brainstorm a list of types of inequality. You could include these types if students don't think of them on their own: economic, health care, education, gender, racial. Explain a specific example to the students: Sometimes men are paid more than women for the same job. Give the students time to work with a partner or small group to choose one type of inequality and think of ways to reduce it.

Grammar: *would rather* and *would prefer* (p. 94)

Lead-in

Ask the students to define what a *charity* is (an organisation to which you give money so that it can give money and help to people who are poor or ill, or people who need advice and support). Ask them if they know any charities. Elicit answers such as Médecins Sans Frontières, the Salvation Army, Task Force for Global Health, World Vision, Habitat for Humanity International, Save the Children and Goodwill Industries International. Ask them to work in pairs and think of examples of other charities. Listen to their ideas as a class. Continue the discussion by surveying the class to see if anyone has ever donated to a charity.

A 2.06

- See the Student's Book for the **audioscript**.
- Refer the students to the photo. Have the students read the questions.
- Play the audio and have the students read along. Then elicit the answers from the class.

Answer

No, he isn't. He'd prefer to start his own campaign.

NOTICE!

- Direct the students' attention to the **Notice!** box.
- Have them find and underline all the examples of *prefer* and *rather* in the conversation.
- Ask the students what kind of verb follows each example.

Answers

A base form verb + *to* (or an object) follows *prefer*.
A base form verb follows *rather*.

B

Form & Function

- Have the students read the conversation again, paying attention to *prefer* and *rather*.
- Point out that the table presents the function and form and gives examples of *would ('d) rather* and *would ('d) prefer*. Remind the students there is a difference between expressing their own preferences and someone else's. Make sure the students notice that the phrases can be used in either a positive or negative way.
- Ask the students to complete the table using examples from the text in Ex. A.
- Check the answers with the class.

Answers

1. you'd rather not work through a charity
2. I'd rather get directly involved
3. I'd prefer not to do that.
4. Yes, I'd prefer to do that, too.
5. I'd rather we didn't just donate money
6. I'd rather we took some positive action
7. most people would prefer charities to organise campaigns.

C

- Ask the students to complete the exercise individually.
- Direct the students' attention to the **What's right?** box and make sure they understand that the second sentence is incorrect, because *would rather* is followed by the base form, not by the infinitive (with *to*). Write extra examples on the board if necessary.
- When you check the answers, make sure the students understand why each answer is correct.

Answers

1. start   2. to get   3. to donate   4. didn't organise
5. not to work   6. not raise

D

- Ask the students to read the instructions. Explain that the events listed are common ways that charities earn money or gather donations of items to give away.
- Put the students in pairs and ask them to choose one or more of the events that they feel would be most effective and easy to organise.
- Ask each pair to discuss the reasons for their choice. Give them time to work individually first, thinking of ideas and making notes if they wish. Then allow enough time for discussion.
- Remind them to use *would rather* and *would prefer* in their discussion. Tell them to pay attention to the following verb form.
- When they have finished, ask each pair to present their choice to the class and to explain it.

 Workbook pp. 46–47, Section 2

Reading: biographical profiles (p. 94)

Lead-in

Direct the students' attention to the photos on p. 95 and ask them if they know who the two women are (Angelina Jolie and Shakira). Ask the students what they know about these two women and make a list on the board.

A

- Present the questions in the Student's Book. Give the students time to read the profiles to find the answers to the questions.
- Check the answers. Ask the students to explain what part of the profile helped them find each answer.

Answers

1. Angelina Jolie   2. Shakira   3. Angelina Jolie

B

- Remind the students that reading for details is an important part of studying. Discuss skimming and scanning for details too.
- Put the students in pairs. Give them time to check for the details mentioned in the biographical profiles.
- Check the answers as a class.

Answers

date and place of birth – B
occupation – B
what they studied – A
how they became famous – B
causes they support – B
charities they are involved with – B
how they raise money – N
awards/recognition they received – B
reason why they became involved in humanitarian issues – S

C

- Direct the students' attention to the list of words (1–8). Explain that these are all social-issue words.
- Point out that the part of speech is given for the words and that the definitions provided are formal definitions. Have the students work individually to match the words with their definitions.
- Put the students in pairs to compare their answers before checking the answers as a class.

Answers

1 g   2 c   3 h   4 f   5 d   6 b   7 e   8 a

A fair deal? UNIT 8   73

Extra: discussion

Review the definition for *refugee* (someone who leaves their home country because it is not safe there). Ask the students what might make a place unsafe. Elicit answers such as *war*, *persecution* or *natural disasters*. Extend the discussion by asking the students if any of these would make them relocate to another country.

Extra: vocabulary

Elicit from the students current examples of each vocabulary word. Ask them to write sentences using the vocabulary word and their examples. Provide two examples on the board if students need help getting started: *Many refugees have come from Somalia since the Siad Barre regime collapsed many years ago. There are many people suffering from famine in Somalia and the country needs humanitarian help.*

D
- Give the students time to read the questions.
- Put the students in pairs to discuss answers to the questions before holding a whole-class discussion.

Extra: in your own words

Have the students write a few sentences in their own words about the importance of charity work. Encourage them to use the grammar and vocabulary from this section.

Extra: homework

Ask the students to write a paragraph about a famous humanitarian. If the students need help thinking of someone, provide this list: Ricky Martin, Nelson Mandela, Mother Teresa, Princess Diana, Florence Nightingale, Scarlett Johansson, David Beckham, Ben Affleck, George Clooney, Richard Branson, Sean Penn, Bono.

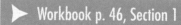 Workbook p. 46, Section 1

Listening: for main ideas (p. 96, p. 71)

Lead-in

Remind the students that they practised listening for main ideas on p. 71.

Give the students time to read the information in the skills panel.

Write these sentences on the board:
1 *It consists of 39 counties.*
2 *For example, Norfolk, Kent and Yorkshire are English counties.*
3 *England is a relatively small country.*

Ask the students which sentence is the main idea (3), a detail (1) and an example (2).

Remind the students that they listened to a lecture in Unit 4, and if necessary remind them what a lecture is (a speech on a topic, often given by a professor or an expert). Point out that in lectures the main ideas are supported by details and examples, and that speakers often use key phrases to help their listeners know what they are going to say next.

A 🎧 **2.07**
- See p. 127 for the **audioscript**.
- Tell the students that they will hear an academic lecture. Have them look at the photos and say what they think the speaker will talk about. Ask volunteers to share their predictions. Do not confirm any answers.
- Play the first part of the lecture and have the students check their ideas.

Answer
The speaker is talking about fair trade.

B 🎧 **2.08**
- See p. 127 for the **audioscript**.
- Explain to the students that they are going to listen to the rest of the lecture. Ask them to read the notes about the lecture. Tell them that as they listen, they should choose the sentence, a or b, which best expresses each main idea.
- Play the audio and give the students time to choose the options.

Answers
Purpose: a   History: b   Labelling: a   Criticism: b

Culture note

Fair trade is a non-profit social movement that exists to help improve conditions for trade in disadvantaged communities. Its goal is to help farmers in developing countries build sustainable businesses and use the free market to their advantage.

C
- Explain to students that they are going to listen to the lecture again to focus on the details. Ask them to read the statements and decide whether each statement is true or false.
- Play the audio once. Play it again if necessary before checking the answers.

Answers
1 T   2 T   3 T   4 F   5 F   6 F

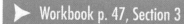 Workbook p. 47, Section 3

Pronunciation: the contracted form of would (p. 96)

A 🎧 2.09
- See the Student's Book for the **audioscript**.
- Explain what a contracted form is in English (words or phrases that have been shortened by dropping letters and then combined). Mention that contracted forms use an apostrophe. Draw attention to the grammar section that covered *would prefer* and *would rather*. Explain that *would* is often contracted.
- Play the audio and make sure the students notice the contracted forms in the second sentence of each pair.

B
- Put the students in pairs to take turns choosing a sentence from each pair to read aloud.
- Circulate to help as needed.

Extra: pronunciation practice
Ask the students to write two sentences with *I would* and two with *I'd*. Then put the students in pairs and have them take turns reading their sentences to their partner. Partners should monitor each other's pronunciation and correct as needed.

Speaking: talking about social justice (p. 97)

Lead-in
Remind the students that throughout this unit they have been reading and hearing about social issues. Explain that everyone has a slightly different idea of what social justice means to them. Ask volunteers to share their idea of social justice. Read the statement in Ex. A to the students: *A fair society helps its poorer members*. Ask them what this statement means to them, making sure that they understand the meaning of *fair* in this context (without prejudice).

A 🎧 2.10
- See p. 127 for the **audioscript**.
- Define *debate* (a formal argument presenting two different opinions or points of view on a particular topic). Ask the students if they have ever watched a debate, such as a presidential debate on television, or watched or participated in a debate at school. Ask what they think might be challenging about participating in a debate. Explain that they are going to hear a person taking part in a debate and explaining why he agrees with the statement, *A fair society helps its poorer members*.
- Direct the students to read the four points. Tell the students that as they listen they should tick the points the debater makes that support his argument.
- Play the audio once and check progress. Play the audio again if necessary.
- Check the answers with the class.

Answer
The following numbers should be ticked: **1**, **3**

B
- Focus the students' attention on the words from the box. Tell them that these words were used in the audio they just heard. Have the students repeat each word or phrase to practise the pronunciation.
- Point out that the part of speech of each word or phrase is given in parentheses. Mention that the students should notice this because it will help them complete the exercise. Have the students fill in the blanks with the vocabulary word that is the closest in meaning to the word or phrase in italics.
- Check the answers with the class.

Answers
1 live on **2** can't afford **3** benefits **4** have the right
5 unemployed **6** have a responsibility

C
- Ask the students to complete each sentence with a word or phrase from Ex. B. Remind them to use the correct form.
- Check the answers with the class.

Answers
1 have the right **2** unemployed **3** can't afford
4 live on **5** benefits **6** have a responsibility

D
- Put the students in pairs and ask them to read the statement about unemployment benefits.
- Choose one student in the pair to be for the statement and the other to be against it. Have the students look at the statement again. Ask them to think of three reasons to support the opinion they have been given. Remind them they must support their answers and that their reasons should be included in their notes.

Alternative
Put the students into AA/BB pairs to think of the three reasons to support their opinion and to make notes about their reasons.

E
- Put the students in pairs. Explain that they should take turns giving their opinion to their partner. Each student should speak for about one and a half minutes. They should use the notes they made to help them stay focused and remember everything they want to say. While one student speaks, the other should listen without interrupting.
- Ask the students to tell the class whether their partners have convinced them to reconsider their opinions. Encourage them to say why or why not.

A fair deal? UNIT 8

Extra: speaking

Organise a class debate on the issue of whether poor people should receive support from the government to buy food and other necessities. Put the students in two groups: those who are for the idea and those who are against it. Give the students a few minutes to share their ideas and prepare their statements. Then have the groups debate the issue.

▶ Workbook p. 48, Section 4

Grammar: noun clauses as subjects (p. 98)

Lead-in

Write these sentences on the board:
1 *The world needs love now.*
2 *What the world needs now is love.*

Focus attention on sentence 1 and ask the students what the subject is (*The world*) and what the verb is (*needs*). Shift focus to sentence 2 and again elicit the subject (*What the world needs*) and the verb (*is*). Tell the students that both sentences mean fundamentally the same thing even though the subject takes different forms. Explain that this unit will explain how nouns can be one word or a clause. Leave the sentences on the board.

A 2.11

- See the Student's Book for the **audioscript**.
- Point out the question and ask the students to answer it after they hear the audio.
- Play the audio once and ask the students for the answer.

Answer

It's difficult for young people to get jobs because employers want people with work experience and students don't have work experience.

NOTICE!

- Direct the students' attention to the **Notice!** box.
- Ask them to find and underline all the examples of *what, how, who* and *where* in the conversation. Ask them what kind of clause the words introduce.

Answers

<u>What's</u> really difficult for them is getting their first job, ...,
<u>What</u> students need is good work experience ...,
<u>How</u> students prepare for work is so important.
<u>Who</u> gets the best job very often depends on ...,
<u>where</u> you get your first job can influence ...
Each word introduces a noun clause.

B
Form & Function

- Ask the students to read the conversation again, paying attention to the noun clauses.
- Draw the students' attention back to the two sentences about love on the board. Point out that although the two sentences mean basically the same thing, the second sentence is more emphatic. Explain that in the second sentence the subject is a noun clause (*What the world needs*) and that the noun clause itself contains both a subject and a verb. Point out that using a noun clause at the beginning gives a sentence stronger emphasis. Ask them to think of times when they might want to be more emphatic.
- Explain that noun clauses like this begin with a question word. Remind them that the whole clause operates as the subject of the sentence and not just one word.
- Refer the students to the table. Point out the two different noun clause forms shown in the table, and explain that different modals such as *could, should, can* and *would* can be used in the second noun clause structure.
- Ask the students to scan the conversation in Ex. A and find one example of each form to write in the table. Have them underline the verb in the noun clause and circle the verb in the main clause. Allow enough time for the students to do this individually and then check the answers with the class.
- Direct the students' attention to the **What's right?** box. Explain that even though noun clauses begin with the question word *What*, they use affirmative subject – verb word order rather than question order.

Answers

1 <u>'s</u> really difficult for them (is) getting
2 students <u>prepare</u> for work (is)
3 you <u>get</u> your first job (can)

C

- Point out that each numbered item in Ex. C is a sentence but that the parts are out of order.
- Ask the students to work individually to put the parts in order, beginning each sentence with a noun clause.
- Have them compare their answers in pairs. Then check the answers with the class.

Answers

1 What young people need are more training opportunities.
2 How you write your job application is very important.
3 Who interviews you makes a big difference.
4 Where you work can affect your self-confidence.
5 What can create a good impression is a positive attitude.

D

Put the students in pairs and ask them to explain to each other what they would do to reduce youth unemployment in their country or city. Point out that they can start with the sentence beginnings provided. Encourage the students to use these and other noun clauses in their discussions.

Extra: homework
Ask the students to write a paragraph about their plan.

 Workbook pp. 48–49, Section 5

Writing: sentence variety (p. 99)

Lead-in
Ask the students to read the information in the skills panel. Point out that just as there are several different ways of saying the same thing, there are several different ways to write the same thing. Explain that variety in writing is especially important because it makes it more interesting for the reader. Tell the students that using the same grammatical structures repeatedly in writing can make it sound repetitive and not academic.

Refer the students to the photo. Ask them if they are familiar with any international aid organisations that offer help in the wake of a natural disaster. To get the students started, suggest the United Nations as one example. (The UN is an international organisation that is committed to peace and security around the world.) Make a list on the board of the organisations and the things the students know about them.

Culture note
The United Nations was founded in 1945, immediately after World War II. Fifty-one countries were involved and their mission was to maintain international peace and security. Although today the organisation is best known for peacekeeping, conflict prevention and humanitarian aid, it also works on issues such as sustainable development, disaster relief and counter terrorism, among others, with the goal of making the world a safer place for future generations.

A
- Direct the students' attention to the extract and the question. Ask them to read the extract silently to find out what problems the writer thinks international aid may cause. When they have finished, elicit the answer from the students.

Answer
The writer suggests that international aid may mean that a country can become dependent on aid instead of developing its own economy.

B
- Tell the students that good writing uses many types of grammar. Ask the students to look at the grammatical structures in the exercise. Review with them the meaning of each of the structures and point out that they should be familiar with all of them.

- Direct the students to read the extract in Ex. A again. Ask them to find and underline examples of the grammatical structures listed and to label each one with the number of the correct structure. Remind them that some sentences have more than one structure.
- Check the answers. Go through each structure in turn and ask the students to give the example or examples of the structure that they found in the text.

Answers
[3] [6] Giving aid to countries that are facing economic problems seems like a good idea. [1] It helps people in a time of crisis. [4] It's important to continue to support very poor people in the world. However, there are also some dangers associated with giving aid. [5] [6] If an aid organisation provides money and food, it can create dependence that is harmful for the local economy. [3] [6] Importing cheap food can also hurt local producers who cannot compete and therefore lose their income. [2] [6] What world aid organisations need to do is provide training that will enable countries to develop their own economies. [7] When a country has all its aid supplied in the form of money or food, it can easily become dependent. [3] Providing medical care and education is a much better way of helping other countries. [5] If all countries have access to good healthcare and education, they can develop the ability to become independent participants in the global market.

C
- Refer the students to the sentences and ask them to rewrite them using the words given. Remind them to use the grammatical structures in Ex. B.
- You could put the students in pairs to rewrite the sentences together.
- Check the answers with the class.

Answers
1. Providing aid to countries that are at war is not right.
2. If we don't provide aid, people will suffer.
3. What we should do is make people work for the aid they receive.
4. It's fair to give suffering people money or food.
5. We should get the government to increase the size of aid payments.
6. Aid, which we provide to many countries, has both advantages and disadvantages.

D
- Tell the students that they will write two or three paragraphs explaining their own opinions of international aid. Direct their attention to the two points and tell them they can choose to write about one or both of these topics, or another topic regarding international aid.
- Remind the students that they should use different grammatical structures in their sentences in order to make their paragraphs more interesting. Circulate while the students are working and give help as needed.
- Collect their papers and correct any errors.

Alternative

After the students complete their paragraphs, put them in pairs for a peer review. Ask the partners to check each other's sentences and correct errors. Collect the papers and correct any remaining errors.

Extra: Homework

Ask the students to write the paragraphs for homework to be collected in the following class.

 Workbook p. 49, Section 6

LifeSkills: understanding rights and responsibilities (p. 100)

Step 1: Understand what rights and responsibilities are. (Ex. A)
Step 2: Decide what rights and responsibilities are valid in a given environment or situation. (Ex. B, Ex. C)
Step 3: Be aware of rights and responsibilities in different contexts. (Ex. D, Ex. E)

Lead-in

Read the target skill aloud and invite the students to tell you what they think *understanding rights and responsibilities* means.

Draw attention to the document in the photo, and ask the students what it is (an official document that gives an overview of human rights). Invite the students to say what connection they think this document might have to the title. Ask the students if they can name any other official documents. Expect answers including government documents, school documents or legal documents. Make a list on the board.

Then **highlight** the three-step strategy to develop the skill of *understanding rights and responsibilities*.

Culture note

The United Nations offers a Universal Declaration of Human Rights. The document has a preamble and 30 articles (an article is a part of a legal document or agreement that deals with a particular point). The Universal Declaration of Human Rights was adopted by the UN General Assembly in 1948 after World War II. Part of the reason for its writing was so that the rights of every individual would be protected everywhere.

Extra: discussion

Extend the discussion about other types of legal documents. Ask the students to think of examples for each category of legal documentation they listed earlier. For example, legal documents might include visa applications, business contracts, licences or agreements.

A

- Ask the students to read the definitions. After they have finished, hold a class discussion about what is meant by 'rights' and 'responsibilities'.

Possible answers

Rights are the freedoms we enjoy and the things we can choose to do.
Responsibilities are the obligations we have and the things we have to do.

B

- Have the students read the statements about parents' and children's rights and responsibilities. Make sure the students understand all the vocabulary.
- Put the students in pairs. Ask them to discuss each statement and decide whether it is a right or a responsibility or both. Encourage them to discuss whether they agree or disagree with each statement and to tick the appropriate box. Remind them that partners might not always agree with each other and that this is OK.
- When the students have finished, discuss the answers as a class. Invite the students to share whether they agree or disagree with each statement and take a class poll. Ask the students if opinions might change if their role changes. For example, ask them if they think their ideas might change if they actually become a parent.

C

- Have the students work with the same partners as in Ex. B to add two more rights / responsibilities for both parents and children. Direct their attention to the sample conversation and encourage them to use these expressions in their discussion.
- When the students have finished, put each pair with another pair to compare their ideas. Circulate while the students are discussing and then listen to their ideas as a class.

Extra: discussion

Ask the students to think of two rights or responsibilities for other roles. For example, they could list rights and responsibilities for teachers, students, siblings, employees, employers, friends, other relatives, etc.

D

- Draw attention to the photos. Ask the students what they think is represented by the two photos. Elicit that the young man dressed in an 'alternative' way represents freedom of expression or the right to dress however we want, and that giving money to a homeless person represents the responsibility to take care of others in society. Continue the discussion by asking the students if they agree or disagree with what these photos represent and if they have ever expressed themselves the same way.
- Ask the students to work with the same partner as before to consider their society as a whole. Have them make lists of the rights and responsibilities they believe citizens of their country have. If the students have trouble thinking of ideas, suggest *money, work, politics, the law, freedom to do / from something, helping other people* as ideas. Provide *vote in general elections* and *pay taxes* as examples of a right and a responsibility in the UK. Draw attention to the list in the Student's Book and encourage them to fill it out or to make their list in a similar way.

E

- Write *What we all have a right to do is …* and *What we all have a responsibility to do is …* on the board. Explain that these are noun clauses that the students can use as subjects as they share their ideas with the class.
- Invite pairs to share their lists with the rest of the class. Take a class poll to determine whether they came up with more rights or more responsibilities.

F

- Put the students in pairs to discuss the questions. Have them think about the domain of **Self and Society** as they talk about how they feel and what they have learned.
- Combine the pairs to form groups of four and have them brainstorm a list of things they have learned, and a list of things they would like to learn, about their rights and responsibilities.
- Have a class discussion and write the students' ideas about what they would like to learn on the board. Ask how easy or difficult it might be to learn about each one.

REFLECT

- Discuss the question with the whole class. Ask the students to say what they feel are the most useful points they learned from this lesson, and how the skill of *understanding rights and responsibilities* might be useful in the domains of **Study and Learning** and **Work and Career**, either now or in the future.
- Elicit the following ideas: *actively seeking out rules and regulations, talking with others about their civic duties,* etc.

Extra: discussion

Ask the students whether they are also aware of their responsibilities when they insist on their rights. Invite individuals to share their thoughts.

RESEARCH

- Go through the task and check that the students are clear about what they have to do.
- Suggest that the students research citizens' rights and responsibilities in several different countries in order to compare and contrast them. Depending on class time and availability of computers, this could be done in class rather than outside of class.
- Have them share their findings in class. Lead a class discussion about how citizens' rights and responsibilities are similar and different around the world.

Language wrap-up (p. 102)

For notes on how to approach the exercises in the Language wrap-up section, please see page 9.

Class test

- Ask the students to do the exercises in test conditions, and give a time limit (e.g. 20 minutes).
- Check answers with the class and deal with typical errors or problems.

1 Vocabulary

- Ask the students to read the whole paragraph for general understanding and to gain an idea of the context before filling in the blanks with the words or phrases from the box.

Extra: vocabulary

Put the students in two teams. Ask them to write ten sentences using the vocabulary words. Tell them their sentences will be a quiz for the other team. Circulate to help as needed. Collect their sentences. Type them into a quiz leaving a blank where the vocabulary word should be. Distribute the quizzes to the opposite teams during the next lesson.

2 Grammar

A

- Ask the students to read each sentence through first before completing the exercise. Encourage them to say each sentence silently to themselves before deciding on their answers.
- When checking the answers with the students, remind them or elicit that *would rather* and *would prefer* can have one of two functions: expressing the subject's preference about their own actions; and expressing a preference about the actions of the subject and someone else (or someone else alone).

B

- Remind the students that they may need to add words when rewriting the sentences since there is a verb in the noun clause and in the main clause.
- When checking the answers, point out that noun clauses can begin with a variety of question words, such as *what, who, when, how* and *where*.

A fair deal? UNIT 8

Extra: discussion

Put the students in small groups. Ask them to discuss whether they agree or disagree with each of the sentences used in Ex. B in Grammar. Ask them to support their answer with a reason or example for their opinion.

Speaking workshop: proposing a solution (p. 103)

Lead-in

Ask the students to share some world problems they think need to be addressed. Elicit answers such as *poverty, hunger, the economy*. Tell them this workshop will focus on how to propose solutions to problems.

Explain that proposing solutions is an important concept in academic studies. Give examples of assignments such as writing a problem/solution essay or giving a presentation about a problem and its solution.

Alternative

Ask the students to think of problems specific to the city where the school is located. Put the students in small groups to share their ideas.

A 2.12

- See p. 128 for the **audioscript**.
- Ask the students to look at the photo and read about the problem. Check that they understand the problem.
- Tell the students they will listen to someone proposing two solutions to the problem. Ask them to complete the notes as they listen.
- Play the audio once. Play it again if necessary. Then discuss the answers with the class.

Answers
Solution 1: Control rent increases
Solution 2: Provide low-rent housing

B

- Ask the students to read the descriptions of what the speaker did. Ask them to listen as you play the audio again and tick the things the speaker did in the presentation.
- Play the audio again. Repeat only if necessary.
- Check the answers with the class.

Answers
The following items should be ticked: restates the problem in her own words, suggests two solutions, adds details to support each solution, makes a concluding statement.

C

- Explain that the students will now propose solutions to a different problem. Ask them to read the problem, then check that they understand it. Then give them some time to think of possible solutions. Encourage them to decide on two solutions to present to the class.
- Remind the students that they should restate the problem in their own words, add details to support their solutions and make a concluding statement.
- Allow enough time for each student to prepare. Circulate and help as necessary.

D

- Schedule enough time for each student to present their solution proposal to the class. Each student should talk for about one minute.
- When everyone has finished, take a class poll on which solutions stand out as the best.

How are you doing?

- Ask the students to read the statements and tick the ones they believe are true.
- Ask them to discuss their talk with another student in the class and identify things they could improve on next time.

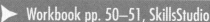 Workbook pp. 50–51, SkillsStudio

UNIT 9 COMPETITIVE EDGE

The expression *competitive edge* refers to the advantage a person or company has over their competitors. *Competitive* means trying to be more successful than others and an *edge* is an advantage that makes someone or something more successful than other people or things.

Unit plan

Unit opener	(p. 104)	20 min.
1 **Grammar:** gerunds after prepositions	(p. 106)	40 min.
2 **Listening:** to experts' opinions	(p. 107)	30 min.
• Vocabulary: scientific nouns and verbs		15 min.
3 **Pronunciation:** nouns and verbs with different pronunciation	(p. 107)	15 min.
4 **Speaking:** paraphrasing	(p. 108)	30 min.
5 **Grammar:** verb + gerund	(p. 109)	40 min.
6 **Reading:** understanding text organisation	(p. 110)	30 min.
• Vocabulary: expressions of emotion		15 min.
7 **Writing:** a description	(p. 111)	30 min.
LifeSkills: synthesising information (Study and Learning)	(p. 112)	50 min.
• Optional downloadable *LifeSkills* lesson (Self and Society)		50 min.
• Optional downloadable *LifeSkills* lesson (Work and Career)		50 min.
Language wrap-up	(p. 114)	15 min.
Writing workshop	(p. 115)	20 min.
Video and downloadable video worksheet		45 min.

Unit opener (p. 104)

Lead-in
Ask the students to look at the unit title and the photos and to predict what the unit will be about. Ask the students if they know anyone who is competitive and whether they think this is a good quality. Encourage them to expand on their answers and give examples. Direct the students' attention to the points in the unit objectives box and go through the information with them. To get your students to think about the skills being developed in this unit, ask them to look at the questions in the cogs.

Reading: understanding text organisation
- Ask the students what they like to read. Elicit answers to the questions and ask them what factual topics interest them and why.

Speaking: paraphrasing
- Make sure the students understand that paraphrasing is saying the same thing but using different words. Ask them to answer the question in pairs. Then discuss different situations as a class.

LifeSkills: synthesising information
- Ask the students if they know what *synthesising* means (combining different ideas into a single piece of work). Explain how this is important in academic studies because the students will have to combine information they learn. Elicit ideas in answer to the question.

Common European Framework: unit map

Unit 9	Competence developed	CEF Reference (B2 competences)
Grammar	can use and understand preposition + gerund structures	Table 1; Table 2; Sections 5.2.1.2; 6.4.7.7; 6.4.7.8
Listening	can understand an expert's opinion	Table 1; Table 2; Sections 4.4.2.1; 4.4.3.1; 4.4.3.5; 4.5.2.2
Pronunciation	can correctly pronounce nouns and verbs spelled the same (homographs)	Section 5.2.1.4
Speaking	can paraphrase a text	Table 1; Table 2; Sections 4.4.1.1; 4.4.1.3; 4.4.3.1; 4.4.3.5; 4.4.4.1; 4.5.2.1; 5.2.3.2
Grammar	can use and understand verb + gerund structures	Table 1; Table 2; Sections 5.2.1.2; 6.4.7.7; 6.4.7.8
Reading	can understand the way texts are organised	Table 1; Table 2; Sections 4.4.2.2; 4.4.2.4; 4.5.2.2
Writing	can write a description of a reality TV show	Table 1; Table 2; Sections 4.4.1.2; 4.5.2.1; 5.2.1.1; 5.2.1.2; 5.2.1.6; 5.2.3.2

A

- Ask the students to look at the six photos and captions of competitions from around the world. Give them a few minutes to work individually to rank them from the strangest to the least strange.
- Put the students in small groups to discuss the questions.
- Ask group members to share answers on behalf of their group. Remind the students there is no correct ranking.
- Ask the students if they know of any other unusual competitions. Brainstorm as a class and see who can come up with the most unusual ones. Provide examples, e.g. cheese rolling in the UK; running while carrying your wife in Finland. Extend the discussion by asking the students if they would participate in any of these competitions.

Extra: discussion

Ask the students if they are familiar with the *Guinness Book of World Records* (a reference book that lists world records in both human and natural world achievements). Write these facts on the board and see if the students think they are true or false. (They are all true according to the Guinness World Records available at www.guinnessworldrecords.com, but change the details to make some of them false.)

The most people extreme ironing underwater is 173 (achieved by de Waterman Diving Club (Netherlands) in Oss, the Netherlands, on 28th March 2011).

The largest air guitar ensemble was 2,377 participants, and it took place in Highland, California on 22nd September 2011.

The longest beard measured eight feet and two and a half inches on a man named Sarwan Singh, who lived in Canada. It was measured in 2011.

The longest limbo skating is 180 feet and 5.35 inches. It was achieved by Li Mingfen in Beidaihe District, Qinhuangdao City in China on 7th May 2010.

The farthest distance that a mobile phone has been thrown by a male competitor is 314 feet and 5 inches. This was achieved by Chris Hughff at the 2007 UK Championships.

The greatest distance flown in a wing suit is 16.71 miles. This was achieved by Shinichi Ito in Yolo County, California, on 26th May 2012.

Culture note

Extreme sports are growing in popularity. Extreme sports are activities that are considered very dangerous because they usually involve high speeds, great heights or specialised equipment or outfits. They are also called action sports or adventure sports. Examples include freeflying, wakeboarding, skydiving and rock climbing.

There is a television channel devoted to extreme sports: Extreme Sports Channel (ESC). This television channel started in 1999 in Amsterdam and is now available in over 60 countries and in 12 languages.

The X Games is an annual sports event that focuses on extreme sports. The first X Games event took place in 1995 in Rhode Island in the United States. Like the Olympics, athletes compete for gold, silver and bronze medals. They also win prize money.

B

- Put the students in small groups. Ask each group to develop a new and unusual competition to present to the rest of the class. Set a time limit.
- After the presentations, take a class vote to see which idea is the best. If circumstances allow, have the students present to other classes and let outside students be the voters.

Grammar: gerunds after prepositions (p. 106)

Lead-in

Ask the students to look at the photo. Ask them to comment on whether or not they have snowboarded or would like to snowboard. Extend the discussion by surveying the class to see how many students think snowboarding is dangerous. Ask the students to support their answers.

Point out that different personality types may prefer certain activities over others. Explain that they will read an article about different personality types.

A

- Ask the students to read the question and the title of the text. Give them time to read the text, keeping the question in mind.
- When everyone is finished, ask for their ideas about people they know. Then refocus their attention on the photo of the snowboarder. Ask them if they think the snowboarder is Type A, B, C or D (probably A).

NOTICE!

- Direct the students' attention to the **Notice!** box.
- Ask the students to reread the text and underline the gerunds that follow prepositions. Then ask for the answer to the question.
- Make sure the students know the form and function of a gerund (*-ing* form; serves as a noun). Explain that the *-ing* ending makes a gerund look like a verb, but it acts like a noun. Write these sentences on the board to illustrate the *-ing* as a verb and a noun: *I go swimming in the summer. Swimming is my favourite sport.*

Answers

The following words should be underlined:
Paragraph 1: competing, having, doing; Paragraph 2: going, telling, working; Paragraph 3: having, getting, organising, making; Paragraph 4: doing, following, sticking, making.
We form gerunds by adding *-ing* to verbs.

B

Form

- Have the students read the text again, paying attention to the use of gerunds. Point out that a preposition plus gerund can follow both verbs and adjectives and that certain combinations are very common. Tell them they will use examples from the text to complete the table.

- Review the forms in the table. Give the students time to write the appropriate phrases from the text in the correct places in the table.
- Check the answers.
- Direct the students' attention to the **What's right?** box. Ask why the two incorrect sentences are wrong (in the first, *seeing* is necessary because the verb follows an adjective + preposition; in the second, *see* is necessary because the infinitive follows *would like*). Explain that it is easy to confuse when to use a gerund and when to use an infinitive. You could write some other incorrect sentences on the board for the students to correct.

Answers

verb + preposition + gerund	adjective + preposition + gerund
look forward to	fond of
care about	bored with
insist on	good at
worry about	interested in
object to	responsible for
	happy about
	capable of

C

- Go over the instructions. Have the students focus on using the appropriate preposition with each verb or adjective. Encourage them to look at the table if they need help as they work.
- Check the answers with the class.

Answers

1. about using / in, communicating
2. to having
3. of telling / in listening
4. about competing
5. with doing / about doing (*to do* would also be correct after *happy*)
6. to learning / about making
7. for organising
8. of concentrating

D

- Tell the students they will now determine personality types for each other.
- Put the students in pairs to ask each other the questions in Ex. C and to discuss their answers. Ask them to determine their partner's personality type. Refer them to the text in Ex. A and to the example to help them decide.
- If time allows, ask individual students to present their findings to the class.

Extra: grammar practice

Ask the students to choose a personality type from Ex. A and write two or three sentences to describe it. Encourage them to use a verb or adjective + preposition + gerund in their descriptions (for example, *A Type A person is someone who gets excited about competing in games*, etc).

Extra: homework

Ask the students to write a short paragraph about whether they agree or disagree with their partner's opinion about their personality, and to explain why or why not.

▶ Workbook p. 52, Section 1

Listening: to experts' opinions (p. 107)

Lead-in

Write the word *moderator* on the board. Elicit what the students think the definition of a *moderator* is (someone who is in charge of a discussion or meeting between people with different opinions). Ask the students to describe their experience listening to panel discussions or debates where there may have been a moderator. Ask them what makes listening to experts difficult, for example, speakers are hard to understand, vocabulary is challenging. Tell them that they will practise by listening to two experts give opinions in this section.

A

- Put the students in pairs. Have them look at the question and the photo.
- Explain that making predictions about a discussion before listening can help them understand the content better. Ask them to brainstorm things they think the speakers might mention. Do not correct them at this point.

B 2.13

- See p. 128 for the **audioscript**.
- Tell the students they are going to hear a moderator and two experts (both educational psychologists) talking. Play the audio once. Ask the students to listen to see if any of their ideas are mentioned.

Answers

Speakers give opposing theories on the effects of competition on young people.
Dr Carson mentions studies that have concluded that competition is bad, specific effects of competition on winners and losers, and alternatives to competition.
Dr Banks mentions studies that support the idea that competition is necessary and how it helps to prepare children to handle negative experiences and failure as adults.

C

- Ask the students to listen again and to take notes on the main arguments.
- Play the audio more than once if necessary.
- Put the students in pairs to compare notes.
- Discuss the answers with the class.

Competitive edge UNIT 9

Possible answers

Dr Carson:
- Personal worth is measured by winning.
- Few people can become winners.
- Competition makes children anxious and unable to concentrate.
- 'Winners' become aggressive and feel ashamed when they don't win.
- 'Losers' get discouraged and stop trying.
- Cooperative activities create high self-esteem and satisfaction.

Dr Banks:
- Competition is healthy and necessary for children.
- Competition is a fact of life.
- There's no proof that competition is bad for the majority.
- Children have to experience failure in order to handle failure as adults.
- Competition helps young people develop important skills.

D
- Put the students in small groups. Ask them to say which speaker they agreed with more and why.
- Encourage the students to use their notes.

E
- Refer the students to the table. Have them complete it with nouns and the infinitive of the verbs.
- If possible, have the students use a dictionary to check their answers. Then check the answers with the class.
- Point out that several of the words are the same in the verb and noun forms.

Answers
1 test 2 study 3 research 4 proof 5 theory
6 experiment 7 measure 8 conclude

F
- Ask the students to complete the sentences with the correct form of a word from Ex. E. Point out that there may be more than one correct answer.
- Check the answers with the class.

Answers
1 test
2 experiments/studies
3 proven/proved/researched/tested/studied
4 concluded
5 measurement
6 research
7 experiment
8 proof

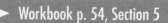 Workbook p. 54, Section 5

Pronunciation: nouns and verbs with different pronunciation (p. 107)

A 2.14
- See the Student's Book for the **audioscript**.
- Point out that even though the verbs and nouns are spelled the same, they are pronounced differently.
- Play the audio once and ask the students to tell you which syllable is stressed in nouns and verbs (the first syllable in nouns; the second syllable in verbs). Then play it again for the students to repeat each word.

B 2.15
- See the Student's Book for the **audioscript**.
- Put the students in pairs and ask them to practise saying the sentences.
- Play the audio so the students can hear the correct pronunciation. Then have them say the sentences again.

Extra: pronunciation
Give the students extra words to practise (or ask the students to brainstorm their own lists). Some words to use include: conduct, conflict, object, progress, project, subject, reject, suspect.

Speaking: paraphrasing (p. 108)

Lead-in
Ask the students to read the information in the skills panel.
On the board, write these sentences: *The idea that humans use 10% of their brain has been proven false by recent technology. Although not all parts of the brain are active at the same time, functional magnetic resonance images (fMRI) show several brain areas at work for any given activity.*
Tell the students that there are shorter and easier ways to say these sentences. Ask them to make suggestions. Give an example: *It is a myth that humans use 10% of their brain. Imaging technology shows that more than one area of the brain works at any given time.*

A
- Direct the students' attention to the instructions and go over the four ways to paraphrase.
- Ask the students to read the short text and to identify which technique is being used for each numbered part of the paraphrase.
- Check the answers with the class.

Answers
a 2 b 3 c 1 d 4

B
- Put the students in pairs. Explain the task to the class, making sure they all understand the instructions before they begin.
- Check the answers with the class.

Possible answers

a) Change words to different parts of speech, e.g. a noun to a verb:
If we use / Using; problem-solving or information recall / solving problems or recalling information

b) Use synonyms (words that have the same meaning as other words):
generate / create; related to / connected with; frequently / often

c) Change the word order or the sentence structure and add or delete words as necessary:
… it will generate more neurons and axons / … causes it to create more neurons and axons; The implication of this may be that the more frequently we play competitive sports and games, the more we want to play them, which may make us more competitive. / … it's possible that competing a lot makes us want to compete even more.

d) Use different connectors, or break a long sentence into two sentences:
… it will generate more neurons and axons related to those activities, which improves brain function and causes us to perform better. / … causes it to create more neurons and axons connected with those activities. Our brain functions more effectively, so …

C 🎧 **2.16**
- See p. 128 for the **audioscript**.
- Put the students in pairs. Tell them they will listen to two people talking about a study on peer support among young adults. Ask them to paraphrase what each person says.
- Play the audio once and check progress. Play the audio again if necessary.
- Put the pairs together in groups of four to compare their paraphrases.
- Have a class feedback session and write good ideas and examples on the board.

D
- Ask the students to choose a short text or paragraph from a text in Units 1–8.
- Put the students in pairs and ask them to paraphrase the text they chose for their partner.
- Direct the students' attention to the examples in the **How to say it** box and encourage them to use these expressions when asking for clarification.

Extra: homework

Have the students paraphrase a paragraph from a book of their choice. Ask them to submit the original and the paraphrase.

▶ Workbook p. 55, Section 6

Grammar: verb + gerund (p. 109)

Lead-in

Ask the students if they watch any reality television shows. Ask them to name any they can think of. Make a list on the board. If the students are not familiar with any, suggest a few to give them an idea of the variety: *Survivor* (contestants are isolated in the wilderness and compete for cash), *Strictly Come Dancing* (celebrities pair up with professional dancers to compete), *The Bachelor* (a dating game show), *Project Runway* (a fashion designing competition), *MasterChef* (a cooking competition).

Draw attention to the photo of the young man lying on the sofa. Ask the students to describe him. Elicit answers such as *lazy, tired, bored, happy*. Ask the students if they ever do what this young man is doing and what they watch on television.

A 🎧 **2.17**
- See the Student's Book for the **audioscript**.
- Play the audio and have the students read the conversation as they listen, keeping the question in mind.
- Ask them to quickly say whether or not Sandra dislikes all reality shows and why.

Answer

No. She likes reality shows that have competitions.

Extra: pronunciation

Put the students in pairs to read the conversation and then let them listen to compare themselves to the speakers.

NOTICE!
- Direct the students' attention to the **Notice!** box.
- Ask the students to notice the phrases that are underlined in the conversation. Ask them what verb form follows each underlined phrase.

Answer

the gerund (*-ing*) form

B

Function
- Ask the students to read the conversation again, paying attention to the verbs in the underlined phrases. Remind the students that they are already familiar with many verbs that are followed by gerunds.
- Have the students read the conversation again and complete the rule. Then check the answer with the class.

> **Answer**
>
> perception

Form

- Present the four forms in the table.
- Ask the students to complete the table using the appropriate underlined phrases from the conversation.
- Check the answers with the class.
- Direct the students' attention to the **What's right?** box. Elicit that *watch* is incorrect in the first sentence because it is in the infinitive instead of the gerund.

> **Answers**
>
> 1 trouble   2 (more) fun   3 watch   4 see   5 observe
> 6 feel   7 their time   8 my life   9 at home

> ### Extra: grammar practice
>
> Put the students in small groups to write two sentences for each form. Circulate as the students work to make sure the students understand the different forms. Invite groups to share their sentences with the rest of the class.

C

- Have the students choose an appropriate verb to complete each question. Remind them to use the verb in the correct form. Let them know there is more than one possible answer for some of the questions.
- Check the answers with the class.

> **Answers**
>
> 1 sitting/lying   2 spend/waste   3 have; spend/waste
> 4 watching/seeing   5 understanding   6 hear/see

D

- Put the students in small groups to discuss the questions in Ex. C.
- Listen to some of their ideas as a class.

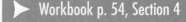 Workbook p. 54, Section 4

Reading: understanding text organisation (p. 110)

Lead-in

Ask the students to read the information in the skills panel. Ask them to guess what kind of text they will be reading (a factual text) and what they expect it to include (main ideas, details and examples).

Point out that the same elements can be found in lectures. Review the fair trade lecture in Unit 8 as an example.

Ask the students if they ever use encyclopedias or other types of reference material. Ask them to share a topic they have read about recently. Ask volunteers to share a fact they learned about the topic.

Ask the students to look at the Student's Book page and predict what they will be reading about and the kind of language involved (the brain, science words and phrases, expressions of emotion).

A

- Ask the students to read the factual text about the competitive brain and to identify the main idea. Put the students in A/B pairs. Tell them to read both theories in the text, but for Student A to focus on the first and Student B on the second, since they are going to explain one theory each.
- When the students finish, ask them to talk about the main idea and to paraphrase the theories that are presented. Remind them to take turns so that Student A paraphrases the first theory and Student B paraphrases the second theory.
- Don't check the answers at this point since the students will repeat Question 2 in Ex. C.

> **Possible answers**
>
> 1 Main idea: The structure and chemistry of our brain may control how competitive we are.
> 2 First theory: Brain chemistry (the amount of hormones and chemicals in our brain) causes us to be more or less competitive; people with high levels of testosterone and dopamine tend to be more competitive.
>
> Second theory: The brain generates more cells for doing something the more we do it, so repetition makes us better at things and success makes us more competitive in those things.

> ### Culture note
>
> Neurochemistry studies neurochemicals and other molecules and how they influence the neurons and how they work in the brain. Neurochemists and neuroscientists research the interactions of molecules and how they affect the nervous system.

B

- Remind the students that noticing details is an important part of reading factual texts. Explain that they will now look back at the text for specific information in paragraphs 2 and 3.
- Ask the students to find and underline the items in the text.

Answers

1 The male hormone testosterone
2 winning causes a rise in testosterone levels, which gives a person a sense of power and success. The desire for this feeling may encourage us to be even more competitive. In contrast, losing appears to cause a drop in testosterone levels, which helps explain the agony of defeat.
3 the chemical dopamine, which is a neurotransmitter that produces a feeling of pleasure.
4 The thrill of victory is caused by a combination of increased levels of testosterone and dopamine
5 'plasticity'. This means that the brain is constantly 'rewiring' or changing its structure.
6 The nerve cells in the brain are called neurons,
7 These dendrites and axons are responsible for transmitting information to and from other cells in the body.
8 if we use our brain for activities such as problem-solving or information recall, it will generate more neurons and axons related to those activities, which improves brain function and causes us to perform better.

C

- Have the students work in the same pairs as they did in Ex. A. Ask them to repeat the paraphrasing activity they did then and to discuss the question.
- Then check and discuss the answers to Ex. A.

Possible answer

It helps you pick out specific important information that you can use in your explanation.

 Workbook pp. 52–53, Section 2

D

- Explain that the students will now focus on vocabulary for emotions. Ask the students to brainstorm a list of emotions to make sure they understand the meaning. Expect answers such as *happy, sad, bored, lonely, excited*.
- Give the students time to answer the three questions.
- Check the answers with the class.

Answers

1 the joy of – 2 the fun of – 3 the thrill of – 1
2 defeat, loss
3 the will to, the desire for/to

Culture note

The phrase 'agony of defeat' is often associated with Vinko Bogataj. He is a ski jumper from Slovenia who was competing at the Ski-flying World Championships in 1970. Due to snowy conditions, Bogataj was going too fast on the ramp. When he tried to stop, he lost his balance and flew off the ramp, flew through the air and crashed into a fence near the audience. Amazingly, he suffered only a minor concussion. That failure was featured on the TV show *Wide World of Sports* in America and billed as the 'Agony of Defeat'.

E

- Put the students in groups. Give them time to discuss the three questions.
- Invite volunteers to share their answers.

Extra: homework

Ask the students to write a paragraph about themselves that answers one of the questions in Ex. E.

 Workbook p. 53, Section 3

Writing: a description (p. 111)

Lead-in

Without giving its name, describe a television show that the students are likely to recognise. Invite the students to guess which show you are describing.

A

- Give the students time to read the description of the reality show *The Island with Bear Grylls*. Answer any vocabulary questions as needed.
- Ask the students to discuss the questions. Encourage them to give reasons for their answers.

B

- Put the students in small groups. Ask them to brainstorm a list of TV programmes that they are familiar with. Have a member of each group write their lists on the board so that all the students have more choices for the rest of the activity.
- Encourage the students to discuss with their group which programme they can all agree is excellent or terrible. Encourage them to make notes about what makes the programme the best or worst.
- Tell each group to work together to write a description of the television programme they chose, modelled on the description in Ex. A.
- Allow enough time for discussion and group writing.

Competitive edge UNIT 9 87

C

- Have the students choose a reader for their group. Ask the readers to present the descriptions to the rest of the class. Have the students vote on the best and worst TV show based on the descriptions.

Alternative

Have the students write their descriptions without mentioning the name of the television show. Ask the other groups to guess what television show is being described.

Extra: discussion

Ask the students to review the lists from Ex. B. If they chose the best to present for Ex. C, then ask them to choose the worst. If they chose the worst to present for Ex. C, then ask them to choose the best.

LifeSkills: synthesising information (p. 112)

Step 1: Gather information from different sources. (Ex. B, Ex. C)
Step 2: Organise relevant information into categories. (Ex. C)
Step 3: Combine the information to produce a new idea or a conclusion. (Ex. D)

Lead-in

Read the target skill aloud and ask the students what they think *synthesising information* means.

Draw attention to the photo and ask the students if they know anything about ginkgo biloba. Ask the students how they might go about researching information about this plant. Point out that they would probably need to use more than one source (an encyclopedia, websites, talk to a specialist, etc).

Then **highlight** the three-step strategy to develop the skill of *synthesising information*.

A

- Present the definition of *synthesising information* and then ask the question. Accept any reasonable answers, but make sure the students include both academic and non-academic situations, for example, when preparing a report or class project, when giving a presentation, when buying a mobile phone – gathering information from different sources before deciding what to buy.

B

- Put the students in groups of four and explain that they are going to participate in an activity that is similar to a project done in university classes. Ask them to imagine that their university professor has asked them to prepare a report about a particular kind of supplement that increases competitive advantage.

- Have the groups read the instructions for the report. Then ask them to discuss the information they need to find out and the types of sources they might need to use. Remind them to paraphrase the language in the instructions.
- Make sure the students understand the supplement and the four components they need to include in their report.

Culture note

The ginkgo biloba is a kind of tree that is native to China. Ginkgos are very large trees and can grow to be over 60 feet tall. In the autumn, the leaves turn bright yellow before falling off within 15 days of changing colour. They usually live for a very long time because they are able to resist disease and the wood can also resist insects. Ginkgos are used as food and medicine. People sometimes take ginkgo supplements.

C

- Ask the students to look at the four texts (A–D). Explain that these are the source information they will use for their research. Ask the groups to choose one text for each group member. Tell the students they are each responsible for following the steps in Ex. C for their reading: underlining the main idea, supporting details and examples; summarising the underlined information; sharing the information with the group to decide which is most relevant to the task in Ex. B and categorising the information (description, claims, evidence, conclusions); and analysing the information and discussing conclusions.
- Direct the students' attention to the examples in the **How to say it** box on p. 113 and encourage them to use the expressions when presenting their reports.
- Answer any questions about the procedure. Give the students sufficient time to follow the steps.
- Circulate as the students are working. Be prepared to address vocabulary or content questions.

Extra: research

Ask the students to research fish oil (omega-3 fats), another food supplement that may increase competitive advantage. Have them include information about what it is and what it is used for. The students should include information about claims made by supplement manufacturers and statistical or anecdotal evidence that supports or refutes the claims. Put the students in groups and give them a few minutes to discuss the information they found.

D

- After the students have completed all the steps in Ex. C, ask them to prepare their group report.
- Have the groups present their reports to the rest of the class. Encourage the other groups to comment and ask questions. Ask the students if their opinion about the supplement has changed, and to explain why or why not.

Culture note

People sometimes take dietary supplements to give their bodies nutrients that they may not be getting naturally. One of the most common types of dietary supplements is multivitamins. Many medical professionals agree that dietary supplements are not needed if people eat a balanced diet.

Culture note

Botany is the scientific study of plants. Botanists study fungi, algae, herbs and all types of plants and flowers. The study of plants is important because a large percentage of the oxygen and food that they produce is necessary for animal and human life.

E

- Put the students in groups to discuss the questions. Ask them to focus on the skill *of synthesising information* in the domain of **Study and Learning**. Have them make some notes in answer to each question.
- Have a class feedback session and write the best ideas on the board. Then check the answers with the class.

Possible answers

1 Putting information into categories can help you present the information in an organised way in your report. You can use this organisation format as your outline and just fill in the main idea (topic sentence) and supporting details for each category.
2 If you have to form some kind of conclusion or new idea, it's never a good idea to use just one source. With only one source, you will just repeat the ideas in that source instead of having your own ideas, and there may be different studies or opinions so it's important to find out about any conflicting information in order to come to an informed conclusion.

Extra: homework

Ask the students to write a summary of their answers to the questions in Ex. E.

REFLECT

- Discuss the question with the whole class. Ask the students to say what they feel are the most useful points they learned from this lesson, and how the skill of *synthesising information* might be useful in the domains of **Self and Society** and **Work and Career**, either now or in the future.

- Elicit the following ideas: *summarising information from multiple sources, combining related reports into one single report*, etc.

RESEARCH

- Go through the task and check that the students are clear about what they have to do.
- Suggest that the students conduct research on a health- or performance-related product that is currently popular.
- Have them share their report in class. Lead a class discussion about the product they researched.

Language wrap-up (p. 114)

For notes on how to approach the exercises in the Language wrap-up section, please see page 9.

1 Vocabulary

A

- Ask the students to read each sentence for general understanding and to gain an idea of the context before filling in the blanks with the phrases from the box.
- When checking the answers with the students, point out that the vocabulary words are related to emotions.

Extra: vocabulary

Ask the students to change the subject of each sentence to create a new sentence with the same vocabulary word. Give an example by changing the first sentence from *Sitting in the garden gives me a feeling of peace* to *Visiting my grandmother gives me a feeling of peace*. Ask volunteers to share their new sentences.

B

- Go over the words in the box. Call on the students to say them aloud and correct pronunciation and stress as needed.
- Encourage the students to read through the whole text before they choose the correct word for each blank.
- Remind the students to use the context to help them choose the correct words and forms.
- Call on individual students to say the sentences, inserting the correct answers. Ask the rest of the class to say whether the sentence is correct or not.

2 Grammar

- Ask the students to read the whole paragraph through first before completing the exercise. Encourage them to say each sentence silently to themselves before deciding on their answers.
- When checking the answers with the students, point out the form of gerunds (*-ing* forms) and how they can follow verbs + prepositions and adjectives + prepositions.

Competitive edge UNIT 9 89

Writing workshop: writing a discursive essay (p. 115)

Lead-in
Hold a brainstorming session with the class. Ask them what types of essays they know of. Elicit answers such as *compare and contrast, cause and effect, describing a process, problem-solution*, etc. Focus their attention on discursive essays. Inform the students that a discursive essay is sometimes called an argument-style essay because it often gives an analysis of a controversial topic. Ask the students to brainstorm a list of topics that might be considered controversial. Accept any reasonable answers.

Alternative
Ask the students if they have ever written a discursive essay and for what reason. Elicit answers such as for classes, for exams or for debates. Encourage the students to share their topics.

A
- Present the topic and tell the students that the writer presents both sides of the argument. Read the assignment and make sure the students understand it.
- If helpful, present the idea of a T-chart and encourage students to list the advantages and disadvantages of sports supplements on either side of the chart.
- Tell the students they should decide which point of view the writer agrees with. Ask the students to explain how they know the answer.

Answer
The last paragraph shows that the writer agrees with the sceptics of supplements.

Culture note
Sports supplements come in many forms. Some of the more popular forms are protein shakes or protein bars. To make a protein shake, a powdered protein is mixed with water or milk. Other sports supplements are available as liquids, capsules or tablets. Some common sports supplements include creatine (which is used for energy) and vitamins and minerals; others may be anabolic formulas that accelerate muscle development.

B
- Refer the students to the four paragraphs and explain that this is a common structure for a discursive essay.
- Ask the students to answer the questions about the essay.
- Check the answers with the class.

Answers
1. Paragraph 1
2. they give a reason (because they contain ingredients that benefit performance) and then give some examples (protein can help build muscle; caffeine can provide extra energy).
3. 1 Not enough research to know whether supplements work, 2 health risks, 3 false advertising; many supplements have too little of the ingredients to have any effect
4. Writer agrees with the sceptics. She starts with the point of view that she doesn't agree with and follows with a list of reasons about the point of view that she does agree with. Her final paragraph summarises that view.

C
- Explain that the students will now write their own discursive essay for the assignment in Ex C.
- Encourage them to make notes to help them plan their essay, including the arguments for and against taking a supplement that can affect memory and learning.
- Have them work in pairs to compare their notes and which content should be included in each of the four paragraphs. Afterwards, check some of their ideas as a class.
- Give the students plenty of time to write their essays. While they are writing, circulate and assist where necessary.

Culture note
Memory is a topic often studied in psychology courses. There are several types of memory. Sensory memory allows people to remember things perceived by the five senses, such as sight. Short-term memory is what people remember in the seconds or minutes after it is learnt. Short-term memory capacity is limited. Long-term memory allows individuals to remember large quantities of content for a long time span (or even over an entire lifetime). Declarative memory requires an individual to make a conscious effort to recall certain information.

D
- Give the students time to write their letter in class or for homework. Remind them to include all the necessary information and all the different parts of a business letter. Remind them to write about 200 words.
- Award an extra mark or marks for including new language and structures from the unit.

How are you doing?
- Ask the students to read the statements and tick the ones they believe are true.
- Ask them to discuss their essay with their partner and identify things they could improve on next time.

Extra: homework
Ask the students to write a discursive essay for a formal evaluative grade.

 Workbook pp. 56–57, SkillsStudio

UNIT 10 RISKY BUSINESS

The expression *risky business* means that a situation involves something dangerous or hazardous. For example, buying a house can be a risky business since it involves a lot of money that might have to be paid back over a period of time. Another example might be investing in the stock market. It can be risky because stock prices may go down instead of up.

Unit plan

Unit opener	(p. 116)	20 min.
1 **Reading:** an opinion article	(p. 118)	30 min.
• Vocabulary: safety and risk		15 min.
2 **Grammar:** expressing ability	(p. 119)	40 min.
3 **Writing:** requesting action	(p. 120)	30 min.
• Vocabulary: expressions with *risk*		15 min.
4 **Grammar:** past modals of deduction	(p. 121)	40 min.
5 **Pronunciation:** reduction of *have*	(p. 122)	15 min.
6 **Listening:** rapid speech	(p. 122)	30 min.
7 **Speaking:** speculating about events	(p. 123)	30 min.
LifeSkills: managing stress (Self and Society)	(p. 124)	50 min.
• Optional downloadable *LifeSkills* lesson (Work and Career)		50 min.
• Optional downloadable *LifeSkills* lesson (Study and Learning)		50 min.
Language wrap-up	(p. 126)	15 min.
Speaking workshop	(p. 127)	20 min.
Video and downloadable video worksheet		45 min.

Unit opener (p. 116)

Lead-in
Ask the students to look at the unit title and the photos and to predict what the unit will be about. Ask the students to give examples of things they consider to be *risky business*. Direct the students' attention to the points in the unit objectives box and go through the information with them. To get your students to think about the skills being developed in this unit, ask them to look at the questions in the cogs.

Listening: rapid speech
- Ask the students the question and give them time to formulate a list of reasons. Have them discuss native speakers they know and rate their rate of speech on a scale from 1–10.

Writing: requesting action
- Ask how many students have written a letter requesting action. What style did they use? Give the students time to talk with a partner. Discuss the answers as a class.

LifeSkills: managing stress
- Ask the students to tick the statement that best describes them. Ask how many students chose each statement. Invite volunteers to share their answer and the reason they chose it. Ask the students to share an example of a stressful situation they have experienced.

Common European Framework: unit map

Unit 10	Competence developed	CEF Reference (B2 competences)
Reading	can understand an article presenting an opinion	Table 1; Table 2; Sections 4.4.2.2; 4.4.2.4; 4.5.2.2
Grammar	can use and understand verbs and expressions of ability	Table 1; Table 2; Sections 5.2.1.2; 6.4.7.7; 6.4.7.8
Writing	can write a letter to request action	Table 1; Table 2; Sections 4.4.1.2; 4.4.3.2; 4.4.3.4; 4.5.2.1; 5.2.1.1; 5.2.1.2; 5.2.1.6; 5.2.2.2; 5.2.2.4; 5.2.3.2
Grammar	can use and understand past modals of deduction	Table 1; Table 2; Sections 5.2.1.2; 6.4.7.7; 6.4.7.8
Pronunciation	can correctly pronounce reduced *have*	Section 5.2.1.4
Listening	can understand rapid speech	Table 1; Table 2; Sections 4.4.2.1; 4.4.3.1; 4.4.3.5; 4.5.2.2
Speaking	can speculate about events	Table 1; Table 2; Sections 4.4.1.1; 4.4.3.1; 4.4.3.5; 4.5.2.1; 5.2.3.2

Risky business UNIT 10

A

- Put the students in pairs. Ask them to look at the photos and captions. Give them time to discuss the questions.
- Listen to their ideas as a class. Point out that answers will vary and everyone might have different opinions. Take a poll to see which job the students think is the most risky.

Possible answers

A firefighter takes a lot of risks because they work in dangerous situations.
An actor might take risks when working on action films.
A politician takes risks with his or her career by making unpopular decisions.
A stock trader takes big risks with their company's money every time they buy stock.
A small business owner doesn't take many physical risks unless his or her business involves extreme physical activity of some kind.

Alternative

Ask the students to look at the photos and captions individually. Have them write a list of risks they associate with each of the professions. Point to each photo and ask volunteers to tell what is risky about it. Encourage other students to add more information. After discussing all of the professions, conduct a poll to see which one the students think is the most risky.

Extra: discussion

Discuss what personality traits people in the occupations in Ex. A probably have. Ask the students what other types of occupations might be appropriate for people with these personality traits. Continue by asking the students which occupation they would choose from the five choices.

Possible answers

Common personality traits include: ability to ignore fear and anxiety, great physical/mental stamina, ability to think creatively, a positive attitude, high energy, a desire to succeed.
Other appropriate jobs include: surgeon, military officer, extreme-sports athlete, manager.

Extra: discussion

Ask the students to brainstorm a list of risky occupations, then write them on the board. Put the students in small groups and assign one occupation to each group. Have the students discuss what the risks of their occupation are with their group. Give the groups a few minutes to debate why they think their occupation is the most risky.

B

- Start a discussion by asking the students if they think they are a risk-taker in general. Tell them that this activity is designed to help determine if they are a risk-taker in all or part of their lives.
- Draw attention to the questions and give the students time to talk with a partner. Check that the students understand the following vocabulary: *caving* (walking and climbing through caves under the ground); *bungee jumping* (jumping from a very high place while attached to a long cord); *helmet* (a hard hat that protects your head); *freelance* (not permanently employed and working for more than one company). Have the students complete the questionnaires individually before talking about the results with their partner.
- Arrange for the students to share their results. Note that there is no single answer to any of the questions. The aim is to encourage critical thinking and for the students to have the opportunity to express and explain their ideas.

Reading: an opinion article (p. 118)

Lead-in

Remind the students that it is a good idea to think about a topic before reading. Before-reading strategies often improve comprehension.

Have the students look at the photo and ask them what it is of (a person standing on a dangerous ledge). Ask them what kind of risk this person is taking. Survey the students to see how many of them would be willing to take the same risk as the person pictured.

Tell the students they are going to read an article about taking risks.

Extra: group project

Ask the students to bring in a photo of an activity they enjoy or would like to learn how to do. Collect the photos anonymously and have the students vote on which they think are most risky. Play a game in which the students try to guess who brought in which photo.

A

- Have the class discuss why they think some people are risk-takers. Ask them to look at the three statements. Give them time to check whether they agree or disagree with each statement.
- Put the students in pairs to compare their answers. Ask volunteers to share their answers.

B

- Ask the students to read the article. Remind them that their objective is to decide whether the author would agree or disagree with the statements in Ex. A.
- Ask the students to compare the writer's answers with their own answers. Hold a discussion about whether the students agree with the points the writer makes.

> **Answer**
> The writer would agree with the statements in 1 and 2, and disagree with the statement in 3.

C
- Direct the students to the list of vocabulary words. Explain that these are all words and phrases associated with safety and risk, but they can also be used in other contexts as well.
- Have the students work individually to match the words and phrases with the definitions, using the context of the article to help them.
- Circulate while the students are working and help as needed. Check the answers with the class.

> **Answers**
> 1 e 2 a 3 g 4 f 5 b 6 h 7 d 8 c

D
- Put the students in pairs to discuss the questions. Encourage the students to support their answers with details and examples.
- Ask the pairs to share their answers with the class.

Extra: homework
Ask the students to write a paragraph about one of the occupations shown in the Unit opener. Ask them to explain how the occupation is risky. Encourage them to use vocabulary from Ex. C.

 Workbook p. 58, Section 1

Grammar: expressing ability (p. 119)

Lead-in
Define *ability* (the fact of being able to do something or the level of skill that someone has in a particular job or activity). Ask the students what their abilities are. Make sure the students know what an *entrepreneur* is (someone who uses money to start businesses and make business deals). Poll the class to see if any students would want to be an entrepreneur.

Extra: Discussion
Ask students to name some well-known entrepreneurs. Some examples include: Sergey Brin and Larry Page (Google), Elon Musk (Tesla), Mark Zuckerberg (Facebook), Estée Lauder (cosmetics), Richard Branson (media, aviation), Steve Jobs (Apple Inc.), Bill Gates (Microsoft), Coco Chanel (fashion). For each of the people the students name, ask what they have done and why they think they have been so successful.

A
- Refer the students to the question and ask them to think about how much they agree with each comment as they read.
- Give the students time to read the article and the two comments.
- Hold a class discussion, asking the students to what extent they agree with each of the comments.

> **NOTICE!**
> - Direct the students' attention to the **Notice!** box.
> - Explain that there are examples of both the ability and the inability to do something in the article. Ask the students to find the expressions and underline them. How many different expressions are there?
>
> **Answer**
> succeed in, good at, able to, capable of, manage to, can, could, incapable of, unable to, can
> There are nine different expressions in the text.

B
Form
- Present the list of phrases in the box. Read them out and make sure the students understand the meaning of all the verbs (*be good at*: to be able to do something well; *manage*: to succeed in doing something, especially something that requires a lot of effort or skill; *succeed in*: to achieve something that one attempted to do; *be able/capable of*: used for saying it is possible for someone to do something; *be unable/incapable of*: used for saying it is not possible for someone to do something). Point out that they will already be familiar with some of these verbs, especially *can/can't*, *could/couldn't* and *be able to*.
- Explain that all of these verbs are related to ability or inability in some way and they can all be combined with other verbs in different ways.
- Refer the students to the table and describe the form of the verbs. Each of the verbs is followed by either an infinitive with *to*, an infinitive without *to* or an *-ing* form. Ask the students to complete the table by writing the verbs from the box in the correct column. Tell them to look back at the text to help them.
- Check the answers with the class.

> **Answers**
> **Verb + infinitive:**
> be able
> be unable
> (not) manage
> **Verb + infinitive without to:**
> can/can't
> could/couldn't
> **Verb + gerund:**
> be capable of
> be good at
> be incapable of
> (not) succeed in

Risky business UNIT 10 93

Extra: grammar note

Point out that *could* can only be used with sense verbs to describe general past abilities. Give examples of sense verbs (*see*, *hear*). Explain that we do not use *could* for one-time finished actions. Write *Last year, Tom could make a profit from the business*. Elicit why this sentence is incorrect (*could* is not used with completed past actions that only occurred once). Elicit the correct sentence: *Last year, Tom was able to make a profit from the business*. **Highlight** that we can use *could* in the negative with this meaning: *However, Harry couldn't make a profit from his business*.

C

- Ask the students to complete the exercise individually.
- Point out that each verb will either be an infinitive with *to*, an infinitive without *to* or an *-ing* verb depending on which verb of ability precedes it. Encourage them to refer to the table in Ex. B as they work.
- Direct the students' attention to the **What's right?** box. Elicit that the first sentence is incorrect since *succeed in* has to be followed by the gerund.
- Check the answers with the class.

Answers
1 Some people are incapable of dealing with risk.
2 How did you succeed in making the business profitable?
3 Jeff is unable to judge the acceptable level of risk.
4 In the end, we weren't able to accept that level of risk.
5 Successful entrepreneurs manage to control risk.

D

- Put the students in pairs to discuss the questions about their potential ability to be an entrepreneur.
- Encourage them to use the phrases from Ex. B (verbs of ability) and from Ex. C on p. 118 (safety and risk vocabulary) during their discussions.
- Invite individual students to share their ideas with the class.

Extra: grammar practice

Ask the students to write a short paragraph about what kind of business they would start if they were an entrepreneur and what they think of their ability to make it successful. Ask them to use verbs of ability and safety and risk vocabulary in their writing.

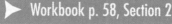 Workbook p. 58, Section 2

Writing: requesting action (p. 120)

Lead-in

Ask the students to read the information in the skills panel.

Ask them to think about a letter to request action and what that is (a letter asking someone to do something or to change the way something is currently being managed). Elicit what characteristics a letter to request action should include (the most important points; a clearly stated description of actions that are being requested; a formal, polite style; a confident attitude that the recipient will respond positively to the requested action[s]).

A

- Direct the students' attention to the photo and ask what it shows (a cave). Hold a class discussion by asking these questions: *Why might people want to go into a cave? / What are the risks associated with going into a cave? / Would you ever go into a cave? / Have you ever been in a cave? What do you think it would be like? / What was it like?*
- Ask the students to read the questions and to keep them in mind as they read the letter.
- Give the students time to read the letter and think about the answers. Check the answers with the class.

Answers
1 Janet West; Citizens for Safety
2 the risks faced by visitors to Bowen Park (one of the caves has long tunnels and deep pools of water that could be dangerous to inexperienced explorers)
3 to explain the general situation and the risks faced
4 to express confidence and request prompt action

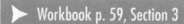 Workbook p. 59, Section 3

B

- Explain that the letter uses several expressions associated with risk. Ask the students to underline all the words or phrases in the letter derived from or including the word *risk*. Then ask them to complete the sentences with one of those words or phrases, changing the form when necessary. Encourage them to use the definitions in parentheses to help.
- Check the answers with the class.

Answers
1 risk assessment 2 at risk 3 risking their lives
4 reduce the risks 5 run the risk 6 high-risk

C

- Ask the students to think of a high-risk situation in their local area. Draw attention to the ideas in the Student's Book. You could brainstorm as a class for other ideas.
- Put the students in pairs. Ask them to choose one situation to discuss using the questions in Ex. B as a guide.
- Ask the pairs to summarise their discussion for the class.

D

- Have the students write a letter of action requesting action from the proper authority. Define *authority* as someone in a position or with the power to change the situation. Tell them to use their ideas from Ex. C and appropriate phrases from Ex. B.
- Ask them to use the format of the letter provided in Ex. A. Their letter should state the problem, contain ideas for solutions to the problem or a statement of what should be done to fix the problem, and express confidence that the recipient of the letter will be able to solve the problem. The letter should be in a formal style, using complete sentences, paragraph divisions and correct punctuation.
- Circulate while the students are working and offer assistance as necessary.

▶ Workbook p. 60, Section 4

Grammar: past modals of deduction (p. 121)

Lead-in

Write the word *deduction* on the board. Ask the students to define this word (something that you know from the information or evidence that is available). Ask the students when they might need to make deductions. Elicit answers such as *figuring out a maths problem, solving a mystery, conducting an experiment, making a hypothesis*. Give an example: *Lin goes to class from 9am until noon. It's 11.30am. Where is she? She must be in class.*

A 2.18

- See the Student's Book for the **audioscript**.
- Tell the students they will listen to a conversation about a daredevil (someone who does dangerous things for enjoyment and does not worry about the risk). Have them read the questions and listen for the information.
- Play the audio and have the students read along. Then discuss the answers with the class.

Answers

They are talking about Felix Baumgartner, who did a skydive from a height of 24 miles (39 kilometres) on 14th October 2012. He may have done this because he loves extreme sports or because he likes to take big risks.

Culture note

Felix Baumgartner is an Austrian daredevil. In 2012, he set the world record for skydiving when he dove 24 miles and reached a speed over 840 miles per hour. He has also jumped from the stratosphere in a helium balloon back to Earth. When he did this, he set records for the highest manned ballooned flight, highest parachute jump and greatest freefall velocity. Other stunts include jumping from Taipei 101, BASE jumping from the Millau Viaduct and base jumping from Turning Torso.

NOTICE!

- Direct the students' attention to the **Notice!** box.
- Ask the students to note the verb form that follows each of the phrases in bold in the conversation.

Answer

a past participle

B

Form

- Ask the students to read the conversation again, paying attention to the phrases in bold.
- Focus the students' attention on the table. Point out that a past modal has the structure: modal + *(not) have* + past participle. Make sure the students understand that past modals of deduction are used to talk about the probability or possibility of something that occurred in the past. Point out that they should be familiar with these modals of deduction in their present form.
- Draw attention to the column headings and elicit that *moderate* means *not very strong*. Have the students complete the table with the modals in bold from the conversation.
- Check the answers with the class.
- Direct the students' attention to the **What's right?** box. Elicit that the first sentence is incorrect since it uses a present modal (*must*) for a past situation.

Answers

1 must have   2 may have   3 might have   4 could have
5 must not have   6 couldn't have   7 can't have

Function

- Ask the students to think about the function of these phrases and complete the explanation by choosing one of the options for each blank.
- Check the answers with the class.

Answers

1 a   2 b   3 b

Risky business UNIT 10

C

- Have the students rewrite the sentences as deductions using past modals. Remind them to use the table in Ex. B to help them. Point out that there may be more than one correct answer.
- Check the answers with the class.

Answers

1 Baumgartner must have felt nervous as he waited to jump.
2 It can't / couldn't have been the first time he'd made a very high skydive.
3 He may / might / could have made a number of practice jumps first.
4 He can't / couldn't have planned it alone and he must have had a team of people behind him.
5 He may not / might not have known he would break the sound barrier.
6 His family may not / might not have wanted him to make the jump.

Alternative

As a class, go over each sentence before letting the students work individually. Identify whether each sentence shows strong probability, moderate probability, moderate improbability or strong improbability. Then have the students work alone or in pairs to write the deductions.

D

- Draw attention to the photo. Ask the students to work in pairs and deduce what happened just before the photo was taken.
- Listen to some of their ideas with the whole class. Correct any errors in the use of past modals of deduction.

 Workbook pp. 60–61, Section 5

Pronunciation: reduction of *have* (p. 122)

A 2.19

- See the Student's Book for the **audioscript**.
- Play the audio. Have the students listen and follow along in the book. Give them time to practise each phrase individually. Ask them to tell you how *have* is pronounced (/əv/).

Alternative

Have the students practise the pronunciation as a group by listening to the phrases in Ex. A and repeating them.

B 2.20

- See the Student's Book for the **audioscript**.
- Play the audio and have the students practise the sentences.
- Monitor progress and check that the students are pronouncing the modals and *have* correctly.

Listening: rapid speech (p. 122)

Lead-in

Ask the students to read the information in the skills panel. Explain that native speakers of every language use rapid speech, and that learning to recognise phrases that native speakers tend to run together will make understanding rapid speech easier.

Ask the students if it is difficult for them to understand native English speakers. Ask them if rapid speech contributes to that difficulty. Ask the students if they ever watch English-language television programmes. Encourage them to talk about characters or shows that are challenging to listen to because of rapid speech.

A

- Direct the students' attention to the photo and see if they know who the man is (David Blaine). Ask if they think he was in danger during the stunt that is pictured. Check that the students understand *stunt* (something dangerous that is done to entertain people) and *electrocution* (killing or injuring someone with electricity).
- Ask the students to read the paragraph and think about whether David Blaine was in real danger during the stunt.
- Put the students in small groups to discuss their opinions about the danger of the stunt.
- Hold a whole-class discussion to compare answers from the groups.

Culture note

David Blaine's real name is David Blaine White. He is an American illusionist and endurance artist. He is famous for stunts such as Buried Alive (he was buried in a plastic box underneath three tons of water under the ground), Frozen in Time (he stood in a block of ice for over 60 hours) and Vertigo (he stood on a pillar without any harness and withstood high winds and cold temperatures for 35 hours).

B 2.21

- See p. 128 for the **audioscript**.
- Explain that the students will hear two people discussing David Blaine's stunt. Point out that they should listen for each person's opinion.
- Play the audio once and check progress. Play the audio again if necessary. Ask the students to state the opinions to check comprehension.

Answers

Nicola believes that it was a genuine achievement and that Blaine ran real risks, whereas Jemma believes that Blaine, as a professional illusionist, created a convincing illusion of risk.

Alternative

Extend Ex. B by asking the students which person they agree with, Nicola or Jemma. Ask them to support their answers by explaining why they agree or disagree.

C

- Ask the students to listen to the conversation again, but this time they should focus on listening for specific examples of rapid speech. Refer the students to the sentences in the list and explain that they will hear one example from each pair. Ask them to check the one they hear.
- Play the audio once and check progress. Play the audio again if necessary. After checking the answers, play the audio again as the students look at the correct phrases, especially if they found the exercise difficult.
- Ask the students if their opinion of David Blaine's stunt changed and what they think about him doing the stunt.

Answers

1 You've got to see it!
2 What do you think?
3 It couldn't have been real.
4 He must have practised a lot of times.
5 I don't know.
6 I'm going to find some photos of it.
7 I don't want to see the photo.
8 I've got to go.

Extra: homework

Ask the students to choose another stunt by David Blaine or Felix Baumgartner (or let them choose a daredevil of their choice) and write a paragraph about it.

 Workbook p. 61, Section 6

Speaking: speculating about events (p. 123)

Lead-in

Write the following verbs of ability on the board: *be good at, manage, be able, succeed in, be capable of, be incapable of, could/couldn't, can/can't, be unable*. Put the students in small groups. Point randomly at the different verbs of ability and have groups call out the correct form that follows each verb (infinitive with *to*, an infinitive without *to* or *-ing* form). The first team to call out the correct answer wins a point. Take the opportunity to review verbs of ability studied earlier in this unit if necessary.

A 2.22

- See p. 129 for the **audioscript**.
- Define *speculating* (considering or discussing why something has happened or what might happen). Draw attention to the photo and ask the students to speculate about what is happening. Use the photo to teach *deck chair* (a chair used outdoors) and *pellet gun* (a gun that shoots small, round pieces of steel or metal).
- Ask the students to listen to the news report. Tell them they should listen for speculations that the reporters make about the event. Play the audio once and check progress. Play the audio again if necessary.
- Check the answers with the class.

Answer

They speculate that he might have wanted to be a pilot but couldn't get a licence, and that he may have taken a gun with him to shoot at birds.

B

- Put the students in small groups. Ask them to discuss why they think the man did this and what they think happened in the end.
- Direct the students' attention to the examples in the **How to say it** box and encourage them to use these past modals and verbs of ability in their discussion.
- Allow time for the discussion. Then listen to the students' ideas as a class, but don't confirm whether they are right or wrong at this point.

C

- Give the students time to read the news story. Remind them that they are reading with the objective of learning if their guesses about what happened were correct. Check that they understand the word *helium* (a gas that is lighter than air and is used to inflate balloons).

Extra: discussion

Invite the students to share their opinions about what Larry did. Ask them if they approve or disapprove, explain why and say if they would ever consider trying a similar stunt.

D

- Put the students in pairs. Present the two headlines and check that the students understand *meteorite* (a piece of rock that has fallen from space and landed on the ground). Explain that the students should speculate about the news story behind each headline.
- Remind the students of the **How to say it** box in Ex.B and encourage them to speculate about the headlines in the same way.
- Ask the students to decide together which story to talk about and to make notes on it.
- Before giving the students the answers, have them complete the Independent Speaking task in Ex. E.

Risky business UNIT 10 97

Answers

The first headline refers to a story that happened in China. Tian Yuchao, a bus driver, saw a bus crash into 11 cars. It was out of control because the driver had a stroke. Tian Yuchao jumped from his own bus and chased the other bus on foot. He finally managed to catch up with it, jump on board and turn off the engine.

Possible answer for the second (invented) headline: Martin Cobb, a six-year-old boy from Surrey, England, had been eating rock cakes in his back garden. When he saw what looked like another rock cake on the ground near the step he was sitting on, he picked that up, and put it in his mouth. The fact that it was so hard shocked him and he breathed in quickly … and swallowed it! But it wasn't a rock cake; it was a small meteorite! It stuck in his throat and he couldn't breathe properly. Luckily, his mum was just coming out of the house and she saw Martin having problems breathing. She ran over to him and slapped him hard in the middle of his back. The meteorite flew out of his mouth and he was able to breathe again.

E

- Put the students in pairs. Explain that they should take turns telling their partner about their news story. Each student should speak for about one and a half minutes. They should use the notes they made to help them stay focused and remember everything they want to say. While one student speaks, the other should listen without interrupting.
- When they have finished, reveal the answers.

LifeSkills: managing stress (p. 124)

Step 1: Recognise the symptoms of and risk factors for stress. (Ex. A, Ex. B, Ex. C)
Step 2: Consider different ways of relaxing. (Ex. D)
Step 3: Develop your stress-management strategy. (Ex. E)

Lead-in

Read the target skill aloud and invite the students to tell you what they think *managing stress* means (*managing*: to succeed in doing something or to organise and control something; *stress*: a worried or nervous feeling that stops you from relaxing). Ask the students to suggest things that they have to manage (homework, after-school job, chores) and how these things might cause them stress (pressure at school, family problems, financial concerns).

Ask the students to think about a time when they were stressed. Invite volunteers to share their stories. Make a list on the board and leave it there for later discussion. Note the broad categories that the students' stressful situations fit into; these are likely to be school, work, family, money. Tell the students that it is important to be able to manage stress in all facets of their life and that this section will help them recognise symptoms, identify ways to relax and help them develop their own strategy.

Then **highlight** the three-step strategy to develop the skill of *managing stress*.

A

- Draw the students' attention to the two questions. Have them read the article with the questions in mind.
- After they have finished reading, ask the students what they think of the advice offered in the article. Ask them to be specific about which strategies they think would work for them, and why or why not.

Alternative

Before reading, preview the symptoms of stress with the class. Ask the students to talk about how stress makes them feel physically and emotionally. Write each suggestion on the board and ask the rest of the class to raise their hand if they have ever felt that way. If the students do not mention the symptoms listed in the article, name them yourself and add them to the list on the board. Again, ask the students to raise their hand if they have ever felt these symptoms.

Extra: discussion

Point out the four ways the author suggests managing stress: avoid, alter, adapt and accept. Put the students in pairs. Have one student make up a stressful scenario. The other student tells how they can avoid, alter, adapt or accept the situation to reduce stress. Then that student makes up another stressful scenario for their partner to manage.

B

- Ask the students to focus on the specific stressful situations listed. Have the students rank them on a scale of 1 (not stressful) to 5 (very stressful).

Alternative

Draw attention to the list of situations on the board from the Lead-in activity. Ask the students to think about any that aren't duplicates of those listed in Ex. B and to rank them from 1 to 5.

C

- Put the students in pairs to compare their answers. Remind them that everyone will have their own opinions and that reactions to stressful situations will not be the same.
- Give the students time to discuss what causes them the most stress and to talk about what they have in common.
- Invite the students to share ideas from their discussions with the whole class.

Extra: discussion

Ask the students to give examples from their personal experience about any of the situations in Ex. B they have faced. Give an example: *I had to make a long trip without my family to attend university. I was travelling 300 miles and taking a bus. This was stressful for me because I had never travelled alone before.*

D

- Tell the students that it is now time to think about strategies to relieve stress. Focus their attention on the six photos and ask them to describe what the people are doing in each one in order to relax.
- Ask the students to respond to each photo with the appropriate phrase and to complete item 7 with their own strategy for relieving stress.

Culture note

Pet therapy or animal-assisted therapy uses dogs or other animals to help people cope with stress or recover from health problems. The goal of pet therapy or animal-assisted therapy is to help someone feel better emotionally. Pet therapy most often includes the use of domesticated animals, such as dogs, cats, fish and hamsters, but other animals that have been used are dolphins and farm animals like horses.

Extra: discussion

Ask the students to state what strategy they listed for item 7. Make a list on the board. Take a vote for each new strategy and see if the students already do this, would like to try this or are not interested in this.

Extra: discussion

Put the students in pairs to compare their answers. Ask them to talk about any ways of relaxing from Ex. D that they would both like to try. Ask them to extend the discussion by comparing things they both would not want to try. Ask each pair to summarise their discussion for the rest of the class.

E

- Ask the students to think about things that cause stress in their own lives and to choose one cause of stress for this activity. Ask them to make notes about how they might use different strategies to cope with the stress.
- Present the example notes showing a cause of stress and different coping strategies and encourage the students to use this example to create their own notes.
- Circulate and help as the students are making their notes. When they are ready, ask the students to share their notes with a partner. Ask the pairs to discuss which strategy or strategies they think would be most effective for each of their situations.

F

- Put the students in pairs to discuss the question, with particular reference to the domain of **Self and Society**. Ask them to think of three reasons why they might be able to manage stress better in the future.
- Have a class feedback session and take a poll on the best reasons for being able to manage stress better.

 REFLECT

- Discuss the question with the whole class. Ask the students to say what they feel are the most useful points they learned from this lesson, and how the skill of *managing stress* might be useful in the domains of **Work and Career** and **Study and Learning**, either now or in the future.
- Elicit the following ideas: *exercising regularly, using calming techniques, setting reasonable expectations for themselves*, etc.

 RESEARCH

- Go through the task and check that the students are clear about what they have to do.
- Suggest that the students research a variety of sources about meditation.
- Have them share their findings in class. Lead a class discussion about what they learned about meditation.

Language wrap-up (p. 126)

For notes on how to approach the exercises in the Language wrap-up section, please see page 9.

1 Vocabulary

- Go over the words and phrases in the box. Call on the students to say them aloud. Correct their pronunciation and stress as needed.
- Encourage the students to read through the paragraph before they choose the correct word or phrase for each sentence. Point out that there is more than one possible answer for some sentences.
- Remind the students to use the context of the sentence to help them choose the correct word or phrase.
- Call on individual students to say the sentences, inserting the correct answers. Ask the rest of the class to say whether the sentence is correct or not.

Extra: writing

Ask the students to write a paragraph describing themselves or describing a famous person they admire. Ask them to use at least six of the vocabulary words or phrases in their writing.

2 Grammar

- Ask the students to read the whole story through first before completing the exercise. Encourage them to say each sentence silently to themselves before deciding on their answers.
- When checking the answers with the students, point out that they can express ability three ways: verb + infinitive with *to*, verb + infinitive without *to* and verb + *-ing* form. Give examples. Also remind the students that past modals of deduction need to be followed by a past participle.

Risky business UNIT 10

Speaking workshop: responding to a question asking for a choice (p. 127)

Lead-in
Ask the students if it is hard for them to make decisions. Draw a table with three columns on the board and label the columns 'Easy', 'Medium' and 'Hard'. Put the students in small groups to list decisions that are easy, medium and hard to make. Allow time for the groups to share answers. Remind them that there may be conflicting answers and that this is OK because everyone has different opinions about what is easy and hard to do.

A 2.23
- See p. 129 for the **audioscript**.
- Explain that being able to respond to questions about choice is important in social, academic and professional settings. Mention that questions like these are also popular on standardised tests, as well as tests that are given in academic courses.
- Point out the information and question in the box. Tell the students they will listen to someone answering this question. Tell them to take notes on the main points the speaker makes.
- Play the audio.
- Put the students in pairs to compare notes. Play the audio again if the students have varying main points.

> **Answer**
> The main points made by the speaker are:
> She would rather do something quiet because 1) quiet activities are more relaxing and less dangerous, 2) her job is active so she wants her free time to be relaxing and 3) quiet activities reduce the amount of stress in her life.

B
- Play the audio again and ask the students to complete the phrases the speaker uses to express her preferences.
- Repeat the audio only if necessary.
- Check the answers with the class.

> **Answers**
> **1** would much **2** much more relaxing than **3** tend to prefer **4** to me more **5** much prefer

Extra: writing
Ask the students to write a few sentences that express their own preferences. They can write about a type of activity they prefer or about any other preference that is relevant to them. Encourage them to use two or three of the phrases they just learned to express the preferences.

C
- Explain that the students will now give their own answer to a question similar to the one in Ex. A. Ask them to read the information and question in the box in Ex. D. To prepare for giving their answer, ask them to make notes to answer the questions in Ex. C.
- Circulate and help as necessary while the students are making notes.

D
- Schedule enough time for each student to present their answer to the question, either in small groups or to the whole class. Each student should talk for about one minute.
- Remind the students that they should include information from their notes and give details and examples in their answer.

How are you doing?
- Ask the students to read the statements and tick the ones they believe are true.
- Ask them to discuss their talk with a member of their group or another student in the class and identify things they could improve on next time.

Extra: homework
For homework, ask the students to write a paragraph telling which profession they think would suit them most and why. Remind them to include details and examples in their writing.

▶ Workbook pp. 62–63, SkillsStudio

UNIT 11 THROUGH THE LENS

The expression *through the lens* refers to images seen through the lens of a camera. This unit focuses on what photos represent to us and how different people perceive them.

Unit plan

Unit opener	(p. 128)	20 min.
1 **Grammar:** verb + gerund/infinitive with a change in meaning	(p. 130)	40 min.
2 **Listening:** a podcast	(p. 131)	30 min.
• Vocabulary: describing photos		15 min.
3 **Speaking:** making comparisons	(p. 132)	30 min.
• Vocabulary: making comparisons		15 min.
4 **Grammar:** connectors of addition / cause and effect	(p. 133)	40 min.
5 **Reading:** understanding text organisation	(p. 134)	30 min.
6 **Pronunciation:** stress timing	(p. 135)	15 min.
7 **Writing:** a memo	(p. 135)	30 min.
LifeSkills: giving and receiving feedback (Work and Career)	(p. 136)	50 min.
• Optional downloadable *LifeSkills* lesson (Self and Society)		50 min.
• Optional downloadable *LifeSkills* lesson (Study and Learning)		50 min.
Language wrap-up	(p. 138)	15 min.
Writing workshop	(p. 139)	20 min.
Video and downloadable video worksheet		45 min.

Unit opener (p. 128)

Lead-in

Ask the students to look at the unit title and the photos and to predict what the unit will be about. Ask the students to give some examples of things they like to take photos of. Ask what they do with their photos, e.g. whether they edit them, how often they post them on social media sites, etc. Direct the students' attention to the points in the unit objectives box and go through the information with them. To get your students to think about the skills being developed in this unit, ask them to look at the questions in the cogs.

Reading: understanding text organisation
- Explain or elicit that within a paragraph there are different types of sentences. Elicit some of the conventional sentence types the students know from studying paragraph structure, e.g. topic sentence, concluding sentence, sentences giving details.

Speaking: making comparisons
- Ask the students to compare two items in the classroom, for example, two different students' backpacks. Write the comparison language the students use on the board. Tell the students that they will practise comparing photos using this language.

LifeSkills: giving and receiving feedback
- Ask the students what it means to give and receive feedback and have them answer the questions. Elicit reasons why it is useful or important to be able to give and receive feedback in our work lives. Ask for examples. Ask how they feel when they receive feedback and what they think helps make feedback easier to accept.

Common European Framework: unit map

Unit 11	Competence developed	CEF Reference (B2 competences)
Grammar	can use and understand verb + gerund/infinitive structures with changes in meaning	Table 1; Table 2; Sections 5.2.1.2; 6.4.7.7; 6.4.7.8
Listening	can understand a podcast	Table 1; Table 2; Sections 4.4.2.1; 4.5.2.2
Speaking	can make comparisons	Table 1; Table 2; Sections 4.4.1.1; 4.4.3.1; 4.4.3.5; 4.5.2.1; 5.2.1.1; 5.2.1.2; 5.2.3.2
Grammar	can use and understand connectors of addition / cause and effect	Table 1; Table 2; Sections 5.2.1.2; 6.4.7.7; 6.4.7.8
Reading	can understand the way texts are organised	Table 1; Table 2; Sections 4.4.2.2; 4.4.2.4; 4.5.2.2
Pronunciation	can correctly apply stress and rhythm	Section 5.2.1.4
Writing	can write a memo	Table 1; Table 2; Sections 4.4.1.2; 4.4.3.2; 4.4.3.4; 4.5.2.1; 5.2.1.1; 5.2.1.2; 5.2.1.6; 5.2.2.2; 5.2.2.4; 5.2.3.2

Lead-in

Ask the students why we take photos and how they are important in people's lives. Ask how often the students take photos and how they prefer to take them (with a camera, mobile phone, etc). If any students do photography as a hobby, ask them to talk about how they became interested in it and to describe the types of subjects they like to photograph and why.

A

- Have the students look at the photos and describe each of the situations.
- Give the students time to tick the situations they have taken photos of.
- Put the students in pairs. Ask them to discuss which of the situations they take photos in, and what they like to take photos of and why.
- Elicit answers from several students and ask individual students to talk about the importance of photographs in their lives.

Culture note

The first photograph was taken of an outdoor view in 1826 by Frenchman Joseph Nicéphore Niépce.

Extra: picture share

Put the students in pairs or groups and have them use their mobile phones to share some of their favourite recent photos, explaining the subject(s) of the picture, where and when it was taken, why they decided to take it, etc.

B

- Ask the students to read the statements and think about whether they agree or disagree and why.
- Put the students in pairs to discuss the statements.
- Lead the class in a discussion of the statements. Call on individual students to give their opinions and to support them with examples and reasons.

Alternative

Write some additional statements and quotes about photography and taking photos on the board to extend the discussion. Put the students in pairs to discuss the quotes and say which ones they like, whether they agree and disagree and why. Here are some possible quotations:

A picture is worth a thousand words. – Anonymous

'There are no bad pictures; that's just how your face looks sometimes.' – Abraham Lincoln

'You don't take a photograph, you make it.' – Ansel Adams

'The camera is an instrument that teaches people how to see without a camera.' – Dorothea Lange

'Taking pictures is savouring life intensely, every hundredth of a second.' – Marc Riboud

Grammar: verb + gerund/infinitive with a change in meaning (p. 130)

Lead-in

Direct the students' attention to the picture. Ask who they think the people are, what their relationships are and when and where they think the picture was taken. Tell the students they are going to read the reaction of one of the people in the photo who is looking at it years later. Elicit some predictions for what the person will say about the photo.

Ask the students how they feel when they see old photos of themselves.

A

- Give the students time to read the text with the instructions in mind.
- Put the students in pairs to summarise the person's reaction to the photo, and to discuss why they think the person feels this way.
- To focus on comprehension of the text, ask the class whether the person's reaction to the photo is all negative and what he feels is positive.

Possible answer

The person is embarrassed by his old-fashioned hairstyle and clothing in the photo. However, he enjoys remembering the happy moments with his family because they are all grown up and have their own lives now.

NOTICE!

- Direct the students' attention to the *Notice!* box.
- Have the students find and underline all the examples of gerunds and infinitives in the text.
- Put the students in pairs to compare answers and discuss the verbs that precede the gerund and infinitive forms.
- Check the answers as a class.

Answer

The following words should be underlined: *being, to look, having, wearing, laughing and having, to stop, to remember, to treasure*
They follow the verbs *remember, try, regret, stop, forget*.

B

Form

- Have the students read the article again, paying attention to the instances of verb + gerund and verb + infinitive.
- Give the students time to complete the table individually with examples from the text. Then check the answers with the class by calling on individual students to read their sentences aloud.
- Direct the students' attention to the *What's right?* box. Elicit that the first sentence is incorrect because it is about a past regret and so the following verb needs to be a gerund.

Answers
1 I'll never forget laughing and having fun …
2 I regret having that style now.
3 I remember being in this photo!
4 You have to remember to treasure …
5 Everyone stopped wearing those years ago!
6 …it's good to stop to think about those days …
7 My dad made us try to look natural, …

Function
- Give the students time to read the pairs of definitions.
- Have the students complete the phrases, writing *gerund* or *infinitive*.
- Put the students in pairs to compare answers. To make sure they understand the differences in meaning, refer to the pairs of example sentences in the table and connect them to the definitions. For example, have the students read the two sentences with *forget* and elicit that in the first example (*I'll never forget laughing and having fun …*) it means he will never lose the memory. In the second example, *Don't forget to show him the photo*, it means the person has to remember to show the photo.

Answers
1 infinitive; gerund		4 gerund; infinitive
2 infinitive; gerund		5 infinitive; gerund
3 gerund; infinitive			

C
- Have the students work individually to complete the sentences using the gerund or infinitive forms. Then check the answers with the class.
- Ask the students to explain their reasons for choosing each form using the descriptions of the functions. For example, in item 1 the infinitive is not used after the past tense of *regret*.

Answers
1 taking   2 having   3 to think   4 to avoid

Extra: grammar practice
Give the students some sentences and tell them to rewrite each one with the same meaning using either the verb + gerund or verb + infinitive. Give the students the verb to use in their rewritten sentence, for example, *I always leave my keys when I leave work. (forget)* – *I always forget to take my keys when I leave work.*
1 John wishes he hadn't spent so much money. *(regret)*
2 Ariel wants to ride a motorcycle. *(try)*
3 Greg has given up eating meat. *(stop)*
4 I have no memory of saying those terrible things. *(remember)*

Answers
1 John regrets spending so much money.
2 Ariel is trying riding a motorcycle.
3 Greg has stopped eating meat.
4 I don't remember saying those terrible things.

D
- Give the students time to reread the questions in Ex. C and to think about their responses. Encourage them to make notes about the topics.
- Put the students in pairs to discuss the questions. Encourage them to support their answers with details and examples and to ask follow-up questions to find out more about their partner's answers. Encourage the students to use the verb + gerund/infinitive forms from Ex. B.
- Elicit responses from the class. Ask the students to talk about how often they look at old photos of their family, and discuss their reactions to the writer's opinion that it is important to 'treasure every moment with your family'.

▶ Workbook p. 67, Section 6

Listening: to a podcast (p. 131)

Lead-in
Ask the students to name any famous photographers they know (e.g. Ansel Adams, Robert Doisneau, Yousuf Karsh, Dorothea Lange, Robert Mapplethorpe, Annie Liebovitz, etc). Ask the class what they think makes a good photographer. Ask the students if they have ever taken an exceptionally good photo and what they think made it special.

Extra: famous photos
Show the class some of the most famous photos of all time (see examples below – images available online) and elicit the students' reactions to them. Discuss with the class what makes the pictures stand out and what kinds of skills a good photographer needs.
Le Baiser de l'Hôtel de Ville (The Kiss) – Robert Doisneau
Abbey Road, The Beatles – Iain Macmillan
V-J Day in Times Square – Alfred Einsenstaedt
Lunch atop a Skyscraper – Charles C. Ebbets
Afghan Girl – Steve McCurry
Migrant Mother – Dorothea Lange

A
- Tell the students they are going to listen to a podcast. Have the students look at the photo and predict what the podcast will be about.
- Elicit some general reactions to the photo of the homeless man. Ask the students what strikes them about the image and what questions they have about it.

B 2.24
- See p. 129 for the **audioscript**.
- Explain to the students that they will hear two speakers during the podcast: Penny and Jack.
- Give the students time to read the partial sentences. Elicit some predictions from the class about what words or phrases might complete the blanks. Alternatively, put the students in pairs and have them predict the missing words or phrases.

Through the lens UNIT 11 103

- Play the audio and have the students complete the sentences.
- Have the students compare their answers in pairs. Then check the answers with the class.

Answers
1 local photographers
2 social media
3 impressed
4 your attention away
5 economic problems

C
- Go over the pronunciation of the words in the box. Call on individual students to say the words aloud. Correct their pronunciation and stress as needed. Elicit that all of the words are connected to the field of photography and are useful for describing photos.
- Give the students time to look at the photos and think about which words belong in which blank. Point out that one of the words belongs in two of the blanks.
- Play the audio again and have the students fill in the blanks.
- Have the students compare answers in pairs before checking the answers with the class.

Answers
1 portrait 2 background 3 focus 4 subject
5 landscape 6 side 7 side 8 foreground

D
- Put the students in pairs. Ask them to decide which photo in Ex. C each of them will describe. Give them time to think about how to describe their photo and allow them to make some notes.
- Have the students take turns describing their photo. Encourage them to be specific and detailed in their descriptions and to add to their partner's descriptions and react to their opinions, saying whether they agree or disagree and why.
- When the pairs finish their descriptions, call on a few individuals to describe their photos for the class.

Extra: homework
Have the students write a paragraph describing the picture they talked about in Ex. D.

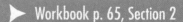 Workbook p. 65, Section 2

Speaking: making comparisons (p. 132)

Lead-in
Give the students time to read the information in the skills panel. Write the words *compare* and *contrast* on the board and elicit their definitions from the class. **Highlight** that *contrasting* means looking for differences, while *comparing* can mean looking for both similarities and differences. Elicit some useful phrases for comparing two or more things and write them on the board.

A
- Direct the students' attention to the photos. Call on individual students to give a brief description of each one.
- Put the students in pairs to compare the photos and make notes about the similarities and differences in the table.
- Combine the pairs to form groups of four and have the students compare answers in their groups.
- Make two columns on the board labeled 'Similarities' and 'Differences' and check answers by having the students come to the board and write their answers in the columns.

Answers
Points of similarity mentioned: both show groups of people; both show people posing for the camera and smiling; both show how people who want to record this moment in their lives.
Points of difference mentioned: the first photo is a family portrait, possibly taken by a professional photographer, while the second shows someone taking a selfie; the first photo is more formal than the second photo; the people in the second photo more natural than those in the first; the first group of people probably want a photo to display at home while the second group want a photo to put online; the second photo is more modern than the first.

B 🎧 **2.25**
- See p. 129 for the **audioscript**.
- Tell the students they are going to hear two people talking about the two photos. The woman, Becky, is talking to a friend and trying to choose one of the photos to illustrate an article she is writing. Ask the students to listen and compare their notes to the points Becca and the man make, and to add any points they missed.
- Play the audio. If needed, pause a few times to allow the students to add to their notes.
- Check the answers. Then ask the students how close their notes were to the points made in the conversation and which points they missed.

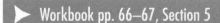 Workbook pp. 66–67, Section 5

C
- Go over the pronunciation of the words and phrases in the box. Call on individual students to read the words and phrases aloud. Correct their pronunciation and stress as needed.
- Give the students time to read the partial sentences and think about which word or phrase might complete each sentence.
- Play the audio again and have the students complete the sentences.
- Have the students compare their answers in pairs. Then check the answers with the class.

Answers

1 alike 2 while 3 similarity 4 whereas
5 point of difference 6 In contrast 7 in that 8 unlike

D

- Put the students in pairs and have them decide which partner will describe which set of photos. Then give them time individually to make some notes comparing and contrasting the photos.
- When they have prepared, have the students take turns comparing and contrasting their set of photos, using the new vocabulary. Ask the students to take notes on their partner's points as they listen.
- To conclude, call on individual students to use their notes to report to the class on the points of comparison their partner gave.

 Workbook p. 65, Section 3

Grammar: connectors of addition / cause and effect (p. 133)

A

- Have the students look at the photo and say whether they think it has been changed or edited in any way.
- Have the students scan the text for unknown words. Answer any questions about unfamiliar vocabulary.
- Give the students time to read the two opinions. Ask them to think about which one they agree with and why. Encourage them to make some notes.
- Elicit responses from several students. Lead a brief class discussion about the common places where edited images are used, e.g. advertising, fashion magazines, on celebrities' websites, etc and the possible effects of this type of picture editing, in particular on young people's attitudes to and expectations about appearance.

NOTICE!

- Direct the students' attention to the **Notice!** box.
- Have the students look through the text and locate the bold words and phrases. Ask them to think about the purpose of each bold word or phrase.
- Have the students match the words/phrases that have similar meanings. **Highlight** that while *result* and *consequence* are interchangeable, *result* can refer to any effect and *consequence* often refers to a negative effect.
- Have them compare answers in pairs before checking the answers with the class.

Answers

Moreover, besides that, furthermore and *in addition to* have similar meanings.
Because of, so, due to, as a result and *as a consequence* also all have similar meanings.

B

Form

- Have the students read the opinions again, paying attention to the words in bold.
- Ask the students to complete the table with the words in bold, referring to the opinions to decide the purpose of each word or phrase.
- Check the answers with the class.
- **Highlight** that some of the connectors in each set must be followed by a comma when they come at the beginning of a sentence. Elicit which ones take a comma (*Also, Moreover, Besides that, Furthermore, As a result, As a consequence, Therefore*).
- Explain that with connectors of cause and effect, the form changes when *of* is used (I didn't study. As a result, I failed my exams. / As a result of not studying, I failed my exams.).

Answers

connectors of addition: moreover, besides that, furthermore, in addition to
connectors of cause and effect: because of, so, due to, as a result, as a consequence

Function

- Have the students read the two rules and decide which one refers to connectors of addition and which to connectors of cause/effect. Have them choose the correct options.
- Elicit the answers from the class and ask the students to support them with examples from the text in Ex. A.
- **Highlight** that some of the connectors in each set are more formal than others. Elicit which ones are typically reserved for more formal situations (*moreover, furthermore, in addition to, as a consequence, therefore*).

Answers

1 addition 2 cause and effect

C

- Direct the students' attention to the **What's right?** box. Elicit that the first sentence is incorrect since *because* is followed by a noun phrase and so *of* is necessary.
- Go over the task with the students. Make sure they understand that they should use the phrases given and add additional words if necessary to rewrite the two sentences as one. They should rewrite each pair in two different ways.
- Give the students time to rewrite the sentences.
- Have the students compare their answers in pairs. Then check the answers with the class.

Answers

1 Because of the fact that they cannot live up to the ideal they see in images, many people get depressed.
2 As a result of not being able to live up to the ideal they see in images, many people get depressed.
3 Models are made to appear more beautiful and, besides that, they are often made to appear thinner.
4 Models are made to appear more beautiful and, furthermore, they are often made to appear thinner.

Through the lens UNIT 11 105

Extra: grammar practice

Add the following two pairs of sentences as an extension to Ex. C.
1 Many people cannot live up to the ideal they see in images. They get depressed. (*and, so*)
2 Models are made to appear more beautiful. They are often also made to appear thinner. (*in addition, being made*)

Answers
1 Many people cannot live up to the ideal they see in images and so they get depressed.
2 Models are made to appear more beautiful and, in addition, they are being made to appear thinner.

D

- Have the students read the questions and think about their responses.
- Put the students in pairs to discuss the questions. Remind them to use connectors of addition and of cause and effect, and to support their opinions with details, examples and reasons.

 Workbook p. 66, Section 4

Reading: understanding text organisation (p. 134, p. 110)

Lead-in

Remind the students that they practised understanding text organisation on p. 110. Give the students time to read the information in the skills panel. Lead a brief class discussion to elicit how understanding the function of sentences can help the students understand a text better (to help them find important information in a text more easily and quickly, to be able to separate main ideas and details, facts vs. opinions, etc).

To lead into the article, ask the students to explain in their own words what a *selfie* is (a photo of yourself taken by you with a digital camera and often uploaded to a social networking site). Elicit some of the reasons why people take selfies and call on a few individual students to share their opinions about the practice of taking selfies and posting them online.

Direct the students' attention to the two photos and call on an individual student to describe the difference. Elicit some of the possible reasons why people took selfies in the past and why they do so today.

Culture note

Recent reports suggest that more than 17 million selfies are uploaded onto social-networking sites each week. At the Oscars ceremony in 2014, Ellen DeGeneres, Bradley Cooper and other film stars tweeted a selfie at the awards ceremony which was retweeted over two million times.

The selfie is now a significant trend that celebrities, presidents and even the pope have joined.

A

- Ask the students to read the article, paying attention to the author's views on selfies. Ask them to think about whether they agree or disagree with the author's views.
- Put the students in pairs to summarise the main points of the article and the author's views. Ideas that they might have are that the author feels that selfies are basically harmless and pointless, and people often use them just to get attention and show how glamorous and exciting their lives are; the author says that selfies have been around since the advent of photography and disagrees with sociologists' notion that they are fuelling people's obsession with looks.
- Elicit responses from several students and ask volunteers to support their ideas with reasons and examples. Encourage the rest of the class to ask questions and share their own opinions.

Possible answers
The author feels that selfies are basically harmless and pointless, and people often use them just to get attention and show how glamorous and exciting their lives are. The author says that selfies have been around since the advent of photography, and disagrees with sociologists' notion that they are fuelling people's obsession with looks.

B

- Give the students time to read the five functions.
- Have them read the article again and match the underlined sentences with the functions. Encourage them to circle any words or phrases in the text that helped them decide the answers.
- Elicit the answers from the class, asking volunteers to explain their choices.

Answers
1 b 2 a 3 e 4 d 5 c

Alternative

Have the students complete the exercise in pairs, talking about their choices as they work and explaining how they know a sentence serves a particular function.

Extra: expansion

With the class, analyse the whole text and discuss the functions of some of the other sentences. For example, the first sentence in paragraph 1 introduces the overall topic of the article. The second sentence presents information that supports or strengthens the first sentence.

C

- Give the students time to read the multiple-choice questions.
- Have them choose the answers. Encourage them to circle the information in the text that helped them decide the answers.
- Call on individual students to tell you the answers and where they found the information in the text.

Answers
1 c 2 a 3 c

D

- Give the students time to read the questions and think about their responses.
- Put the students in pairs to discuss the questions. Encourage them to support their responses with details, reasons and examples.
- When the pairs finish their discussions, go over the questions with the class and elicit a few responses to each one.

▶ Workbook p. 64, Section 1

Pronunciation: stress timing (p. 135)

A 2.26

- See the Student's Book for the **audioscript**.
- Have the students read the instructions and the quotations silently.
- Play the audio once and have the students listen. Remind them to focus on the regular rhythm of the underlined words. **Highlight** that the stressed words are content words – mostly nouns and main verbs that carry the main meaning of the sentence.

B 2.27

- See the Student's Book for the **audioscript**.
- Have the students practise saying the quotations individually, focusing on the correct stress timing.
- Ask for volunteers to say the quotations aloud for the class.
- Play the audio and have the students check their pronunciation.

Extra: quote me

Have the students work in pairs to create their own photography-related quotations. Give them the following sentence stems:
The secret to taking a good selfie is …
A true photographer …
An old family photo is like …
Compared to words, photos …
Have the pairs underline the stressed syllables to indicate the correct stress timing and then practise saying their quotations. Call on the pairs to read their quotations aloud for the class, focusing on the correct stress timing.

Writing: a memo (p. 135)

Lead-in

Explain or elicit a definition of a *memo* and its purpose. Then have the students read the information in the box below Ex. B. Ask them which points they made and any points they missed in their own definitions.

A 2.28

- See p. 129 for the **audioscript**.
- Direct the students' attention to the photo of the worker in the office. Encourage the students to imagine that they are working in an office. The manager calls with some important information.
- Play the audio and have the students just listen. Then play it again and have them take notes on the manager's request. Remind them to write key words and short phrases only, so they don't miss important information.
- Have the students compare their notes in pairs and discuss any differences or missing information.

B

- Tell the students that they are going to use their notes to write a memo in the form of an email to all the staff members. Stress that a memo should be clear and easy to understand and should contain all of the important details that staff members need to know.

Alternative

Before the students begin writing the memo, put them in pairs to summarise and list the important information that should be included in the memo.

- Have the students complete the top portion of the memo first. Then give them time to write the full memo.
- Have the students compare their memos with a partner, discussing any differences between them and pointing out any missing information.

Possible answer

Dear all,

In order to update our website, we'd like to include a photo of everyone. To give the website a modern feel, we'd like you to take a selfie while you're doing something you enjoy. It could be in the kitchen, or bike riding or doing anything that you love to do.

In addition, we'd like you to write a few sentences about yourself: your interests and your hobbies.

Please email it to me before the 22nd. Thank you!

Regards,
Student's own signature

LifeSkills: giving and receiving feedback (p. 136)

Giving feedback
Step 1: Start by making at least a couple of positive comments. (Ex. C)
Step 2: Give the other person a chance to respond. (Ex. E)
Step 3: Use friendly language and positive body language. (Ex. E)

Receiving feedback
Step 1: Listen with an open mind.
Step 2: Ask questions to fully understand the feedback.
Step 3: Stay calm and consider the validity of any criticism.

Lead-in

Read the target skill aloud and invite the students to tell you what they think *giving and receiving feedback* means (telling someone what they are doing well and what they could do better and hearing this from others). Ask them to think of situations in which we might need to give and receive feedback in the workplace.

Ask the students to think about why it is important to know how to give and receive feedback and elicit some of the possible benefits of being able to do these things well. Explain that people who can give feedback well are often well respected and trusted by their co-workers, which leads to positive relationships and the ability to help others develop and grow. People who are good at receiving feedback have the ability themselves to take the advice of others, which often helps them become better workers and better people.

Then **highlight** both sets of three-step strategies for developing the skill of *giving and receiving feedback*.

A 2.29

- See p. 130 for the **audioscript**.
- Tell the students they are going to listen to a conversation between a manager and an employee.
- The manager, Mrs Vaughan, is giving the employee, Paul, feedback on his presentation.
- Have the students reread the three-step strategies at the beginning of the section. Tell them to think about these as they listen for how well Mrs Vaughan and Paul give and receive feedback.
- Play the audio and encourage the students to take notes on how well the speakers do with giving and receiving feedback.

- Elicit responses from several students. Ask individual students to suggest ways the speakers could improve their skills of giving and receiving feedback.

Answers

The manager gives feedback very well. She is understanding and starts by making a couple of positive comments before gently making suggestions for improvement.

Paul receives the feedback badly. He is defensive and tries to blame other people.

Extra: anecdotes

Ask for volunteers to share any experiences they have had with receiving feedback in the workplace, at school or elsewhere. Ask the students how they felt, how they reacted, what they did well and what they feel they could have done better.

B

- Direct the students' attention to the photos and tell them to read the instructions. Explain or elicit the meaning of *public relations company* (a company that helps improve the public's image or opinion of someone or something). Elicit some predictions for what the email will be about.
- Give the students time to read the email. Put the students in groups to discuss the questions.
- Elicit responses from the class.

Answers

1 The two elements that need to be included are visuals and good slogans.
2 The manager wants them to work with their own team first to come up with good ideas and then present their ideas to another team and listen to their constructive feedback.

C

- Have the students stay in their groups. Give them time to read the list of ideas silently.
- Tell the students they are going to discuss and give feedback on each of the ideas, saying what they like and what they don't like about them. Remind them that the point of the activity is to practise giving feedback, so they need to consider how they are presenting their opinions about the ideas.
- As they discuss and critique the ideas, encourage the students to share their own ideas and give feedback on one another's ideas. Remind the students to make notes of any other ideas that come up.

D

- Have the groups begin planning their local tourism campaign. Remind them of the elements they need to include according to the manager's email.
- Circulate during the students' discussions and make sure all the students are participating.
- Remind the students to write their plans in the space provided or on a separate paper.

E
- Tell the students they are going to present their plans to another group and receive feedback on them, as well as giving feedback on the other group's plans.
- Give the groups time to read the instructions.
- Combine the groups and nominate one Group A and the other Group B.
- Remind the students to explain how each element of the plan will help boost tourism.
- Direct the students' attention to the examples in the *How to say it* box and encourage them to use the expressions as they give and receive feedback.

Alternative
Encourage the students to write down the feedback they receive from the other group so they can apply it to improve their plans in the next exercise.

F
- Have the students separate into their original groups again.
- Give them time to review their feedback and decide how to improve their plans.
- Have the groups take turns presenting their plans to the class. Encourage the groups to ask for further feedback from the class and encourage the rest of the class to ask questions and give appropriate feedback.

G
- Have the students work in small groups to discuss feedback in the domain of **Work and Career**. Point out that item 2 focuses on receiving feedback and ask each group to think of at least three reasons why their reaction to feedback might be different in the future.
- Ask the groups to report to the class and write the most popular reasons on the board.

REFLECT
- Discuss the question with the whole class. Ask the students to say what they feel are the most useful points they learned from this lesson, and how the skill of *giving and receiving feedback* might be useful in the domains of **Self and Society** and **Study and Learning**, either now or in the future.
- Elicit the following ideas: *helping others solve problems and solving their own problems more quickly and effectively, improving their study habits and academic performance*, etc.

RESEARCH
- Go through the task and check that the students are clear about what they have to do.
- Suggest some business magazines, journals or work-related websites where the students might find information about performance reviews and the types of questions asked.
- Have them share their findings in class. Lead a class discussion about how the images could be improved.

Language wrap-up (p. 138)

For notes on how to approach the exercises in the Language wrap-up section, please see page 9.

1 Vocabulary
- Ask the students to read each sentence for general understanding and to gain an idea of the context before choosing the correct option.

2 Grammar

A
- Encourage the students to say each sentence silently to themselves before deciding on their answers.

B
- Go over the phrases in the box.
- Have the students look back through the unit and review the meanings of the phrases if needed.
- Encourage the students to read through the paragraph before they choose the correct phrase for each blank, and remind them to use the context to help them. Point out that more than one answer is possible for some blanks.

Writing workshop: writing a report (p. 139)

Lead-in
Ask the students what a *report* is and what the purpose is (a written summary of information and recommendations based on research). Ask the students about their experiences with writing reports, in what situations they have had to write them and what about.

Tell the students that they are going to write a report about ways to improve local tourism.

A
- Have the students scan the report for any unknown words. Answer any questions they have about vocabulary.
- Give the students time to read the report, focusing on the problems the writer identifies and the recommendations she makes. Encourage them to take notes as they read.
- Call on individual students to tell you the problems and recommendations.

Answers
Problems identified: the website needs updating and people can't share it on social networks; the images are too formal

Recommendations made: modernise the website with better links to social media; update staff photos using selfies

Through the lens | UNIT 11 | 109

B

- Give the students time to read the questions.
- Have them read the report again and analyse it based on the questions.
- Elicit the answers from the class.

Answers

1. She puts that information at the top of the report, showing who it is to, who it is from and the subject.
2. She uses headings for her paragraphs that show the particular topic she is discussing.
3. Reports like this are usually written for work situations, where people are busy and have limited time. Therefore, it's important that you can see at a glance who the report is for and what topics it covers.
4. The report is very formal because it's written for someone at work.

C

- Have the students read through the whole exercise.
- To help the students get started, elicit some ideas of problems related to local tourism. Encourage the students to choose real problems in their local area, such as traffic, pollution, inconvenient public transportation, etc. Write the problems on the board and elicit a few recommendations for each one.
- Give the students time to make some notes outlining the problems and suggestions for addressing them.

Alternative

Have the students research and write a report about a real problem related to tourism at a famous tourist destination somewhere in the world, for example, related to the negative effects of tourism on the environment and wildlife or on local culture.

D

- Give the students time to write their reports in class or for homework. Remind them to write about 200 words.
- Encourage the students to use new language and structures from the unit in their writing. Award an extra mark or marks for including comparisons, connectors or other vocabulary from the unit.

How are you doing?

- Ask the students to read the statements and tick the ones they believe are true.
- Ask them to discuss their report with another student in the class and identify things they could improve on next time.

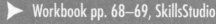

UNIT 12 BRIGHT LIGHTS, BIG CITY

The expression *bright lights, big city* makes us think of the excitement of life in a large city, especially at night. Bright lights can refer to show business in particular, and bring to mind theatres, cinemas and clubs, and the neon lights that attract people to them.

Unit plan

Unit opener	(p. 140)	20 min.
1 **Grammar:** connectors of contrast	(p. 142)	40 min.
2 **Writing:** a letter of complaint	(p. 143)	30 min.
• Vocabulary: formal letters		15 min.
3 **Reading:** a guidebook	(p. 144)	30 min.
• Vocabulary: describing places		15 min.
4 **Listening:** rapid speech	(p. 145)	30 min.
5 **Grammar:** ways of talking about the future	(p. 146)	40 min.
6 **Pronunciation:** connected speech	(p. 147)	15 min.
7 **Speaking:** talking about cities of the future	(p. 147)	30 min.
LifeSkills: recognising and avoiding plagiarism (Study and Learning)	(p. 148)	50 min.
• Optional downloadable *LifeSkills* lesson (Work and Career)		50 min.
• Optional downloadable *LifeSkills* lesson (Self and Society)		50 min.
Language wrap-up	(p. 150)	15 min.
Speaking workshop	(p. 151)	20 min.
Video and downloadable video worksheet		45 min.

Unit opener (p. 140)

Lead-in

Ask the students to look at the unit title and the photos and to predict what the unit will be about. Ask them if they like the excitement of big cities or if they prefer the country. Direct the students' attention to the points in the unit objectives box and go through the information with them. To get your students to think about the skills being developed in this unit, ask them to look at the questions in the cogs.

Listening: rapid speech

- Ask the students about their experiences listening to native English speakers. Ask what they find challenging and elicit any strategies they use to help them, including ones they learned in Unit 10.

Writing: a letter of complaint

- Ask the students if they have ever been dissatisfied with a product or service and whether or not they complained about it. Elicit ways customers can express disapproval and point out that some people write a letter of complaint. Elicit what the students think should be included in a letter of complaint. Then list their ideas on the board.

LifeSkills: recognising and avoiding plagiarism

- Ask the students to explain in their own words what *plagiarism* is (using someone else's words without permission and without giving the original author credit). Elicit reasons why it's important for the students to understand plagiarism.

Common European Framework: unit map

Unit 12	Competence developed	CEF Reference (B2 competences)
Grammar	can use and understand connectors of constrast	Table 1; Table 2; Sections 5.2.1.2; 6.4.7.7; 6.4.7.8
Writing	can write a letter of complaint	Table 1; Table 2; Sections 4.4.1.2; 4.4.3.2; 4.4.3.4; 4.5.2.1; 5.2.1.1; 5.2.1.2; 5.2.1.6; 5.2.2.2; 5.2.2.4; 5.2.3.2
Reading	can read and understand an extract from a guidebook	Table 1; Table 2; Sections 4.4.2.2; 4.4.2.4; 4.5.2.2
Listening	can understand rapid speech	Table 1; Table 2; Sections 4.4.2.1; 4.4.3.1; 4.4.3.5; 4.5.2.2
Grammar	can use and understand different ways of talking about the future	Table 1; Table 2; Sections 5.2.1.2; 6.4.7.7; 6.4.7.8
Pronunciation	can correctly use connected speech	Section 5.2.1.4
Speaking	can talk about cities of the future	Table 1; Table 2; Sections 4.4.1.1; 4.4.3.1; 4.4.3.5; 4.5.2.1; 5.2.1.1; 5.2.1.2; 5.2.3.2

A

- Direct the students' attention to the photos and elicit the general and specific places shown (see below).
- Check that the students understand the meanings of *landmark* (a famous building or object that is recognisable to many people), *tourist attraction* (a popular place for people from other areas to come and visit) and *seat of government* (capital of a state, country, etc).
- Have the students work individually to tick the criteria they think are important in defining a 'great' city. Point out that there are no right or wrong answers and that they may tick as many criteria as they wish. Encourage the students to use the space provided to add their own ideas for features of a great city.
- Call on individual students to share their ideas about what makes a great city. Encourage them to discuss any differences of opinion.

Culture note

The photographs show, clockwise from top right:

Wall Street is a 0.7-mile-long street that runs through the financial district of New York City. It is the home of the New York Stock Exchange, and other major exchanges have or have had headquarters in the area.

The Sydney Opera House, located on Sydney Harbour in Australia, is one of the most famous examples of architectural design. It was designed by Danish architect Jørn Utzon.

The Basilica of the Sagrada Família is located in Barcelona, Spain. It was designed by architect Antonio Gaudí.

Heathrow Airport, 14 miles west of London, began as a small airfield in the 1920s and rapidly expanded into a five-terminal international airport. Today it carries approximately 70 million passengers per year to over 180 destinations worldwide.

King's College in Cambridge, England was founded in 1441 by King Henry VI. Cambridge University is one of the world's most prestigious universities.

The Paris Metro is the rapid transit system of Paris, France. It first opened in 1900. It is the second busiest transit system in Europe, after Moscow, Russia.

Petaling Street, located in Kuala Lumpur, Malaysia, is a Chinatown area with many shops, restaurants and outdoor food stalls.

Extra: class poll

Have the students work in groups to reach a consensus on the top five features of a great city. As they discuss the features, encourage them to support their suggestions and opinions with examples of real cities.

B

- Put the students in groups. Ask the students to think about the capital city or another important city in their country, or ask them to think of a well-known city from around the world.
- Refer them to the criteria they selected in Ex. A and have them use these to consider whether the city they chose should be defined as a 'great' city. Give the students time to think about their answers to the questions and to make notes for their discussion. Point out the model language.
- Give the groups time to complete their discussions. Circulate during the discussions and ask follow-up questions to encourage the students to give more detailed responses.
- Call on a representative of each group to share the group's ideas with the rest of the class.

Extra: research

Ask the students to name cities from around the world and write them on the board. Ask questions to elicit cities in different continents, for example, *Who can name a major city in India? Africa? North America?* Ask the students to choose a city and research online to find out which of the criteria from the list in Ex. A it has. Encourage them to identify any other interesting information they find about the city. On an index card, have the students write the name of the city and a few sentences about why they think it is or is not a great city according to the criteria they identified. Display the cards by continent.

Extra: homework

For homework, have the students write a short essay about a city they have visited. They should describe the city in detail and say what criteria it has from the list in Ex. A.

Grammar: connectors of contrast (p. 142)

Lead-in

Make two columns on the board and label them '+' and '−'. Elicit some statements about the positive points about the town or city where the students live and write them under the '+'. Then elicit some of the negative points and list them under the '−'. For example:

+	−
Our city has a centre for arts and culture.	It doesn't have many parks.

Explain that these are contrasting (differing) ideas about their city. Ask the students to think about how they could combine pairs of sentences like these into one. Give them time to think and then elicit a few examples from individual students. Try to elicit sentences that use connectors of contrast, for example, *Our city has a successful sports team; however, it doesn't have a very big sports stadium.* On the board, list any connectors that the students use.

A

- Direct the students' attention to the photo and elicit some guesses as to which country and city it is. See if anyone can identify the type of tree in the photo and write the name on the board (jacaranda).
- Give the students time to read the travel blog post in order to identify the city.
- Elicit the answer and ask the students to tell you what clues from the text helped them guess the city.

Answer
Pretoria, South Africa

Culture note
Pretoria is a city located in the northern part of South Africa, which serves as the nation's main capital and administrative hub. The city was named after the Dutchman Andries Pretorius, who emigrated to South Africa in the early 1800s from the then British Cape Colony. Pretoria is known as the *Jacaranda City* as a result of the thousands of jacaranda trees that are planted along its streets and in its parks.

NOTICE!
- Direct the students' attention to the **Notice!** box.
- Ask them to find the underlined word and say what the two contrasting ideas are. Discuss the answer with the class.

Answer
feeling OK / the long flight

B

Function
- Ask the students to read the travel blog again, paying attention to the sentences with contrasting ideas.
- Give the students time to think about their answer to the question. Then ask individual students to share their answers with the class.

Answer
To connect contrasting ideas

Form
- Have the students complete the table with examples from the travel blog and answer the two questions. Discuss the answers with the class.
- Direct the students' attention to the **What's right?** box. Elicit that the first sentence is incorrect because *of* is always necessary after *in spite*, and here *of the fact that* is also necessary because it is followed by a clause.

Answers
1 but   2 nevertheless   3 Although   4 even though
5 despite   6 In spite of the fact that   7 although / even though / in spite of / despite   8 but / nevertheless

C

- Give the students time to read the sentences and the answer choices silently, and to think about which connector best fits each one.
- Have the students work individually to select the answers and then compare answers in pairs.
- Check answers by calling on individual students to say the sentence aloud, inserting the correct connector. Have the rest of the class listen for and correct any errors.

Answers
1 In spite of   2 even though   3 Although
4 Nevertheless   5 though   6 but   7 Despite
8 Even though

Extra: grammar practice
Have the students write a travel blog entry like the one in Ex. A about a city they have visited. Encourage them to include at least four sentences that contain connectors of contrast.

D

- Give the students time to read the instructions and think about a place they have visited to use for this activity. Encourage them to make some notes and think about how they can use connectors of contrast in describing it. Go over the model language by giving or eliciting an example sentence using each phrase.
- Put the students in pairs to tell each other about the place they chose. Remind them that they should not tell each other what the city or landmark is, but that they should describe it so that their partner can guess which place they are describing.

 Workbook p. 70, Section 1

Writing: a letter of complaint (p. 143)

Lead-in
Give the students time to read the information in the skills panel. Check that the students understand the meaning of *complaint* (a written or spoken statement expressing dissatisfaction with something).

Bright lights, big city   UNIT 12

Ask the students to think about a negative experience they have had while travelling. Write the following prompts on the board to help them get started: *transportation, hotel/accommodation, restaurant service/food, tours*. Encourage them to make some notes on the experience, what was negative about it, whether they complained and what the outcome was.

Put the students in groups to share their experiences. Then elicit a few anecdotes from the class and ask volunteers to tell you how they felt in each situation.

A

- Ask the students to tell you three adjectives that describe an effective letter of complaint (*formal, clear* and *polite*). Ask why it is important that the letter be clear and polite (you are more likely to get a positive response).
- Direct the students' attention to the photo and elicit the location (Bangkok, Thailand). Tell them they are going to read a letter of complaint from a tourist to a tour company. Elicit some of the aspects of a guided tour that someone might complain about.
- Give the students time to read the letter of complaint. Remind them that they need to underline four complaints and underline the writer's request.
- Check the answers with the class.

Answers

Complaints:
First of all, <u>it lasted only three hours despite being advertised as a five-hour tour</u>, and <u>we didn't visit</u> Wat Pho or the Grand Palace <u>even though these were included on the itinerary</u>. Furthermore, <u>they gave us only 30 minutes at</u> The Golden Mount<u>, but the itinerary said we would have an hour there</u>. Finally, <u>although the tour guide said he spoke good English, he wasn't easy to understand</u>.
Request:
For these reasons, <u>I request a refund for the cost of the tour</u>.

B

- Have the students read the letter in Ex. A again to find out the writer's purpose in each of the three main paragraphs. You could do this exercise in pairs or small groups.
- Check the answers with the class.

Answers

Paragraph 1: To say why he is writing
Details: Date of tour, place of tour, why they booked the tour
Paragraph 2: To explain the problems
Details: Four things that had been promised and what really happened
Paragraph 3: A request for a refund
Details: What he is enclosing with the letter

C

- Give the students time to read the features (1–6) of the letter in Ex. A.
- Have them read the letter again and list the words or phrases the writer used for each feature.
- Have the students check answers in pairs. Then check the answers with the class.

Answers

1 Dear Sir/Madam:
2 I am writing with regard to
3 we were very disappointed
4 First of all, Furthermore, Finally
5 I look forward to hearing from you
6 Yours faithfully

D

- Give the students time to read the instructions. To help them get started, elicit one or two ideas from the class for things that could go wrong during a tour of their city. List them on the board.
- Put the students in pairs to list things that could go wrong on a tour of their city.
- Then have the partners write a formal letter of complaint to a tour company saying what they were unhappy about and what they want the tour company to do. Remind them to write a formal letter and to use the words and phrases from Ex. C as well as connectors of contrast.

E

- Combine pairs to form groups of four and give the students time to read the instructions.
- Review the three characteristics of an effective complaint letter (formal, clear, polite).
- Go over the list of criteria with the class and give some questions to help guide the students for what to look for, for example:

  Paragraph organisation: Does each paragraph have only one topic/purpose?

  Details: Are there enough details in each paragraph to support the purpose and make each point clear?
- Have the pairs exchange and read their letters. Encourage the students to write down their suggestions for how to improve the areas listed.

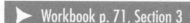
Workbook p. 71, Section 3

Workbook p. 70, Section 2

Reading: a guidebook (p. 144)

Lead-in

Review the idea that we read different types of texts for different purposes and elicit what some of these are (for information in order to do something, to find out news or opinions, to learn information for school or work, to find out about things we are interested in, for pleasure, etc). Have the students look at the title of this section and say what kind of text they will read (an extract from a guidebook) and why they might read it (for information or for pleasure). Ask what way of reading they would use for this kind of text (reading for details).

A

- Direct the students' attention to the photo of Fez, Morocco. Ask whether any students have visited Fez and if so to share a few of their impressions of the city.
- Put the students in pairs. If any students have been to Fez, encourage them to describe the city using statements like those in the table on p. 142 using connectors of contrast. If the students have not visited Fez, encourage them to use the photo and any background knowledge they have to describe what they imagine the city might be like.
- Give the students time to read the extract. Tell them not to worry if they don't understand the words in bold, as they will cover these in the next exercise.
- Have pairs discuss how the description compares to their impressions or guesses about the city of Fez.

Culture note

Fez is the third largest city in Morocco, with a population of about one million. The area in which Fez is located produces wheat, beans, olives and grapes.

B

- Elicit the bold words in Ex. A, correcting the students' pronunciation and syllable stress, and point out that these words are useful for describing places.
- Give the students time to read the definitions and find the matching nouns in Ex A.
- Check the answers by reading the definitions and asking individual students to tell you the correct words.

Answers

1 views 2 heritage 3 heart 4 site 5 trade
6 village 7 settlement 8 alleys

C

- Remind the students that a collocation is two or more words that are frequently used together. Do the first item with the whole class to provide an example.
- Have the students complete the noun collocations with words from Ex. B. Remind them that more than one combination may be possible. If the students need help, refer them to the text in Ex. A to confirm the answers.
- Check the answers with the class.

Answers

1 village / settlement 2 village / settlement 3 alleys
4 site 5 views 6 heritage 7 trade 8 heart

Extra: homework

Have the students write sentences or a full paragraph using the vocabulary and collocations from Ex. B and Ex. C. They should write one sentence for each vocabulary item, choosing an appropriate collocation for each. Encourage them to describe a place in their city or one they have visited and to include connectors of contrast.

D

- Give the students time to read the instructions and the model conversation. Tell them to think of a city they can describe well using the new vocabulary and collocations. Allow them to make some notes if they wish.
- Put the students in groups and have them take turns describing their cities. Encourage them to use words and phrases from Ex. C where possible. If they need help getting started, refer them again to the model conversation.

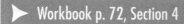 Workbook p. 72, Section 4

Listening: rapid speech (p. 145, p. 122)

Lead-in

Remind the students that they practised listening to rapid speech on p. 122. Give the students time to read the information in the skills panel. **Highlight** that even without understanding every word, they can usually understand enough to get the main gist of a conversation. However, if they panic they will stop listening and lose the opportunity to understand anything at all.

Remind the students that in Unit 10 they listened to two people talking about magician David Blaine, using rapid speech. Ask the students if they remember what one difficulty is in understanding rapid speech (understanding words that are run together). Say the following phrases and ask the students to remember or figure out what each one means: *gonna* (going to), *gotta* (have got to), *coulda* (could have), *wheredya* (where do/did you), *whadya* (what do/did you), *kinda* (kind of).

A

- Have the students look at the photos and tell you where they think they were taken. Elicit the students' guesses but do not confirm yet whether or not they are correct.

Bright lights, big city | UNIT 12 | 115

Answers

All were taken in different areas of London (Southall, Neal's Yard, Chinatown, Brixton Market)

B 🎧 2.30

- See p. 130 for the **audioscript**.
- Explain to the students that they are going to listen to four short extracts from a guided tour and match each extract with one of the photos in Ex. A. Remind them that they should listen for key details and ignore anything that is too fast to understand.
- Play the audio once and have the students listen and look at the photos. Then give them time to match the photos with the extracts. Check whether the students need to listen one more time.
- Have the students compare answers in pairs. Then check the answers with the class. Ask the students what clues they heard that helped them get the answers.

Answers

Extract 1: B   Extract 3: C
Extract 2: D   Extract 4: A

C 🎧 2.31

- See p. 130 for the **audioscript**.
- Explain to the students that they will hear the same extracts from the guided tour, this time including some comments and questions from tourists.
- Give the students time to read the statements. Remind them to stay focused on the key details of the listening and ignore any parts of the audio that they don't understand.
- Have the students mark their statements true or false and then compare answers in pairs.
- Check the answers with the class.

Answers

1 F   2 T   3 T   4 F   5 F   6 T

Extra: false to true

Have the students rewrite the false statements in Ex. C to make them true.

Answers

1 The woman doesn't think the architecture looks much like Mexico.
4 They have Chinese food for lunch.
5 The last stop on the tour is Southall.

D

- Put the students in pairs.
- Play the audio again and then have the students discuss with their partner what they understood and talk about any parts they didn't understand.
- Ask the pairs whether there were any parts both partners didn't understand. Ask whether the students were able to stay focused even when they missed portions.

- Remind them again of the importance of focusing on what they do understand rather than panic about what they don't understand.

▶ 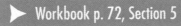 Workbook p. 72, Section 5

Grammar: ways of talking about the future (p. 146)

Lead-in

Refer the students to the photo and elicit where they think it is. Ask them to guess what time period it is. Ask them to refer to specific items in the photo to support their guesses.

A

- Before the students read the article, give them time to scan it for unknown words/phrases (carbon-neutral city: a city where the amount of carbon dioxide and carbon monoxide produced are designed to protect the environment, for example, trees are planted and people use less electricity; solar power: power from the sun; hydrogen power: power from a zero-emission fuel). Put them in pairs and have them ask their partner about any words they don't know and share information about the words and phrases they do know. Go over the words with the whole class and make sure all the students understand their meanings.
- Have the students read the article with the questions in mind. Ask them whether they would like to live in a similar city and elicit their explanations for why or why not.
- Remind the students that *will* refers to something definite and *may/might* refers to a possibility.

NOTICE!

- Direct the students' attention to the **Notice!** box.
- Have them reread the article and underline the verb forms used to refer to the future.
- Have them compare answers in pairs. Then check the answers with the class.

Answers

are moving, will have, is going to function, won't be, will travel, might also have, will be finishing, may be
The present continuous can be used in either the present or the future.

Culture note

Abu Dhabi is the capital of the United Arab Emirates. Its rapid development and urbanisation, coupled with the relatively high average income of its population, has transformed it into the metropolis it is today.

Although it's one of the world's largest producers of oil, Abu Dhabi has actively tried to diversify its economy in recent years through investments in financial services and tourism.

B
Function

- Have the students reread the text in Ex. A, paying attention to the references to the future.
- Ask them to complete the rules with the phrases from the box and complete the examples with phrases from the text.
- Have the students compare answers in pairs. Then check the answers with the class.
- Direct the students' attention to the language box below the table. **Highlight** that the future continuous is often used when imagining future actions: *By this time next week, I'll be lying on a beach in Rio.*
- Point out that the future continuous is commonly used with future time expressions, such as *when* and *(by) this time tomorrow / next week*, etc. Call on a student to read the two example sentences aloud.
- Direct the students' attention to the **What's right?** box and explain that when using expressions like *this time tomorrow*, it is correct to use the future continuous. The second sentence using future simple is incorrect in this situation.

Answers
1 may, might or will 2 will have 3 may be 4 going to
5 is going to 6 present continuous 7 are moving
8 future continuous 9 will be finishing

C

- Give the students time to read the sentences and consider the answer choices.
- Have the students work individually to choose the correct options. If they find this difficult, refer them to the explanations of function in the table in Ex. B.
- Check the answers with the class by calling on students to read the sentences aloud, inserting the correct verb tenses.

Answers
1 I will be working 2 I'm going 3 will visit
4 will be getting ready 5 might be working
6 is flying 7 will look 8 I'll be driving

D

- Give the students time to read the instructions and the list of time expressions. Point out the model conversation. Encourage the students to think about their future plans, hopes and wishes. Encourage them to make some notes if they like.
- Put the students in pairs and have them discuss what they think they will be doing in their lives at the points in time listed. Circulate during the students' discussions and check that they are using future forms correctly.
- Elicit some responses from individual students and encourage the rest of the class to ask follow-up questions to find out more information and to keep the conversation going.

▶ Workbook p. 73, Section 6

Pronunciation: connected speech (p. 147)

A 2.32

- See the Student's Book for the **audioscript**.
- Give the students time to read the list of phrases and compound words. **Highlight** that in each phrase/noun the ending consonant sound of the first word is the same as the initial consonant sound of the second word.
- Play the audio once and have the students listen. Ask them to tell you what happens to the final consonant sound in each word (it is held for a longer time and there is no space between the two words). Then play the audio a second time and have the students repeat each phrase.
- Put the students in pairs and have them practise saying the phrases using connected speech.

B 2.33

- See the Student's Book for the **audioscript**.
- Give the students time to read the sentences and think about how the connected speech will sound in the underlined phrases.
- Play the audio and have the students repeat the sentences.
- Have the students practise the sentences. Correct their use of connected speech as needed.

Speaking: talking about cities of the future (p. 147)

Lead-in

Elicit some ideas from the class about what cities might be like in the future. Give some categories, for example, buildings, homes, cars, aircraft, parks, roads, etc. Ask how they think these things will be different in the future. List the students' ideas on the board.

A

- Give the students time to read the instructions and the guide for their notes. Go over the meaning of *environmentally responsible* (not doing activities that harm the environment).
- Have the students work individually to complete their notes using the guide provided.
- Put the students in pairs to compare ideas. Then elicit some ideas from the class.

B 2.34

- See p. 131 for the **audioscript**.
- Explain to the students that they are going to hear three people talking about how they imagine cities of the future will be. Have them read the statements.
- Play the audio once and have the students match the speakers with the statements. Check whether they need to hear the audio again.

Bright lights, big city UNIT 12

- When you check the answers, elicit what clues the students heard that helped them to match the speakers with the statements.
- Call on individual students to say whether any of the speakers mentioned some of the same points the students listed in their notes in Ex. A.

Answers
Speaker 1 b
Speaker 2 c
Speaker 3 a

C
- Put the students in pairs to discuss the statements in Ex. B. Remind them that they need to say which ones they most agree with and discuss any they disagree with, and say why.

D
- Put the students in pairs. Have them look back at their notes in Ex. A and their ideas from Ex.C. Explain that they should use their notes to talk to their partner about their vision of cities of the future, and that they need to speak for about one and a half minutes. While one student speaks, the other should listen without interrupting.
- When they have finished, ask volunteers to share their ideas with the class.

LifeSkills: recognising and avoiding plagiarism (p. 148)

Step 1: Understand what plagiarism is. (Ex. A, Ex. B)
Step 2: Learn to recognise plagiarism in your own work or others' work. (Ex. D, Ex. E)
Step 3: Learn strategies for avoiding plagiarism. (Ex. C, Ex. E)

Lead-in
Read the target skill aloud and invite the students to tell you what they think recognising and avoiding plagiarism means.

Give or elicit examples of reasons why it is important to be able to recognise and avoid plagiarism (so as not to get into trouble for going against school policies, to give proper credit to researchers and scholars).

Then **highlight** the three-step strategy to develop the skill of recognising and avoiding plagiarism.

A
- Ask the students to read the definition of *plagiarism*. Then ask them to tell you what plagiarism means in their own words. Elicit or point out the verb *plagiarise*.
- Have the students read the discussion questions and think about their responses.
- Put the students in groups to discuss the questions.
- When the groups finish their discussions, call on a representative from each group to share their responses with the class.

B
- Give the students time to read through the quiz questions and think about their responses.
- Put the students in pairs to complete the quiz. Encourage them to give examples and information to support their reasons for their answer choices.
- Combine the pairs to form groups of four and have the students compare answers. Then check the answers with the class.
- Discuss each situation in the quiz. For the questions to which the answer is *no*, elicit examples of what the students could do as an alternative, for example, include source information for a diagram they use.

Answers
1 Yes **2** Yes **3** No **4** Yes **5** No

C
- Elicit some of the students' experiences of how they have avoided plagiarism in their own schoolwork in the past. Have the class give you other ideas for how they might avoid plagiarism in the future. **Highlight** that using select information from other sources is OK and is an excellent way to support the content in a written report or research paper, as long as sources are properly credited.
- Go over the list of strategies with the class. Model the pronunciation and have the students repeat each strategy.
- Give the students time to match the strategies with the definitions. Then have the students compare answers in pairs.
- Check the answers with the class. Ask the students which strategies they have used before and whether any of the ideas are new to them.

Answers
1 c **2** d **3** a **4** b

Extra: class writing project
Provide the students with a few paragraphs of copyrighted informational text. Put the students in four groups and give one of the strategies for avoiding plagiarism to each. Give the groups a few minutes to write a few sentences using their strategy to present the information. Then have the groups take turns sharing the information with the class.

D
- Give the students time to read the extract and the four summaries and think about which summary plagiarises the original.
- Put the students in pairs to discuss which summary they think is plagiarism. Tell them to give specific examples from the text to support their opinions.
- Direct the students' attention to the examples in the **How to say it** box and encourage them to use the expressions in their discussions.
- Discuss the answer with the class.

Answer

The writer of text 2 plagiarises the original text because although he/she has changed a few of the words, the wording is still very similar and the paragraph contains exactly the same information, in the same order, as the original.

E

- Have the students stay in their pairs and discuss how the writers of the other texts avoided plagiarism. Have them identify the strategies from Ex. C that the writers used.
- Combine the pairs to form groups of four and have the students compare answers. Then check the answers with the class.

Answers

Text 1: paraphrasing: The text contains some of the same info as the original, but the focus is on the changes and the problems cities have. The writer doesn't discuss advantages of urbanisation and doesn't mention Africa or Asia.
Text 3: referencing/citing: The writer names the article and author and specifically discusses the original article.
Text 4: quoting: The writer uses a direct quote from the author of the original article and references his name.

F

- Put the students in groups to discuss plagiarism. Have the students focus on the domain of **Study and Learning**. Ask them to think about how other students they know might have plagiarised, either accidentally or deliberately.
- Have the groups share their ideas with the class and give further examples of how to avoid plagiarism.

REFLECT

- Discuss the question with the whole class. Ask the students to say what they feel are the most useful points they learned from this lesson, and how the skill of *recognising and avoiding plagiarism* might be useful in the domains of **Self and Society** and **Work and Career**, either now or in the future.
- Elicit the following ideas: *using existing research and information that is useful for supporting their own work on reports and in memos, maintaining integrity and being respectful of others' work*, etc.

RESEARCH

- Go through the task and check that the students are clear about what they have to do.
- Suggest some possible travel- and tourism-related websites or magazines for the students to explore. Have the students do research and make notes on the city of their choice.
- Have them share their findings in class. Lead a class discussion about the techniques they used to avoid plagiarising.

Alternative

Have the students do research and write a short report individually. Put the students in pairs and have them take turns reading their report and showing concrete examples of how they avoided plagiarising. For example, *Here I used quotation marks to show the words I took directly from one of the sources.*

Language wrap-up (p. 150)

For notes on how to approach the exercises in the Language wrap-up section, please see page 9.

1 Vocabulary

- Go over the words and phrases in the box. Point out to the students that they will be using these to fill in the blanks, whereas they will be choosing the correct noun options.
- Encourage the students to read through the whole email before they decide on their answers.
- Remind the students to use the context to help them.
- Have the students complete the task individually and then compare answers in pairs.
- Call on individual students to say the sentences, inserting the correct answers. Ask the rest of the class to say whether the sentence is correct or not.

2 Grammar

- Point out to the students that they will be filling in the blanks with the correct future form of the verb (in parentheses), whereas they will be choosing the correct connector options.
- Ask the students to read the whole diary entry through first before completing the exercise. Encourage them to say each sentence silently to themselves before deciding on their answers.
- When checking the answers with the students, point out that the future continuous is generally used with a time expression, such as *by the time I graduate, when the summer holidays arrive*, etc.

Speaking workshop: giving a short presentation (p. 151)

A 2.35

- See p. 131 for the **audioscript**.
- Tell the students that they are going to listen to someone from Dallas, Texas talking about how she thinks the city will be different in the next century.
- Give the students time to read the questions. Elicit some predictions from the class about what the speaker will say.
- Play the audio once. Allow the students to make some notes on the questions if they like.
- Check whether the students need to hear the audio again.
- Have the students compare answers to the questions in pairs. Then discuss the answers with the class.

Bright lights, big city | **UNIT 12**

> **Answers**
> 1 No, she says a lot of things will be similar.
> 2 entertainment and going out, architecture, transportation
> 3 most changes: transportation; least changes: entertainment and going out

B

- Go over the headings and examples. Elicit one or two more examples for each purpose from the class.
- Play the audio again and have the students write the additional expressions they hear for each of the purposes.
- Elicit the answers from the class.

> **Answers**
> Contrast: however, but, in spite of, nevertheless
> Reason or result: because (of), as a result, so
> Opinion: I think, I believe, I'm sure

Extra: brainstorm

Put the students in groups to brainstorm additional words and phrases for each of the purposes in the table in Ex. B. Have the groups share their words and phrases with the class by using them in a sentence that describes a city.

C

- Check the format of the exercise and answer any questions.
- Check that the students understand that they will be talking about three aspects of their city. They will be discussing things they think will and won't change and giving reasons for their opinions.
- Give the students time to prepare and make notes for their presentations. Remind them that they will not be able to read from their notes during their presentations, so encourage them to write brief bullet points as opposed to writing their presentation out in full.
- Remind them to use words and phrases for expressing contrast, reasons and results, and opinions. Offer an extra mark or marks for including future verb tenses or new vocabulary from the unit.

Extra: research

Encourage the students to read local news articles and local government websites and use the information, for example, about a city-planning project, to support their opinions about future changes in their city. This will give them an opportunity to practise their new strategies for avoiding plagiarism as they will need to cite references in their presentations.

D

- Put the students in small groups and have them take turns giving their presentations. Remind them not to read from their notes but to try to look up and make eye contact with the audience. Each student should talk for about one minute.

How are you doing?

- Ask the students to read the statements and tick the ones they believe are true.
- Ask them to discuss their presentations with a member of their group and identify things they could improve on next time.

 Workbook pp. 74–75, SkillsStudio

AUDIOSCRIPT

UNIT 1

Who do you think you are?

1.01

I = Interviewer, D = Dylan

I: Today I'm talking to Dylan Drummond about how he defines who he is. Dylan is 28 and married. He's Scottish, and he lives in Nagoya in Japan.
Dylan, how long have you lived in Japan?

D: For almost two years.

I: When you were living in Scotland, which factors were most important to your sense of personal identity?

D: Well, my social group was always very important to me. My friends always played a bigger part in creating my identity than my family, I'd say.

I: Why do you think that was?

D: I think it's because we grew up together and shared the same life goals. And we dressed the same, followed fashion, you know. That was very important to me when I was younger.

I: What about other aspects of your life?

D: I was always really interested in music and belonged to my local bagpipe band. That was a big part of who I was and I loved taking part in shows. It made me very proud to be Scottish.

I: I see. Did anything else influence your personal identity?

D: Erm … I'd say that my career has helped me define who I am. Social status was never particularly important to me, but I always wanted to have a good career. I was very pleased when I finally qualified and could call myself an architect.

1.02

I = Interviewer, D = Dylan

I: OK, Dylan. Let's move on to talk about your life now and how moving to another country has affected your sense of identity. Was it a shock to move to Japan?

D: Oh, yes, in many ways. My wife is Japanese – we met at university – and so she tried to prepare me for life here, but it was still a shock at first. Everyone faces culture shock when they move to a country that's so different, and of course it affects who you are.

I: And how would you say you've changed?

D: I've definitely become more aware of other people's opinions. In Scotland, I just did what I wanted to, but here people pay much more attention to what other people think. You have to be careful not to shock the neighbours!

I: So are the most important identity factors on your list the same as they were when you were in Scotland?

D: No. Well, my friends are still important, of course, and we stay in touch through social media, but other things have changed. For example, my music is not a main factor in who I am any more.

I: And why has that changed?

D: The type of music I played was very Scottish and there's no similar tradition here in Nagoya. But that's been replaced by other interests, such as photography, and I belong to the local camera club.

I: That's interesting. So apart from your hobbies, what things do you consider most important to your identity now?

D: Well, back home, my family background was not really a big part of my identity. My family wasn't particularly close, and as we grew up, my brother and sister and I didn't really keep in touch very much. Here in Japan, it's very different. Family values are much more important, and I've learnt to respect the idea of family far more. My wife and her family have taught me a lot, and it's interesting to see how living here is affecting the identities of our two young children.

I: I'm sure it's going to be interesting to watch them grow up. Dylan, thank you very much for talking to us today.

D: My pleasure.

1.03

A = Anna, S = Sean, B = Bettina, M = Matt

A: How important is it to be an individual, to express your personal identity? Sean?

S: I think it's really important to be yourself. If we don't have a strong sense of our own identity, then it's as if we were all made in a factory.

B: Well, yes, to a certain extent, but don't you think we have to respect the people close to us, like our family?

S: Yes and no. Family members should respect each other, but that also means respecting each other as individuals. I don't think your family should ever force you to dress or act in a certain way.

B: I'm sorry, but I just don't think that's true. I think parents have the right to expect their children to conform to certain family values.

M: And what about at work? For example, you have really long hair, Sean, but if you get an office job, that might not be appropriate.

S: I just don't think a job should force you to go against who you are. I would never take a job that wouldn't let me be myself.

B: I'm afraid I can't agree. People have to make compromises. My older brother was always saying that he would never change because of a job, and he would make fun of people who did. But then he got an office job and he had to start wearing a suit!

A: Sean, do you think you lose your individual identity if you change your hair or clothes?

S: Well, you don't change who you are, but you're letting other people put pressure on you to do what they want you to do.

Audioscript 121

M: In a way, you're right, but if you think life is going to be exactly the way you want it, you're just going to be disappointed.

B: I couldn't agree more. And it isn't sensible to do things that offend other people just to show how individual we are.

S: Yeah, but …

UNIT 2
Global views

1.06

Speaker 1:
I think that globalisation is having a beneficial effect. I mean, it's easier for countries to export goods and that means some of the world's poorer countries can develop their economies. In some Asian countries, there's been huge economic growth in recent decades and the standard of living has increased dramatically.

Speaker 2:
But is that always the case? It seems to me that multinational companies increase their profits by, like, setting up factories in poorer countries because the workers aren't paid very much. I think it's unfair that there's such inequality; the company owners become millionaires, while the majority of people live in poverty.

Speaker 3:
That's a good point. And multinational companies are completely taking over – you know, you see the same fast-food restaurants, coffee shops and supermarkets wherever you go. And small independent companies don't stand a chance.

Speaker 4:
Yeah, I completely agree. I kind of think it's sad that regional cultures are disappearing and countries are becoming more similar to each other. The same music and films dominate popular culture everywhere and it all starts to look the same.

Speaker 5:
I know what you mean, but don't you think that globalisation also has some positive effects? For example, it's so much easier to communicate with people in other countries. The internet facilitates information sharing and … well … that helps everyone.

1.07

I = Interviewer

I: Everyone agrees that people are becoming increasingly interconnected through the use of social media. We can communicate with more people and we can communicate wherever we are. But what do people actually think about it? What do they think are the advantages and disadvantages? We're here in a local shopping centre to find out.

Hello. We want to know what people think about social media. Do you use any sites regularly, and what are their advantages and disadvantages?

A: Oh yeah, I love using social media – my favourite is Twitter. The best thing about it is that I can send short messages all day long and I get tons of messages from my friends, so it's like a conversation going on all the time.

I: How about you? Do you use a lot of social media?

B: Yes, I like to share pictures and videos on Flickr. It's really great because when I went on holiday to India last summer, I could show my friends all the fascinating places I was going to. It's getting easier and easier to send and share information. I think it's great.

I: Excuse me. What do you think about social media?

C: I don't use it very much. I think there are lots of advantages, but I think it's too easy for people like companies and advertisers to get hold of your personal information. It's not a good idea to put all that stuff on the web – you just don't know how they're going to use it, do you?

1.09

1 There are many **vast** new emerging markets.
2 We **do** want to take part in the global conversation.
3 There's a rapid **pace** of development.
4 Large companies can **drain** skilled workers.
5 There is a new international **coal** agreement.

1.10

This is a photo of a modern-looking café that is popular with young people. There are lots of people in the background and the café looks really busy. In the foreground is a group of three young women, sitting in a row. The young woman on the left is using her laptop and the young woman in the middle is on her tablet. They're both smiling, so they're probably not studying. Maybe they're reading emails from friends, or maybe they're watching videos. The young woman on the right is on her mobile phone and she's using a tablet at the same time. She's smiling too, so she's probably chatting to a friend. They're sitting close together so they probably know each other, but they aren't talking or looking at each other at all. They all seem to be very involved with their electronic devices.

UNIT 3
Fame and fortune

1.11

In the late 1990s, an American journalist called James Ulmer devised a scale to find out how valuable film stars are to any film they work on. It takes into account factors such as talent and willingness to promote a film. He called it 'the Ulmer Scale', and it is widely used in the industry. But now this term is being used to rank celebrities in terms of how famous they are. So, at the top of this scale are people on what is called the 'A-List'. Those are people who have been very famous for a long time, like Daniel Day-Lewis, as well as the hottest stars of the moment, such as Keira Knightly. A-listers are often famous celebrities like actors or singers, but they can also be people who are not exactly celebrities, but who are famous. For example, they might run a global company – like Bill Gates. Or they could have broken a world record, such as Usain Bolt, or written a best-selling novel – someone like J K Rowling.

And then further down this list are the celebrities who aren't quite as well-known – the B-listers. They tend to be famous in their own country or profession, but may not be known to the general public around the world. A good example would be someone like, uh, Leona Lewis. She won the *X Factor* in the UK and is also well-known in Europe, but she isn't an international star – at least not yet. Or they might be people who are famous, but not in an 'I'm-a-celebrity-look-at-me!' kind of way. These are people who have done incredibly important things, such as discover a cure for a disease, or come up with an amazing new invention, like Sir Tim Berners-Lee, who invented the World Wide Web, but who don't get on the front pages of celebrity magazines.

And the ones who are even less valuable on the social scene are, of course, the C-listers. This group might include people who've done something like appearing on a reality TV show, causing a scandal somewhere or just inheriting a fortune. They might not really have a particular talent, but we see them in the media a lot.

Of course, the whole idea of using the Ulmer Scale for ranking people in terms of their social value is completely subjective, based on opinions and not on any real factors, but it's interesting to many people anyway.

1.14

Conversation 1

A: I sometimes feel sorry for celebrities. Imagine being chased by the paparazzi every time you left the house.

B: You feel sorry for them? Really? Most of them seem happy with the publicity when it suits them!

A: Well, what I meant was, it can't be easy living in the public eye, that's all.

Conversation 2

C: I think a lot of very famous people lose a sense of reality, don't you?

D: I'm not sure I understand what you mean …

C: What I'm trying to say is that they forget how to behave in a normal way.

Conversation 3

E: It seems to me that rock stars and celebrities are never happy.

F: Of course they are! You're not telling me that these people wake up in the morning worrying where their next million is coming from?

E: Maybe I'm not making myself clear. I'm not necessarily talking about money. Look at the number of famous people who have personal problems when they're at the peak of their careers.

Conversation 4

G: Downsides? Yes! Imagine having all that fame and all that money and not knowing who your real friends are anymore. I think being famous must be awful. I'd hate it.

H: Seriously?

G: OK, maybe I should rephrase that. I wouldn't hate *all* of it, but I don't think it'd be easy …

Conversation 5

I: So you're saying that celebrities don't enjoy their fame?

J: Actually, that's not what I meant. I didn't mean that celebrities never look for fame. A lot of celebrities love all that attention. But I was talking about famous people who don't really enjoy the celebrity part of their jobs. You know, the ones who always try to avoid reporters and photographers. They really just want to have normal lives, and they're not going around looking for attention.

I: Oh, right. I see what you're saying.

Conversation 6

K: It's people like Jay-Z and Beyoncé I feel really sorry for. I mean, all that pressure to perform, to keep your fans happy, to try and keep the paparazzi off your back long enough to spend time quietly with your family. I think fame comes at a price. Put it that way.

L: Did you say that you felt sorry for them?! I think it would be great! You'd have loads of money, a private jet, you could do anything and go anywhere.

1.15

T = Tanya, E = Elaine, B = Bob, Ev = Evan

T: Good morning, everyone. We're here today to discuss my proposal to cut the Lifestyle and Entertainment section from the paper. Who would like to start the discussion?

E: I'm afraid I disagree. We get dozens of letters to the editor each week with comments about articles in the L&E section. In fact, last week we got 50 letters related to that section. If L&E disappears, we're going to get lots of complaints.

B: Yes, but we get hundreds of letters about the news stories and editorials, far more than we get for L&E. We have to cut something, and I agree with Tanya that L&E should go. People want to read real news.

Ev: I don't know. Do we have good data on who our readers are? Tanya, I know you gave us some facts and statistics on newspaper readership, but those are generalisations for the whole country. I'm not sure the numbers would be the same for our local paper. I think people in our community want a newspaper that offers a variety of content.

E: Yes, and also, several national surveys have shown that when young people *do* read the newspaper, they tend to read the L&E sections. If we cut that section, we'll lose any young readers that we have!

B: But look at the facts, Elaine. First, the population is getting younger. Second, newspaper sales are getting smaller. I think the reason is that most young people do not get their news from newspapers.

T: OK. You all have some good points. Why don't we investigate further before making a decision? Let's talk to a large sample of our subscribers and find out who reads the paper and what they read. Here's what we want to know: First, how many people in the family read the paper, and how old are they? Second, what sections of the paper does each person read? Based on that information, we can decide whether to cut the L&E section, or any other sections. Do you agree?

B: Fine. I'll design the survey and we can discuss it at the next meeting. Now, is there any other business?

UNIT 4

Ups and downs

1.16

Good morning, and welcome to today's lecture. This is the third in this series of psychology lectures, and today we're going to be looking at happiness, or more specifically, the relationship between wealth and happiness. Does having more material wealth increase or decrease your happiness?

1.17

Good morning, and welcome to today's lecture. This is the third in this series of psychology lectures, and today we're going to be looking at happiness, or more specifically, the relationship between wealth and happiness. Does having more material wealth increase or decrease your happiness?

It would seem to be common sense that more money will make us happier. Most of us aim to increase our income throughout our lives, to enable us to buy more material goods, such as a car or our own home, or provide the resources to raise a family and so on. And we think that all of this will make us happy. If we didn't think money would make us happy, why would anyone try to get rich?

Well, as expected, the results of an international study confirm the idea that, in general, people with higher incomes feel more satisfied with their lives. This was the case when comparisons were made between people in different countries, as well as between different income groups within the same country.

However, other surprising research has indicated that people with higher incomes are not necessarily happier than those who earn less.

Although these two studies seem to contradict each other by saying, on one hand, that wealthier people are more content, and on the other hand, that wealthier people aren't happier, both offer some very interesting insights into the connection between wealth and happiness. Nevertheless, the first thing to consider is the possible explanations for the differences in the findings of these two studies.

The most crucial factor is the terminology used. Quite simply, 'satisfaction' and 'happiness' are different things. Various factors have an influence on happiness, and 'satisfaction' is just one element of happiness.

So why do people with higher incomes experience lower levels of happiness? A recent study has investigated this question. Research suggests that in addition to satisfaction, another element of happiness is enjoying the simple things in life, like a beautiful sunny day or a good coffee. People with lots of money can purchase lots of positive life experiences, like exotic holidays and expensive meals, and as a result, they may enjoy everyday pleasures less.

Another issue is thought to be …

1.22

A = Alex, L = Luke

A: How was the workshop you went to last week?

L: Oh, yeah! The positive thinking workshop? Yes, well, I was really sceptical at first. I mean, how can someone teach you how to be positive? But I thought, why not give it a go?

A: And? Are you happier?

L: You know, it was better than I thought it would be … to start off with, we all had to think of one aspect of our lives that we want to improve. I chose the problem I had at work, you know, about that promotion? If I'd taken that extra training course, I would've been promoted! But because I hadn't taken the course, they gave the job to someone else.

A: Yeah, that was a tough situation.

L: So, when we had chosen our situation, we had to explain it to a partner and explain all the reasons why it was bad and why it was absolutely impossible to do anything about it.

A: OK …

L: And then I had to swap roles with my partner, and he had to pretend to be me and explain my situation to me as if it was his problem.

A: I see! But how does that help?

L: Well, that's the interesting part. Every time he said a negative thing, I had to say something positive.

A: Hmm … and did that work?

L: Well, it was a bit strange hearing someone talking about my problem. But after a while, it did make me think about it in a different way, and I came up with one or two ideas about how to change things.

A: And did they work?

L: I don't know yet – I'm going to try them out today!

A: Well, good luck – and tell me how it works out!

1.23

Although many people believe that money is the key to happiness, I don't really agree. Personally, I think family and friends are more important. There are two main reasons why I think this.

First of all, it's clear that a person can have lots of money and plenty of 'stuff' – they can own houses and cars and nice clothes – but in the end they are not necessarily happier. Let me give you an example. My friend's grandfather worked for a big financial company. He had a good position there and made a lot of money, but he spent all his time working and never had time to enjoy the money he made or spend any time with his family or friends. When he was old, no one came to visit to him, and he became very lonely and depressed.

My second reason is that money is very temporary but friends and family last a lifetime. For example, I once had a neighbour who had a lot of money, but one day her house burnt down in a fire. She lost all her possessions. Just like that. But friends and family are always there for you whether you are up or down. Relationships with other people are therefore more important to happiness, in my opinion, because they last longer. They aren't necessarily damaged by things like economic crises, or losing your job.

To sum up what I've been saying, I don't believe money can bring us happiness by itself. Spending too much time worrying about money just takes time away from your relationships with family and friends who are more likely to make you happy in the long run.

UNIT 5

Something in the water

1.26

RH = Radio host, J = Jenny

RH: This week is Stop Water Poverty week. My guest today is Jenny Bryant, spokesperson for the charity Water Watch. Jenny, first, please tell us generally what water poverty is, what Water Watch does and what appeal you're making this week.

J: Sure. Hello. There are 884 million people in the world living without access to clean water, and 5000 children die every day because of this. A lack of sufficient clean water to meet your basic needs is known as water poverty. Water Watch aims to prevent water poverty and provide communities worldwide with clean drinking water, but we can't do it without your help. As you said, this week is Stop Water Poverty week, and we are making an appeal to the public to donate money. Even a small donation can make a huge difference to people's lives and help in the fight against water poverty.

RH: What are some of the specific goals of Water Watch?

J: Well, Water Watch has several different goals, Lucas. The primary purpose of the organisation is to prevent water poverty, of course, but we also work to improve hygiene, education and the standard of living of the people in the regions we are active in.

RH: OK, so what does that mean in practical terms?

J: Well, for example, in many parts of Africa, girls don't get access to an education because they have to travel long distances in order to collect water for their families. And as adults, women spend up to 12 hours per day searching for water or looking after children who are sick because of diseases caused by water pollution. So we're investing money to increase the number of taps in these areas. The aim is that no villager should be further than half a mile from their nearest source of clean tap water and that no child should die from a disease that's easily preventable.

RH: And is there a reason why our attention is being drawn to this now with Stop Water Poverty week?

J: Yes, absolutely! Climate change has made a bad situation much worse. The amount of rainfall has been affected by rising temperatures so that many parts of the world see no rain from one season to another. Some areas are experiencing severe drought, and this can cause famine because farmers cannot grow enough food to feed all the people in the region. In areas that do experience a regular rainy season, there have been floods, and crops have been badly damaged. So famines can be caused by too little water or too much water. There's an urgent need to act quickly to end this crisis. That's where the public comes in …

RH: OK. I was just going to ask you what people can do to help.

J: Water Watch is a charity. It doesn't receive any government funding. The only money we get is from public donations. In order to prevent many, many more people from dying, we need to raise £25 million. This seems like a lot, but there are around 25.5 million households in the UK, and if every one of them donated only £1, we'd reach our target. We are also looking for more volunteers. We already have about 3500 volunteers around the world, but we need more! Training is offered to all our volunteers whether they are actively working in the affected countries or offering their services here. You can give a donation or sign up to volunteer on the Water Watch website, or call us at 0800 …

1.27

A: Wow, I was really moved by that documentary about water pollution. I think we should do something to help Pure Water Action. They're doing amazing work for people who don't have access to clean water.

B: Yeah, I agree. Let's get involved! I'd suggest donating some money to Pure Water Action.

A: Well, we don't have much money at the moment, so we wouldn't be able to donate very much. We could try to raise money, though.

B: OK. How would we do that?

A: Well, we could get sponsored by people to run a marathon or something and then send the money. Maybe that would take too long to arrange, though. There's always a jumble sale. You know, we could ask people to donate things like household items, books, clothes, unwanted gifts, that kind of thing, so that we can sell them. Then we send the money we make to Pure Water Action.

A: I'm not sure we could charge much for stuff if it wasn't in good condition. What if we do some volunteering instead?

B: Yeah. Volunteering's another option – and you'd feel more involved in the whole issue. Do you know much about what they expect you to do?

A: Not really, but we could find out.

B: Yeah. Let's look online …

1.28

My family – my husband, my five children and I – live in a small village in Ethiopia. There are about 30 people who live here. Most of the men are farmers. My day starts at about 5am. I get my eldest daughter, Ashmi, out of bed. Her job is to go and collect the water from our nearest waterstand, which is two kilometres away. It takes her about two hours because she often has to wait while other villagers get the water they need. When she gets home with the water, I can begin making the tea and the food for the family's breakfast. Ashmi is very young, so she can carry only 10 litres of water at a time. Sometimes I ask her to get extra water in the evening, especially if it hasn't rained and my husband needs water for washing. As for washing ourselves and our clothes, well, I go with Ashmi and the baby twice a week to the river and we wash there. It's not very clean, but we don't have enough water from the waterstand for all our needs.

UNIT 6

Living traditions

1.30

I = Interviewer

Interview 1

I: Excuse me. I'm doing some interviews for KT FM. Can I talk to you for a minute?

A: Yeah, sure. What about?

I: We want to know if people think it's important to maintain traditions.

A: Do you mean like traditional weddings and things like that?

Ir: Yes. Do you think traditions are an important part of our society?

A: Well, I think they used to be more important, but I think a lot of people, especially young people, don't really care about a lot of old traditions.

I: What about you, personally?

A: No, I'm not into all that traditional stuff, like formal weddings.

I: Why not?

A: They're not relevant to today's society. Young people aren't used to dressing formally and going through rituals that don't make much sense to them. We want to do things in more creative, interesting ways.

I: OK, thanks for sharing your opinion.

A: That's OK.

Interview 2

I: Do you think it's important for society to maintain traditions?

B: It depends on what you mean. We need traditions, but they can't stay the same. All traditions in all societies change over time, and I don't think we can expect new generations to keep doing things in exactly the same way they were done in the past.

I: So you don't object to changes in traditions like weddings, graduation ceremonies, or other traditional ceremonies?

B: No. I'm a university lecturer, and every year I love seeing what the students do at the graduation ceremony. They do some pretty non-traditional things, but the essence of the ceremony, the joy of it, stays the same. Each generation has to make the tradition relevant to themselves and to their lives.

I: Thank you for your comments.

B: You're welcome.

Interview 3

I: How important do you think it is for a society to maintain certain traditions from generation to generation?

C: I think that traditions are one of the things that give society, and groups within a society, a sense of history and continuity.

I: And do you think young people feel the same way? I mean, are they interested in maintaining traditions?

C: Some are, but for the most part, no. Look at the city history festival, which we've had every year in this city for the last 40 years. Young people aren't interested in it. They think it's boring. Nowadays, young people avoid getting involved in anything to do with history or traditions. It's a shame because the traditions will be lost soon.

I: Thank you for your opinions.

C: That's all right.

Interview 4

I: Do you think traditions are important and should stay the same, or is it OK for old traditions to change or disappear?

D: Well, I know that most people my age aren't really interested in keeping traditions, but I think it's important.

I: Why is that?

D: Traditions are important in order for our society to maintain its identity, and also so that there are connections and similarities between one generation and another. For example, if I were getting married, I would want to have a really traditional wedding, just like my parents' wedding, you know, with a white dress and dancing and everything. I suppose some people might think that was old-fashioned, but that's what I believe and that's what I'm used to.

I: Thanks for talking to me.

D: You're welcome.

🎧 1.34

Speaker 1

I had never thought about personal rituals, but I suppose I do have some. For example, I allow myself to eat exactly three biscuits while I watch the news in the evening. That's because I love biscuits, but I have to be careful not to eat the whole packet! What else? Oh, before I go to bed, I always have to plan out the next day. If I don't, I don't sleep well. I write down the things I have to do the next day. In the morning, I go over my list, and that makes me feel prepared for the day.

Speaker 2

Let's see. I do have some rituals, I think. I always go through my post while I eat breakfast, and I line it up in three piles – bin, urgent things and other things. Of course, I don't do anything about it, but at least I feel organised! Oh, and I always get a coffee at the same café on my way to work every day. I get the same thing every day – a large latte. I drink it on the way and I finish it just as I arrive at the office.

Speaker 3

My working life can be very varied, and every day can be different, but I do have one ritual. You might think it's a little strange, though! OK, here it is … I always put on all of my work clothes for the next day before I go to bed. Well, I mean I try on the clothes to see how they look. I don't sleep in them!

🎧 1.35

Well, let me see. Both photos show something connected to the idea of tradition. While the first photo is of a traditional meal, the second is of a traditional dance. One thing the photos have in common is that they both show people doing an activity together. In the first one it's a family, while in the second they might be from the local village or neighbourhood. The photos are similar because in both of them the people are enjoying themselves in a traditional way. In the first, they might be eating special food to celebrate a festival. In the second, it might be a dance they do on a particular day of the year. In contrast to the first photo, the second photo shows people in unusual costumes, which is probably a kind of traditional dress. The first photo is a more relaxed situation and the people are wearing their usual clothes.

I think these traditions are important to these people because they remind them of their history, either their family history or their national history. These traditions bring them together and remind them what they have in common with each other and with other people around them.

UNIT 7

Designed to please

RH = Radio host, **T** = Tony, **M** = Marianne

RH: OK … we're talking about celebrity designers. What do you think of celebrities who bring out their own ranges of products? We've got our next caller on the line, and it's Tony. Hi, Tony. What do you want to say?

T: Hi. I just wanted to say that I'm not a big fan of celebrity designers. I just don't really rate them very highly. These days, it seems that anyone whose career takes off decides to produce a line of clothes or a perfume. Look at people like Lady Gaga or Gwen Stefani. They might be great singers, and yes, they are trendsetters when it comes to fashion, but does that mean they can come up with good ideas? It doesn't. I also think that some of them are cheating the public in a way. I think a lot of the time they don't even draw up the designs themselves. Somebody else does it and the celebrity just puts their name on it.

RH: Thanks for your opinion, Tony. Next, we've got Marianna on the line. Marianna, I think you've got a different opinion.

M: Yes, I disagree with the last caller. I think it takes real talent to create new designs that catch on, and some celebrities have that talent. Look at Victoria Beckham, for example, or Penélope Cruz. Millions of young women look up to them for what they've achieved. When you're famous, you spend a lot of your time thinking about producing the right look, and that means you understand the effects that clothes have on people and you know about the latest trends. Even if a celebrity doesn't actually create a design, they choose it because it fits their style. And if you like that person's style, then you can look like that, too.

RH: OK. Well, thanks for all your calls. We'll hear some more of your opinions after the next song.

2.05

I've been here for nearly two years now. Before I started here, I'd been working in much smaller companies, and they didn't really have an annual performance review. You know, a meeting where they ask you how you feel about what you've done well. Here, though, they rate your performance every two years, and I'm really not looking forward to it. I've been talking to some of the others and I know they're going to ask me about things like leadership and showing initiative. I'm really not sure what I'm going to say in answer to that. I need to come up with some good ideas over the next few weeks.

There's a conference next week. I don't really want to go, but maybe it would be a good opportunity for me to show initiative. I'm not sure how, though. There must be lots of ways. I need to think of a few and then go to my boss with some suggestions.

And the following week we've got to attract new clients. But how? The managers really didn't give us very much guidance on that. I'm sure they're waiting to see how we do on that task just before our performance reviews. So I need to come up with something good. But what?

UNIT 8

A fair deal

2.07

Good morning, and welcome to today's lecture about fair trade. I'd like to start by saying a little about what the fair-trade movement is, before looking at its history, its successes and criticisms of the system.

2.08

Fair trade is an attempt to avoid exploitation and inequality in business between the developed and the developing world. The developed world relies on products from developing countries and spends huge amounts of money on products like tea, coffee and sugar. The companies selling these products make plenty of money, but very often the people who actually produce them live in poverty. In other words, the farmers who grow coffee or tea only receive a very small part of the price you pay in the supermarket. Buying fair-trade products means that the people who produce them receive a fair price.

The next point I'd like to discuss is the change in focus of fair trade. From the 1960s until the 1980s, fair trade was mostly about buying handmade objects, such as traditional fabrics or jewellery. However, by the 80s, many of these objects started to seem old-fashioned. At the same time, international prices of products like coffee and tea were falling, making life very difficult for the producers. Most fair-trade organisations shifted their focus to agricultural products, and today, fair-trade products include not only tea and coffee but also cocoa, honey, bananas, sugar and cotton.

Now, let's move on to how fair trade works. You are probably familiar with the way fair-trade products are labelled. Each has a symbol that shows that they have been approved by an organisation, so the buyer knows they are making a fair-trade purchase. The most familiar to most people is the organisation simply called Fairtrade. The key point about the symbols is that they allow fair-trade products to be easily identified in supermarkets. Customers don't have to wonder which coffee is fair trade and which isn't, and they don't have to go to a special shop. They can buy their fair-trade coffee at the same time as they buy their other groceries. This has made fair-trade products much more popular, and the organisation works with 1.3 million people in more than 70 developing countries.

Let's turn our attention now to some of the criticisms of fair trade. Producers may benefit in the short term, but some economists say that fair trade actually makes the situation worse in the long term. They argue that fair-trade products introduce a high price for goods such as coffee. This encourages the producers to grow more, so then there is too much coffee, and the price generally drops. This makes life even harder for the coffee producers.

Now, I'd like to look in detail …

2.10

If we want our society to be fair, we have to help poor people. I believe this for three main reasons.

First of all, a fair society is one where everyone has enough food. Some people live on very little money every day and they can't afford to buy enough food for their families. The government should provide benefits so that no one goes hungry. We should all have the right to enough food.

Second, we should remember that anyone can lose their job and then be unemployed. In a fair society we take care of the poor because we know that one day we could be in that situation ourselves. We should help people now so that we can get help when we need it.

Finally, we all have a responsibility to help the next generation. Many children are born into poor families. In a fair society we should give them the chance for a good education. In that way, the society of tomorrow will be better off than the society of today.

🔊 2.12

The problem is that the rents in her city are very high. She complains that the rents go up every year and soon she won't be able to afford to live in the city.

This problem is very common in many cities. In my opinion, there are a couple of ways to solve this problem. First, landlords need to stop raising the rent so much. I think it would be good to limit their increases to just one or two per cent per year. Also, they should have to explain why they want to increase the rent. If they don't have a good reason, the rent should stay the same.

Secondly, what the local authorities should do is use taxes from rich people to provide low-rent housing for people who are on low incomes. Then people can save up enough money to buy their own homes, instead of spending everything on high rents.

These are two possible ways to solve the problem of high rents in the city.

UNIT 9

Competitive edge

 2.13

M = Moderator, Dr C = Dr Carson, Dr B = Dr Banks

M: Hello, everyone, and welcome to the third session of the Conference on Healthy Children. Our two guest speakers this morning are Dr Jane Banks and Dr Leo Carson. They are both educational psychologists, and they will present opposing theories on the effects of competition on children and adolescents. After their presentations, they will take questions. Dr Carson?

Dr C: Good morning. We all know that competition is a fact of life, but is competition healthy? Recently there has been an increase in the number of studies that have led me to conclude that competition is terrible, especially for children. Think about it: in our society, personal value is measured by how many competitions a person wins – in sports, for jobs, to get into the best universities. Schools award gold stars or other prizes for top marks in exams and tests, so even getting an education becomes a competition. Very few people can be winners, and if you are not a winner, what are you? A loser. Competition makes children anxious and unable to concentrate well. 'Winners' become more aggressive, and they often feel ashamed or angry when they don't win. 'Losers' become discouraged and often stop trying because they feel that they won't win anyway. The solution? We need to experiment with ways to teach children to work *with* others, not against them. Cooperative games and projects produce feelings of high self-esteem and the satisfaction of being part of a group. Thank you.

Dr B: Good morning, everyone. My colleague has some legitimate concerns about competition, and I agree that there are some negative effects when competition is taken to extremes. However, I would argue that there is, in fact, healthy competition and that it is necessary for children to grow into well-rounded adults. As Dr Carson mentioned, competition is a fact of life. We compete in sports, for jobs – even for the person we want to marry! While it's true that competition can produce anxiety and damage self-esteem in some young people, there is no proof that competition is bad for the majority of people. In fact, a number of psychologists have conducted research and recorded results that indicate that when children are not allowed to experience failure, they respond very negatively to failure later on. Competition helps young people develop important life skills such as problem-solving, recognising strengths and weaknesses, creating strategies and, perhaps most importantly, knowing how to win and how to lose. Thank you.

🔊 2.16

Speaker 1:

I read an interesting study on how young adults' success in both sport and education is affected by the amount of peer support they receive. When young adults receive praise and encouragement from their teammates or classmates, there's an increase in self-esteem, which results in higher motivation, which in turn, results in higher achievement. The conclusion is that praise has a positive effect, even when the person's performance wasn't great.

Speaker 2:

I'm not convinced. There are plenty of other studies that indicate the opposite, which is that excessive praise has no effect, or even a negative effect, on performance. We all know when we've done well, and if we haven't, then having people say 'Well done!' is actually insulting. There is also a theory that too much praise results in decreased effort. If people are praised for basically just turning up, then they start to think that's good enough and they stop trying to improve.

UNIT 10

Risky business

 2.21

N = Nicola, J = Jemma

N: Hey, Jemma, did you hear that David Blaine almost got electrocuted?

J: Nicola, he's an illusionist! He's really good at making people think he's risking his life when he isn't.

N: No, this really happened! Here's the video. You've got to see it!

J: OK, OK, play it.

N: Look, that's a million volts passing through him. What do you think?

J: It couldn't have been real. He must have practised a lot of times before they filmed it. And what's that metal suit he's wearing?

N: I don't know. He looked scared to me. I'm going to find some photos of it.

J: OK, but I think it was all fake. He might have found a way to just get the electricity to go right around him.

N: Look! Here's a photo after the stunt. See? He needs help walking! And I heard that the doctors at the hospital found that he'd developed an irregular heartbeat. Look at how exhausted he is!

J: I don't know, but I don't want to see the photo. Look, I've got to go.

128

2.22

R1 = Reporter 1, R2 = Reporter 2

R1: Wait 'til you see this next clip, just in from Jane McCormack. Here we go …

R2: What's that guy doing?

R1: Well, apparently he managed to ascend to an altitude of 16,000 feet in a deck chair by tying balloons to it.

R2: Are you kidding?! Why would anyone want to do that?! Look, he even took his lunch with him!

R1: Who knows why people do the things they do? He may have always wanted to be a pilot, but couldn't get a licence.

R2: So he decided to fly a deck chair. Why did he have a pellet gun?

R1: No idea. He might have wanted to shoot at birds. Stay tuned for the story of Larry and his deck chair, right after the commercial break.

2.23

In general, I would much rather do something quiet than an exciting extreme sport. There are three main reasons for that. First, I find quieter activities much more relaxing than extreme sports because of the danger involved in activities such as mountain climbing. Unlike some people, I don't like the idea of putting my life at risk for no reason. Relaxation for me means reading a book or watching TV, not risking serious injury. The second reason I tend to prefer quieter activities is that my job is very active – I work outdoors with horses. I might have had a hard week, so on my days off, I like to watch films or meet friends, and I don't really have the energy for extreme sports. Finally, quieter activities appeal to me more because they reduce the amount of stress in my life. Some people like the excitement that more stress brings, but I don't. I much prefer to do activities that don't cause me more stress.

UNIT 11

Through the lens

2.24

J = Jack, P = Penny

J: Hello, and welcome to *Click*, the number 1 photography podcast, with all the latest news from the world of photography, and this is Episode 23, with me, Jack Wood, as usual.

P: And me, Penny Green. So, what have you been up to this week, Jack?

J: It's been such a busy week, Penny. I did a very special wedding shoot, and I'm going to be talking a little bit more about that later, and I attended the opening of an exhibition of local photographers. Wow, I was blown away by the level of talent we have in our local area!

P: I know! It's easy to think that photography these days is all selfies and snapshots on social media, isn't it? But some people are really putting a lot of effort into their work. Did you have a favourite?

J: There were lots of great shots in the exhibition, including some fantastic landscapes of the local area, but I think the one that really impressed me the most was a picture by a local woman, Judy Anderson. It's a portrait of a local homeless man. In the foreground you can see his dog, and on the left-hand side a small sign. The man, the dog and the sign are all in focus, so you can see them clearly and that's where your eye is drawn. In the background, there are people moving around, but it's out of focus, so you can't really tell what's happening. That means they don't take your attention away from the subject – this man who lives on the streets. The photographer has managed to capture his expression and, for me, it makes me wonder about what his story might be, where he came from, how he ended up on the streets. It also says a lot about the recent economic problems that we've been facing around here, so it's like a piece of local history.

P: That sounds really interesting, and I believe that exhibition runs until the end of the month, so go along to the Mayweather Gallery to see some great examples of local work. Now, Jack, tell us about this wedding. I thought you said you'd never do another wedding.

J: Ha. I did, but this one was a little different.

2.25

K = Kumiko, B = Becky

K: Hi, Becky. What've you got there?

B: Oh, just a couple of photos for an article I'm writing. I need to choose one to go with the article, which is called 'The Art of Photography'. I'm just comparing them and trying to choose.

K: Well, the two photos are alike because they're photos of groups. The first is a family portrait and looks like it's been taken by a professional, while the second shows someone taking a selfie with their friends. Everyone's taking selfies these days!

B: Yeah, that's right. And I talk about the selfie phenomenon in my article. Another similarity is that the people are posing for the camera and smiling in both photos. However, maybe the first situation is a little formal for my article, whereas the second situation is much more informal. The people in the second photo seem more natural than in the first, and that would fit with the article well. Another point of difference is the reason they're having their photo taken. The first group of people probably want a photo they can put on the wall at home. In contrast, the second group want a photo they can send to friends or put online to show people what a good time they're having. I think the second one's going to suit the article better, isn't it?

K: Yes, I think so. Both photos are similar in that the people want to record this moment in their lives, but the second one is more modern. It'll appeal to younger people, unlike the first one. I'd go for the photo of people taking a selfie.

2.28

Hi, this is Erica. I just wanted to see if you could send a memo around to everyone about the images for the website. We've decided to do things a little bit differently this year, so instead of having a professional photographer, we're going to get everyone to do a selfie, you know, to give the website a much more modern feel. They need to take a shot of themselves in a situation that means something to them – in the kitchen, cooking or out on their bike, that kind of thing. And they should email it to you, so you can check it before we use it. In addition to that, we need them to write a few sentences about themselves, their interests and hobbies, just to give the website a human face. Can you ask them to do that, please? Oh, and we need everything before the 22nd of the month. Thanks! Bye.

2.29

Mrs V = Mrs Vaughan, P = Paul

Mrs V: Thanks for coming in today, Paul. I just wanted to give you some feedback on your presentation the other day. Now, don't worry! The first thing to say is that everyone thought you did a very good job, particularly since you had such a limited time to prepare.

P: OK … thanks.

Mrs V: And we thought you had some very good ideas. We liked your suggestions for increasing sales. You've given us something to think about. What did you think about the presentation?

P: Um … well … I thought it went OK, you know. I mean, I did my best and I really didn't have very much time to prepare for it because the last speaker dropped out.

Mrs V: Yes, I understand that. Now, I'd like to move onto one or two ideas to improve your presentations in the future. There's always room for improvement, and I've made a few notes. First of all, you seemed pretty nervous. It's important to relax and be confident, you know.

P: That was because of the rush to get things done. It was Damian's fault, really. He was giving the presentation, then he felt ill, and so I had to quickly …

Mrs V: Yes, as I said, we understand that. Still, just try to relax a little bit more next time. Besides that, there were one or two problems with the technology. I know computers can be tricky, but you didn't seem to have any idea how to solve the problems.

P: It's that IT woman, Sylvia. She never explains things to me, and I keep asking her for more help. I don't think I should have to work it out for myself.

Mrs V: Well, I know Sylvia is very busy with a lot of people. All I'm saying is that I'd like you to be more familiar with the computer next time. I think that's all. Thanks again for coming to see me, and I look forward to your next presentation.

P: Oh, OK. Great. Thanks.

UNIT 12

Bright lights, big city

2.30

G = Guide

Extract 1

G: You're going to want to take some photos here, I imagine. It's one of the most colourful areas in London. It's called Neal's Yard, and as you can see, all of the windows and doors, and some of the buildings, are painted bright, happy colours. I think it looks a bit like some photos I've seen of Mexico, with all those brilliant colours!

Extract 2

G: Brixton Market. The market started up in the late 19th century, and today it's the best place to buy African and Caribbean goods and produce. A lot of African and Caribbean immigrants live in this area, and apart from the market, there are lots of nice restaurants and shops where you can get things from those countries.

Extract 3

G: Yes, that's the great thing about London; you can visit several countries in different parts of the world all in the same day! It's almost lunchtime now. Would you like to have some of the best Chinese food in the world? This is the place for it – Chinatown, London!

Extract 4

G: I'm glad you liked the Chinese food. OK, big change of scenery here. This area is called Southall. As you probably know, London has a very large Indian population, and many people from India live in this area.

2.31

G = Guide

G: You're going to want to take some photos here, I imagine. It's one of the most colourful areas in London. It's called Neal's Yard, and as you can see, all of the windows and doors, and some of the buildings, are painted bright, happy colours. I think it looks a bit like some of the photos I've seen of Mexico, with all those brilliant colours!

A: Yes, it does kind of remind me of Mexico, with all the little shops and bright colours.

B: I don't know. The colours do look like what you'd see in Mexico, but the architecture is completely different, of course. You're right that it doesn't really look like London, but not that much like Mexico, either.

[…]

G: We're in a very different area of London now, called Brixton. I think you'll very much enjoy seeing Brixton Market. As you can see, it's an enormous street market …

B: Oh, that's amazing. What did you say it's called?

G: Brixton Market. The market started up in the late 19th century, and today it's the best place to buy African and Caribbean goods and produce. A lot of African and Caribbean immigrants live in this area, and apart from the market, there are lots of nice restaurants and shops where you can get things from those countries.

[…]

A: Oh, look at this! Looks like we've travelled from Africa to China!

G: Yes, that's the great thing about London; you can visit several countries in different parts of the world all in the same day! It's almost lunchtime now. Would you like to have some of the best Chinese food in the world? This is the place for it – Chinatown, London!

B: Great! Of course, we have amazing Chinese food in LA, but we've got to try Chinese food in London, right?

A: Yeah, sounds good!

[…]

G: I'm glad you liked the Chinese food. OK, big change of scenery here. This area is called Southall. As you probably know, London has a very large Indian population, and many people from India live in this area.

A: It's so interesting 'cause LA is a pretty international city – a lot of people from China and all over Latin America, especially, but London seems to have folks from everywhere! In this area, I feel like I'm actually in India!

G: Of course, India was a British colony for many years, so people from India have been coming to live here for a long time. There are also lots of families from Pakistan, Bangladesh and other Asian countries.

B: I think that's what makes London such a fascinating city. Every area is different, with different food, different languages, everything.

G: Oh, yeah. Name just about any country, and there are people here from there!

....

2.34

A: Whenever I think of cities of the future, I think of some of the futuristic cities that already exist or that some countries will be building in a few years. The main characteristic of all of these cities is that they are environmentally responsible. One example is Pangyo in South Korea. It's an eco-friendly planned community near Seoul. It has lots of green areas and it is extremely energy efficient. I think Pangyo and communities like it will be the models for the cities of the future. The emphasis is going to be on creating cities that are carbon neutral and use natural sources of energy like the sun and the wind. This has to happen if we want to continue living on the Earth. We all like modern conveniences like air-conditioning and cars; nevertheless, if we don't make our cities greener they may become uninhabitable in the near future.

B: By the 23rd century, I think most city dwellers will be living below ground. I don't say that because I think it's a good idea, but I think all of the world's biggest cities will be too crowded and there'll just be nowhere else to go. I imagine that future cities will have enormous areas that serve different purposes. So, for example, there might be a large central area with office buildings, shopping centres and things like that. There will be tunnels that go from the business centre to different areas where people live. I'd like to think some cities above ground will stay as they are in spite of the fact that people no longer live there. These cities could become memorials to the past. Maybe people will even go on holiday there and talk about how they didn't like the climate or the food, or how strange life in the past was!

C: My idea of a city of the future is really just the same as a city of the present day – except there'll be lots more people, more cars and fewer green places to escape to. I honestly don't think that 200 years into the future we will be driving flying cars or living in underwater cities. However, I think the spaces we live and work in will definitely change. Gardens may disappear completely, and more and more people will be moving into small houses and flats. The biggest change is going to be in rural areas. In fact, there won't be any rural areas anymore, just a lot of mega-cities with suburbs between them. Farms are going to disappear, so all of our food will be artificial. I'm really glad I won't be around to see it!

....

2.35

I live in Dallas, which is already a very modern city. Of course, lots of things will be changing between now and the 22nd century, mostly because of new technologies that we can't even imagine yet. However, I think that many things will be pretty similar to the way they are now. I'm going to talk about three areas: entertainment and going out, architecture and transportation.

I'm starting with architecture because that relates to the whole appearance and lifestyle of the city. We already have lots of skyscrapers in downtown Dallas, and I believe those buildings will still exist in the next century because they're very functional. I mean, there are lots of buildings still around from the last century, right? I think the main change will be that more and more people will want to live in the city, and as a result, the downtown area will get much bigger. The new buildings will probably all be built from environmentally friendly materials. I think they'll renovate old buildings, so they will be much greener. I'm sure that houses and apartments will all be 'green' and 'smart' by the 22nd century, but apart from that, I don't think there will be any huge changes in architecture.

The area that I imagine may have the least changes is entertainment and going out. The main changes in this area will definitely be related to new technologies. For example, movies might be holograms so that you feel that you're actually in the movie instead of just watching it on a screen. Sort of like 3D but even more real! In spite of the new technologies, I don't think people are really going to change what they like to do for entertainment. People will still be going to the movies, going out to eat and go dancing or to listen to music.

The area of transportation is where I believe the biggest changes may happen. We already have a light rail system in Dallas, but I think it will grow to cover a larger area, and it will become much faster. Nevertheless, I think people will still have cars; people in Texas love their cars! But I imagine that car designs are going to change a lot. The other day I saw a prototype of a car that can fold up to fit into a very small parking space! I'm also sure that cars will be completely automatic by then, so drivers won't actually drive. They'll just programme their destination and the car will drive itself. Finally, there will be no need for oil or gasoline because all vehicles will run on natural resources.

Audioscript 131

WORKBOOK ANSWER KEY

Unit 1

Section 1
Exercise A
1 Text 1: d
  Text 2: a
2 Text 1: b
  Text 2: a, c
Exercise B
1 F 2 F 3 T 4 T 5 F 6 T

Section 2
Exercise A
1 social group
2 life goals
3 family values
4 sense
5 family background
6 social status

Section 3
Exercise A
1 Lisa Adams
2 Lisa Adams
3 Mark Owens
4 Lisa Adams
5 Mark Owens
6 Mark Owens
Exercise B
6 I couldn't agree more.
1 Yes and no.
4 In a sense, you're right.
5 Well, yes, to a certain extent, but …
2 I'm sorry, but I just don't think that's true.
3 I'm afraid I can't agree.

Section 4
Exercise A
✓ 1, 3
What's right?
I had to wear a uniform when I was at school.
Exercise B
1 was wearing
2 didn't have
3 did have
4 didn't look like
5 had never worn
6 put on
7 did feel

Section 5
Exercise A
1 V 2 V 3 N 4 A 5 A 6 A 7 N

Exercise B
1 make sense of
2 sense of humour
3 sensible
4 common sense
5 sensitive
6 sense
7 sensitive

Section 6
Exercise A
1 P 2 P 3 PP
What's right?
I was always taking pictures to express myself.
Exercise B
1 I used to try to be part of the 'cool' group.
2 I would always do what my friends told me to do.
3 I was always behaving irresponsibly.
4 I never used to have a strong sense of my own identity.
5 I would never feel confident.
Exercise C
1 would work/used to work
2 would never help/never used to help
3 was always doing/always used to do/would always do
4 was always making sure/always used to make sure/would always make sure
5 would never take time off/never used to take time off

SkillsStudio
Exercise A
1 there are many
2 more than one
3 three
Exercise B
1 F 2 C 3 A 4 E 5 D
Exercise C
1 d 2 c 3 a 4 b 5 b 6 a
Exercise D
Students' own answers

Unit 2

Section 1
Exercise A
1 the economy
2 the service industry
3 trade
4 communications

Exercise B
Speaker 1 e, d, a
Speaker 2 c, a, d
Speaker 3 d, b, e
Exercise C
1 well
2 kind of
3 like
4 I mean
5 you know

Section 2
Exercise A
1 d 2 b 3 f 4 a 5 e 6 c
Exercise B
1 multinational
2 economic growth
3 dominate
4 profits
5 regional
6 facilitates

Section 3
Exercise A
1 have
2 are you seeing
3 think
4 are
Exercise B
My girlfriend and I had (1) ~~seen~~ **been seeing** each other for three years when her company offered her a job in the Shanghai office. It was (2) ~~being~~ an amazing opportunity, so she moved there last September, and we (3) ~~are not seeing~~ **haven't seen** each other very often since then. It isn't (4) ~~being~~ ideal, but there are a lot of ways to keep in touch. And we've just got engaged, so I (5) ~~'m thinking~~ **think** that old saying, 'absence makes the heart grow fonder', might just be true!
What's right?
I am/I'm thinking of applying for a transfer to the Stockholm office next year.

Section 4
Exercise A
1 c 2 e 3 a 4 b 5 f 6 d
Exercise B
a 2e, 3a, 5f
b 1c, 4b, 6d
Exercise C
1 a 2 b 3 b 4 a 5 a 6 b 7 b

What's right?
Multinational companies are becoming more and more dominant.

Section 5

Exercise A
1 support
2 promote
3 campaign
4 generate
5 value
6 sustain
7 participate
8 boost

Exercise B
1 a 2 b 3 b 4 c 5 c 6 a
7 b 8 c

Section 6

Exercise A
1 Dear Mr Moreno,
2 Thank you for your interest in
3 Could you let me know
4 You will be required to attend
5 I look forward to meeting you
6 Regards
7 Klaus Steinmann, Director, globe4u

Exercise B
(1) ~~Hi Klaus!~~ **Dear Mr Steinmann**,
(2) ~~Thanks so much~~ **Thank you** for your email.
I would prefer to work in June rather than August and I'm available to come in to discuss the work on 5th May at 10 am. (3) ~~Just tell me~~ **Could you let me know** if there's any preparation that I can do for the meeting?
(4) ~~See you then.~~ **I look forward to meeting you**.
(5) ~~With love~~, **Regards**,
(6) ~~Miguel~~ **Miguel Moreno**

SkillsStudio

Exercise A
c

Exercise B
2 The harm that tourism can do to the environment.
1 What an ethical tourist is.
4 How to be an ethical tourist.
3 The harm that tourism can do to local communities.

Exercise C
How can tourism harm the environment?
1 There are more carbon emissions from increased air travel.
2 Tourists damage local environment by dropping rubbish.
3 Tourism uses too many natural resources, such as water.
How can tourism harm local communities?
1 Local businesses can't compete with multinational companies.
2 People are forced out of their homes to make way for tourism.
How can we become ethical tourists?
1 Use ethical transportation (trains, boats, bicycles) if possible.
2 Leave excess packaging at home.
3 Make sure your travel operator is ethical.

Exercise D
1 b 2 c 3 a 4 f 5 d 6 e

Exercise E
1 a 2 b 3 a 4 c 5 b

Exercise F
Students' own answers

Unit 3

Section 1

What's right?
She told us she had to work late yesterday.

Exercise A
2 had never tried
3 couldn't believe/might meet
4 had to take
5 shouldn't charge
6 would probably never be

Exercise B
1 would/will
2 might
3 couldn't
4 had planned
5 would
6 could
7 has to/had to
8 could
9 should

Section 2

Exercise A
1 fortune
2 record
3 scandal
4 invention
5 company
6 a cure
7 novel

Exercise B
a 6 b 4 c 2 d 7 e 5 f 3 g 1

Section 3

Exercise A
1 b 2 c 3 a

Exercise B
1 b; Times Education Supplement
2 b; childhood obesity
3 a; He thinks that one part of the government is investing in food education and healthy school lunches while the other part is promoting junk food and allowing it to be sold near schools.
4 b; TV chef Jamie Oliver
5 c; 16th May
6 a; He believes that it's important to teach children how to cook because it's an essential life skill that can help their future health and wellbeing.

Section 4
1 a 2 a 3 a 4 b 5 b 6 a
7 b 8 a

Section 5

What's right?
They said she would never be famous but years later she became a big star.

Exercise A
1 O 2 O 3 O 4 N 5 O

Exercise B
a 1, 5 b 3 c 2 d 4

Exercise C
She said that Jay Z was never going to be a successful rapper.

Exercise D
1 she's probably not going to win/she probably wasn't going to win
2 wants/wanted
3 she's wearing/she was wearing
4 dreams/dreamed
5 isn't/wasn't
6 would never be
7 will cry/would cry

Section 6

Exercise A
1 Actually, that's not what I meant.
2 Fame isn't easy, put it that way.
3 Maybe I'm not making myself clear.
4 Perhaps I should rephrase that.
5 What I meant was, it's complicated.
6 What I'm trying to say is, it's a problem.

Exercise B
1 e 2 a 3 d 4 b 5 c 6 f

Workbook answer key 133

SkillsStudio

Exercise A
1 Winston Churchill
2 Sherlock Holmes, King Arthur, Winston Churchill

Exercise B
1 confusion
2 fictional
3 treasure
4 inspired

Exercise C
1 e 2 d 3 a 4 b

Exercise D
1 f 2 h 3 a 4 g 5 e 6 b

Exercise E
Students' own answers

Unit 4

Section 1

Exercise A
1 F 2 F 3 F 4 T 5 F 6 T

Exercise B
a 3 b 2 c 1 d 7 e 10 f 9 g 6
h 8 i 5 j 11 k 12 l 4

Exercise C
1 c, e, i,
2 d, f, k
3 b, h, j
4 a, g, l

Section 2

Exercise A
Nouns: appreciation, contentment, enjoyment, happiness, pleasure, satisfaction, wealth
Adjectives: content, happy, pleasant, wealthy
Verbs: appreciate, enjoy, satisfy

Exercise B
1 enjoy
2 wealthy
3 satisfaction/pleasure
4 content/happy
5 appreciate
6 happiness/pleasure/contentment
7 pleasant

Section 3

Exercise A
1 when
2 why
3 how
4 where
5 what

Exercise B
1 b 2 c 3 a 4 c 5 b

Exercise C
1 what
2 why
3 when
4 where
5 how

What's right?
I don't know where he went.

Section 4

Exercise A
1 pessimistic
2 depressed
3 state of well-being
4 optimistic
5 in a good mood
6 distracted
7 emotions
8 focused

Exercise B
1 distracted, focused
2 optimistic, pessimistic
3 emotions, state of well-being
4 depressed, in a good mood

Section 5

Exercise A
1 present simple
2 present simple
3 past simple
4 past perfect

Exercise B
1 would have cried, had watched
2 sees, will/'ll tell
3 were, would/'d be
4 had told, could have helped
5 have, help
6 don't take, will/'ll regret

What's right?
If you had/'d told me he was depressed, I would have called him.

Exercise C
Sian: What are you reading?
Lisa: It's an article called *The Key to Happiness*. I (1) **will/'ll** read you some sections if you're interested.
Sian: All right.
Lisa: OK, well, it says that if you (2) ~~wanted~~ **want** to be happy, then be a good friend because, strong relationships are the key to contentment.
Sian: I think that's true. I love spending time with my friends and if I didn't have them, I (3) ~~will~~ **would** be very unhappy.
Lisa: Me, too. It also says that people are usually more satisfied with life if they (4) ~~did~~ **do** a job that they love.
Sian: Yeah, that's true, too. Do you remember last year when I was doing that office job I hated? If I hadn't got a new job in the music store, I (5) ~~will~~ **would/'d** still be miserable.
Lisa: Hmm, and probably the reason I'm not that happy right now is because I don't have a job I enjoy. I think if I (6) ~~have~~ **had** a job that I loved, then I would be more content.
Sian: I totally agree. So, stop reading that article and check out the job listings instead!
Lisa: Good point!

Section 6

Exercise A
1 Your donation was so generous.
2 I would also like to express my gratitude for …
3 Thanks again from all of us here.
4 I am writing to thank you for …

Exercise B
1 I am writing to thank you for
2 Your donation was so generous
3 I would also like to express my gratitude for
4 Thanks again from all of us here.

SkillsStudio

Exercise A
1 pessimistic
2 optimistic
3 optimistic

Exercise B
1 23, 69
2 Speaker 3

Exercise C
1 b 2 e 3 d 4 a 5 c 6 f

Exercise D
1 high
2 agrees
3 declining
4 doesn't say
5 low
6 disagrees
7 increasing
8 doesn't say
9 high
10 agrees
11 declining
12 agrees

Exercise E
1 a 2 a 3 b 4 b 5 c 6 d

Exercise F
Students' own answers

Unit 5

Section 1

Exercise A
1 e 2 d 3 a 4 c 5 b

What's right?
Dozens of homes were damaged by the flood.

Exercise B
1 was first built
2 was awarded
3 has been transformed
4 are being added
5 is now called
6 was designed
7 hadn't been abandoned
8 was redesigned
9 has been visited
10 is still being used

Exercise C
1 is located
2 was built
3 was given
4 are painted
5 has recently been decorated / was recently decorated
6 has recently been planted / was recently planted
7 are always served
8 had been cleared away

Section 2
Exercise A
1 c 2 a 3 b
Exercise B
1 a 2 b 3 a 4 b 5 a 6 a

Section 3
Exercise A
c
Exercise B
1 range from ... to ...
5 market ... as ...
2 to make ... worth ...
3 put up against ...
4 as much about ... as ...
Exercise C
1 **ranges from** €2.00 **to** €3.50
2 **market** bottled water **as** something
3 **as much about** helping the planet **as** our own convenience
4 **put** bottled water **up against** other products
5 **To make** a simple bottle of water **worth** that kind of money

Section 4
Exercise A
1 collecting
2 putting
3 displaying
4 is
5 giving
6 take
7 hand

Section 5
Exercise A
1 *for* + gerund
2 *in order (not) to* + base form
3 *so as (not) to* + base form
4 *so (that)* + (pro)noun + clause
5 *to* + base form
Exercise B
1 for
2 to / in order to / so as to
3 for
4 To / In order to / So as to
5 so / so that
6 So as not to / In order not to

What's right?
Everyone must drink water to stay healthy.

Section 6
Exercise A
1 water pollution
2 famine
3 hygiene
4 flood
5 water poverty
6 drought
7 disease
8 climate change
Exercise B
1 water poverty
2 water pollution
3 hygiene
4 diseases
5 climate change
6 floods
7 droughts
8 famine

SkillsStudio
Exercise A
2 Water footprinting – a new approach to water conservation
Exercise B
2 The total volume of fresh water used to produce goods and services
Exercise C
1 ...most of us know the concept of the carbon footprint.
2 There is, however, another global environmental issue that requires urgent international attention: water resources.
3 As a way of drawing society's attention to the nature and scale of the problem, scientists have developed the concept of the 'water footprint'.
4 Water footprints can be calculated for specific goods and products.
5 Water footprints have also been calculated for each nation, with the result that we can compare international water consumption.
Exercise D
1 c 2 b 3 a 4 c 5 a
Exercise E
Students' own answers

Unit 6

Section 1
Exercise A
1 'm used to
2 get used to
3 got used to
4 get used to
5 wasn't used to
6 got used to

Exercise B
1 am/'m getting used to
2 to get used to
3 am/'m used to
4 am/'m used to
5 to get used to
6 am/'m used to
What's right?
I'm used to travelling for my job.

Section 2
Exercise A
1 b 2 a 3 b
Exercise B
Speaker 1 b
Speaker 2 d
Speaker 3 c
Speaker 4 a

Section 3
Exercise A
1 fresher
2 initiation
3 mascot
4 high-ranking
5 ritual
6 symbolic
Exercise B
1 ritual
2 initiation
3 symbolic
4 fresher
5 mascot
6 high-ranking
Exercise C
1 freshers
2 initiation
3 ritual
4 mascot
5 high-ranking
6 symbolic

Section 4
Exercise A
1 Did he invite you to go to his graduation party?
2 I advise you not to be late for morning exercises.
3 The principal ordered the students to be quiet.
4 They expect the freshers to arrive on time for the ceremony.
Exercise B
1 us not to worry
2 us to review
3 us to get
4 us to use
5 us not to bring
6 us to come / us to go
What's right?
They even ask us not to work too hard.

Section 5
Exercise A
1 e 2 d 3 f 4 c 5 g 6 b
7 h 8 a
Exercise B
1 go through
2 plan out
3 put on
4 writing down
5 go over
6 cross off
7 line up
8 clean out

Section 6
Exercise A
The following sentences should be underlined.
I just returned from a walk in the woods, every New Year's Day I put on my walking boots and walk in the same place.
I like it, it means I go back there every year on the anniversary of his death and remember him.
I have a personal ritual for when I am worried, I buy a balloon.
This reminds them that I'm thinking about them, it reminds them that they aren't going through life alone.
Now, every morning, I remember my promise, I put on my ring.
I don't have any rituals, now I'll try to start one.
Exercise B
Suggested answers. (Note that the semi-colon, the full stop and the word *and* could be used in any of the sentences, but the following answers show the ways to use all the options.)
1 I just returned from a walk in the woods. Every New Year's Day I put on my hiking boots and walk in the same place.
2 I like it, because it means I go back there every year on the anniversary of his death and remember him.
3 I have a personal ritual for when I am worried; I buy a balloon.
4 This reminds them that I'm thinking about them, and it reminds them that they aren't going through life alone.
5 Now, every morning, I remember my promise when I put on my ring.
6 I don't have any rituals, but now I'll try to start one.

SkillsStudio
Exercise A
1 Monkey Buffet Festival (C)
2 Cheese-Rolling Festival (A)
3 La Tomatina (E)
4 Up Helly Aa (B)
5 Konaki Sumo Festival (D)

Exercise B
1 d 2 h 3 f 4 c 5 a 6 e
7 b 8 g
Exercise C
1 c 2 h 3 b 4 f 5 e
Exercise D
1 Monkey Buffet Festival, Thailand, A large picnic is held for the many monkeys that live locally.
2 Cheese-Rolling Festival, England, Competitors race to see who can catch a large round cheese as it rolls down a hill.
3 La Tomatina, Spain, A large food fight happens where people throw overripe tomatoes at each other.
4 Up Helly Aa, the island of Shetland, Scotland, There is a parade with torches and a boat is then burned. Then there is entertainment in venues across the town.
5 Konaki Sumo, Japan, Two Sumo wrestlers hold two babies. The first baby to cry is the winner.
Exercise E
Students' own answers

Unit 7

Section 1
Exercise A
1 top-quality
2 template
3 manufacture
4 miniature
5 unique
6 innovative
7 affordable
8 personalised
Exercise B
1 unique
2 innovative
3 template
4 miniature
5 manufacture
6 affordable
7 top quality
8 personalised

Section 2
Exercise A
1 c 2 f 3 a 4 b 5 d 6 e
What's right?
He designs affordable, comfortable children's clothes.
Exercise B
1 Dolce and Gabbana's
2 girls', boys'
3 company's closing
4 designers' mothers'
5 designer's and CEO's

Exercise C
1 star's
2 celebrities'
3 X
4 sister's
5 husband's
6 site's
7 X
8 X
9 X
10 Adidas'
11 Gucci's

Section 3
Exercise A
✓ 1, 4, 5, 6, 8
Exercise B
1: If you're like most people, the thought of painting the walls doesn't exactly fill your heart with happiness and joy. (paragraph 1)
4: … babies cry more in yellow rooms. (paragraph 2)
5: … blue interiors can lower blood pressure and reduce your heart rate. For this reason, many people choose this relaxing colour for their bedrooms. (paragraph 3)
6: … create an exciting atmosphere and get people talking … especially at night … (paragraph 4)
8: … brings together the best qualities of blue and yellow. (paragraph 5)

Section 4
Exercise A
1 out 2 off 3 with 4 up
5 on 6 to
Exercise B
1 brought out
2 coming up with
3 drew up
4 caught on
5 took off
6 look up to

Section 5
Exercise A
1 had ended
2 had been drawing up
3 had opened
4 had been
5 had been waiting/had waited
6 had been coming up with
What's right?
She didn't show anyone her designs until she had finished them.
Exercise B
1 had made/had been making
2 had changed
3 had attended/had been attending
4 had noticed
5 had asked
6 had thought

Section 6
Exercises A and B
1 I was hoping
2 I was thinking we
3 I wanted to suggest
4 I was wondering

Exercise C
1 I wanted to ask your opinion about painting the bathroom blue.
2 I think we should buy a new rug to match the colour of the sofa.
3 I was hoping my mother would help us by coming up with an idea of how to decorate the baby's room.
4 I was wondering if Maria had any suggestions for an interesting design for the kitchen.

SkillsStudio
Exercise A
a to amuse readers with stories about the building's problems

Exercise B
1 gawk
2 dispute
3 ray
4 context
5 overcast
6 spire
7 awning
8 glare
9 suspend
10 scorch

Exercise C
a 2 b 4 c 5 d 1 e 6 f 3

Exercise D
Students' own answers

Unit 8

Section 1
Exercise A
1 poverty
2 ambassador
3 philanthropic
4 humanitarian
5 refugee
6 injustice
7 underprivileged
8 foundation

Exercise B
1 refugee
2 poverty
3 injustice
4 ambassador
5 underprivileged
6 philanthropic
7 foundation
8 humanitarian

Section 2
Exercise A
1 Sam would prefer not to take part in the demonstration tomorrow.
2 ✓
3 They would prefer donations not to be sent by mail.
4 ✓
5 We would rather she didn't volunteer anywhere dangerous.
6 We'd prefer not to collect donations until tomorrow.

What's right?
I'd rather donate time than money.

Exercise B
1 not to receive
2 gave
3 went
4 not to transport
5 invest
6 to see

Section 3
Exercise A and B
a 3 b 2 c 1

Exercise C
Main idea 1 b
Main idea 2 a
Main idea 3 c

Exercise D
1 doesn't make
2 sell
3 70
4 the USA
5 Overseas Needlepoint and Crafts Project
6 North America
7 50
8 2006

Section 4
Exercise A
1 d 2 f 3 a 4 b 5 e 6 c

Exercise B
1 has the right to
2 can't afford to
3 unemployed
4 benefits
5 have a responsibility to
6 live on

Section 5
Exercise A
1 b 2 a 3 a 4 b 5 b 6 a

What's right?
What the charity needs is …

Exercise B
1 What people need is a way to feed themselves.
2 Who receives the most aid is uncertain.
3 Where we send donations this year is undecided.
4 What we do is distribute baskets of food.
5 How we support our community is important.
6 What's best is to donate money direct.

Section 6
Exercise A
1 c 2 a 3 g 4 e 5 d 6 b 7 f

Exercise B
1 Discovering how many homeless people there are in your area may surprise you.
2 What they really need is your support to help them get back on their feet.
3 But it's not always easy to know how to get involved in charity work.
4 If you volunteer in some way, you could make a significant contribution.
5 Charities, which often need volunteers, may be the main source of funding for local homeless shelters.
6 You could think of new and exciting ways of getting people to donate money to the charity.

SkillsStudio
Exercise A
a Because he wanted to show the US government how it can help deal with violence in the Democratic Republic of Congo.

Exercise B
1 Rosie
2 Paul

Exercise C
1 b 2 c 3 a 4 b 5 a 6 b 7 c 8 b

Exercise D
1 f 2 a 3 g 4 b 5 d 6 c 7 e 8 h

Exercise E
1 join
2 hear
3 respond
4 disagree
5 point
6 agree

Exercise F
a 1, 3
b 2, 5
c 4, 6

Exercise G
Students' own answers

Unit 9

Section 1
Exercise A
1 about, to
2 at, about
3 by
4 about, in
5 about, about

What's right?
As a parent, I object to having beauty contests for children.
Would you like to play football in the park on Sunday?

Exercise B
1 looking
2 interested
3 capable
4 object
5 insist
6 happy
7 bored
8 excited
9 responsible

Section 2
Exercise A
b, d

Exercise B
a 2   b 3   c 1   d 4

Exercise C
a 2   b 3, 4   c 1

Section 3
1 a feeling of
2 a desire to
3 the agony of
4 the fun of
5 the will to

Section 4
Exercise A
Every evening, millions of families around the world sit at home **watching** reality TV. We know we shouldn't waste time **watching** these programmes, but we have a good time **laughing** at them. They're harmless fun. Or are they? According to a recent survey of girls aged 11–17, those who like to watch reality TV are more competitive than the girls who don't. They are more likely to agree with statements such as, 'You have to lie to get what you want', 'I have a hard time **trusting** other girls' and 'It's normal for girls to gossip and compete with each other'. However, the effects of reality TV were not all negative. Sixty-two percent of the girls who watched reality said they found themselves **learning** about new things and important issues.

What's right?
Olympic athletes spent years preparing for this opportunity.

Exercise B
1 have trouble
2 performing
3 listening
4 spend
5 sit
6 find
7 solving
8 thinking

Section 5
1 Research
2 prove
3 studies
4 researching
5 conclusions
6 theory
7 experiments
8 measure
9 tested

Section 6
Exercise A
1 a   2 b   3 a   4 a

SkillsStudio
Exercise A
1 should not
2 should not
3 should

Exercise B
1 c   2 a   3 b, d   4 b   5 a

Exercise C
1 F   2 T   3 NM   4 NM   5 F   6 T

Exercise D
Students' own answers

Unit 10

Section 1
Exercise A
1 be exposed to
2 dare to
3 failure
4 freedom
5 play it safe
6 risky
7 security
8 take a chance

Exercise B
1 freedom, security
2 risky, took a chance
3 are/'re exposed to, play it safe
4 dared to, failure

Section 2
Exercise A
1 G   2 G   3 I   4 B   5 G   6 B
7 I   8 I   9 G

Exercise B
1 a   2 c   3 c   4 a   5 c   6 a   7 b

What's right?
You have to be capable of taking risks to run your own business.

Section 3
Exercise A
1 a   2 b   3 c

Exercise B
a We would like you to consider …
b We are writing to draw your attention to a problem we noticed …
c We are confident that you will take prompt action regarding this matter.
d We would like to mention that we are happy with …

Exercise C
Dear Mrs Carter,
3 (1 d) <u>We would like to mention that we are happy with</u> the decision to install a lift in the shopping centre because it is very useful for elderly people like myself and saves us having to climb the stairs! (2 c) <u>We are confident that you will take prompt action regarding this matter.</u>
2 (3 a) <u>We would like you to consider</u> taking the following action:
- Close off the lift so that children can't play in it.
- Fix the lift as soon as possible.

1 (4 b) <u>We are writing to draw your attention to a problem we noticed</u> in the new shopping centre – the lift is broken and children were playing in it, which is dangerous.

Section 4
Exercise A
1 f   2 d   3 b   4 a   5 c   6 e

Exercise B
1 risk their lives
2 risky
3 risk assessment
4 reduce the risks
5 run the risk
6 at risk

Section 5
Exercise A
1 SI   2 MP   3 SP   4 MP   5 SI
6 SI   7 MP

Exercise B
1 must have
2 couldn't have
3 may have
4 could have
5 might have
6 must have

Exercise C
1 can't have been
2 might have fallen off
3 might have thrown
4 could have had
5 may not have seemed
6 could have been

What's right?
He couldn't have thought it was risky, or he wouldn't have done it.

Section 6
Exercise A
2

Exercise B
1 T 2 F 3 T 3 T

Exercise C
1 Did
2 must have
3 got to
4 kind of
5 want to
6 don't know
7 could have
8 got a

SkillsStudio
Exercise A
1 third
2 Nepal
3 1955

Exercise B
b his most recent expedition and his motivation for climbing mountains

Exercise C
2 Joe's climb up Mount Kanchengjunga
1 Facts and figures about Mount Kanchengjunga
5 Joe's plans for the future
3 The dangers associated with Mount Kanchengjunga
4 The reasons why Joe loves climbing

Exercise D
1 c 2 f 3 a 4 e 5 b 6 d

Exercise E
1 put up/raise their hands
2 8586 m, third
3 higher/taller, easier
4 southwest
5 avalanches and bad weather
6 More than 20%
7 doesn't think/doesn't agree/disagrees
8 rewarding

Exercise F
Students' own answers

Unit 11

Section 1
Exercise A
1 F 2 A 3 D 4 C 5 B
Exercise B
1 C 2 A 3 F 4 D 5 B

Section 2
1 landscape
2 subject
3 left-hand side
4 foreground
5 right-hand side
6 portrait
7 background
8 out of focus
9 in focus

Section 3
1 similar in that
2 similarities
3 whereas
4 unlike
5 similar
6 while

Section 4
Exercise A
1 b 2 a

Exercise B
1 A 2 A 3 C 4 A 5 C 6 A
7 C 8 C 9 A 10 C 11 C
12 C 13 A

Exercise C
1 because
2 As a consequence,
3 So,
4 because
5 because of
6 In addition to
7 Therefore,

What's right?
Lots of people want to be thinner because of selfies.

Section 5
Exercise A
1 b 2 f 3 e 4 c 5 h 6 g
7 d 8 a

Exercise B
1 To explain a similarity between two things: 2f, 6g, 8a
2 To explain a difference between two things: 1b, 3e, 4c, 5h, 7d

Exercise C
1 S 2 D 3 D 4 D 5 D 6 S
7 D 8 S

Section 6
Exercise A
1 c 2 g 3 f 4 b 5 j 6 e 7 d
8 i 9 h 10 a

Exercise B
1 to inform
2 driving
3 meeting
4 to reply
5 to fix
6 to buy
7 eating
8 swimming
9 seeing
10 to get

What's right?
I forgot to hand in my assignment this morning.

SkillsStudio
Exercise A
1 negative
2 negative
3 positive

Exercise B
1 a 2 b 3 a 4 b 5 a 6 a
7 a 8 b

Exercise C
1 B 2 B, D 3 A 4 C 5 A, D
6 B, D 7 B, C 8 A

Exercise D
Students' own answers

Unit 12

Section 1
Exercise A
1 however
2 but
3 Although
4 despite the fact
5 despite
6 Nevertheless

Exercise B
Correct: 4, 5
Incorrect:
1 Rio was great; however, we didn't get to visit Sugarloaf Mountain./Rio was great. However, we didn't get to visit Sugarloaf Mountain.
2 I love travelling for pleasure, but I really don't enjoy business travel.
3 Although it was very crowded, we enjoyed visiting the Louvre Museum in Paris.
6 Things have cost a little more than we'd expected. Nevertheless, we've had a fantastic vacation./Things have cost a little more than we'd expected; nevertheless, we've had a fantastic vacation.

What's right?
Despite arriving / the fact that we arrived an hour late, my flight to Chicago went well.

Workbook answer key 139

Exercise C
1 Despite/In spite of
2 However/Nevertheless
3 Although/Even though
4 Although/Even though
5 However/Nevertheless
6 Despite/In spite of
7 although/even though
8 However/Nevertheless

Section 2
1 disappointed, c
2 Dear, a
3 Furthermore, d
4 hearing, e
5 concerning, b
6 Yours faithfully, f

Section 3
Exercise A
A 4 **B** 3 **C** 1 **D** 5 **E** 2
Exercise B
Paragraph A: b
Paragraph B: a
Paragraph E: c
Exercise C
1 Dear Sir/Madam
2 I am writing concerning
3 we were very disappointed with it
4 First of all
5 Furthermore
6 Finally
7 For these reasons
8 I enclose
9 I look forward to hearing from you
10 Yours faithfully

Section 4
Exercise A
1 trade
2 heart
3 views
4 alley
5 heritage
6 village
7 site
8 settlement
Exercise B
1 heart
2 settlement
3 trade
4 heritage
5 village
6 site
7 views
8 alleys

Section 5
Exercise A
1 plans for the future
2 travel
3 members of her family
4 shop
Exercise B
1 China
2 history and architecture
3 the centre
4 Chinese cooking
5 He wants to find a job.
6 working at a local bookshop

Section 6
Exercise A
1 d **2** b **3** c **4** a
What's right?
By the time this concert ends, the trains and buses won't be running.
Exercise B
1 may be
2 are leaving
3 will prevent
4 may sink
5 may become
6 will be experiencing
7 are going to build
8 will be

SkillsStudio
Exercise A
1 D **2** A **3** B **4** C
Exercise B
4 limited resources
3 overcrowding
2 climate change
1 pollution
Exercise C
✓ limited resources, overcrowding, pollution
Exercise D
1 d **2** a **3** c **4** b **5** d
Exercise E
✓ 1, 2
Exercise F
Students' own answers